Bienvenue

GLENCOE FRENCH 1B

Bienvenue

Conrad J. Schmitt

Katia Brillié Lutz

GLENCOE

Macmillan/McGraw-Hill

New York, New York   Columbus, Ohio   Mission Hills, California   Peoria, Illinois

Printed in the United States of America.

Send all inquiries to:
Glencoe Division, Macmillan/McGraw-Hill
15319 Chatsworth Street
P.O. Box 9609
Mission Hills, CA 91346-9609

ISBN 0-02-636578-2 (Student Edition)

ISBN 0-02-636579-0 (Teacher's Wraparound Edition)

2 3 4 5 6 7 8   AGH   98 97 96 95 94 93

Photography

Front Cover: Curt Fischer

Abad, Charlie/La Photothèque SDP: 328-329, 347/5; Alan/Option Photo: 241; Antman, M./Scribner: xML, xiTR, 20B, 23, 235, 268/3, 281, 286, 287, 306, 314/1, 314/2, 314/3, 315/5, 316, 338, 347/3, 362T, 377, 385, 416, 423, 468, 470, 470, 478, 483; Arnold, Peter/Peter Arnold: 362B; Bayer, Carol/La Photothèque SDP: 369/6; Bilow, Nathan/Allsport: 368-69/2, 368/3, 368/4; Blatty, Michael: 31, 237; Bohin, Jean-Luc/Explorer: 418/2, 485; Cardoche, Christian/Option Photo: 322R; Carle, Eric/Bruce Coleman: 245/4; Chadefaux, A./Agence TOP: 08; Château d'Agneaux Hôtel, Éliophot, Aix-en-Provence: 456BR; Cogan, Michel/Agence TOP: 475; Cogan, Michel/Rapho: 393/4B; Collection Lausat/Explorer: 430L; Costa, Samuel/Explorer: 242; Cuny, Christian/Explorer: 323TL; Cuny, Christian/Rapho: 244/2; Ducasse, François/Rapho: 392/1; Duomo: 292-293/2, 335, 336, 345, 347/4, 360; Dupont, José/Explorer: 323BL; Eshet, Zviki/La Photothèque SDP: 368/1; Fagot, Patrick/Explorer: 292/3; Fischer, Curt: ixTR, xii, xiv-1, 2, 5, 9, 10-11, 18, 20T, 21, 26, 28, 29T, 33, 240, 248-249, 257, 261, 263, 264T, 267, 268/2, 269/4, 271, 285, 288T, 305, 317, 340, 380, 394, 396-397, 418-419/1, 418/3, 441, 450T, 467, 486; Francis, Jalain/Explorer: 411; Freed, Leonard/Magnum: 405; Gaveau, Alain: ixML, ixBR, xTR, xiii, 6, 12, 15, 17, 272-273, 296-297, 308, 310, 312, 313, 320, 342, 364, 372-373, 383, 388, 406, 414, 417, 432-433, 440, 456TR, 458-459, 471, 474, 476, 480-481/1, 481/4; Geiersperger, Walter/Explorer: 323BR; Geopress/Explorer: 413; Gérard/Vandystadt/Allsport: 244/1; Gile, Michel/Rapho: 455/3; Giraudon/Art Resource, New York: 428, 429T; Gschiedle, Gerhard/Scribner: 230, 268-269/1, 280; Guichoaua, Yann/Allsport-Vandystadt: viii; Holmes, Robert/Photo 20-20: 365, 369/5; Hôtel de Paris, Cannes: 456L; Hôtel Idéal Mont Blanc: 456M; Institut Pasteur: 426, 427M, R; Iundt, Dimitri/ATS: 292/1; Jeffrey, David/The Image Bank: 3; Lausat Collection/Explorer: 430L; Lefeuvre, Eric/Allsport: 293/5; Lenfant, J.P./Allsport: 243; Library of Congress: 431; M., Joana/La Photothèque SDP: 245/5; 346-47, 367; Machatshek, Charles/Photothèque: 370; Madison, David/Duomo: 339; Martel, Olivier/Rapho: 291; McCurry, Steve/Magnum Photos: 322L; Menzel, Peter: 266, 419/4, 454/2; Petit, Christian/Allsport: 290; Pinheira, Christine & J.C./Option Photo: 30; Planchenault, Gérard/Allsport-Vandystadt: xBR; Rega/Rapho: 314-315; Renard, Éric/Agence Temp Sport: 293/4, 346/2; Romanelli, Marc/Image Bank: 415; Rossiaud, Alain/La Photothèque SDP: 226-227; Sallaz, William R./Duomo: 422; Sanson, Nanette/Superstock: 350-351, 366; Scala/Art Resource, New York: 409, 429B; Schafer, Horst/Peter Arnold: 327R; SNCF: 24-25, 27, 29B; Streshinsky, Ted/Photo 20-20: 247, 442; Testelin, Xavier/Rapho: 392-393/2; Thom, Robert/Institut Pasteur: 427R;

Thomas, Marc: xiBR, xiML, 246, 264B, 283, 288B, 332, 348, 358, 376, 382, 391, 447, 450B, 473; Tovy, Adina/Photo 20-20: 244-245/3; TPH/La Photothèque SDP: 270; Vanni/Art Resource, New York: 407; Viollet Collection/Roger Viollet: 325, 430R; Walter/Rapho: 7, 390; Watts, Ron/Westlight: 444; Weiss/Rapho: 269/5L; Wolf, Alfred/Explorer: 392/3L, R, 427L; Wood, Kent/Peter Arnold: 327T; Wysocki, Pawell/Explorer: 393/4T, 315/4, 323TR.

Special thanks to the following for their assistance in photography arrangements: Philippe Boulze, Air France; Guy Martin, Le Grand Véfour Restaurant; Lycée Henri IV, Paris; Groupe Scolaire Sainte-Anne, Paris

Illustration

Abadie, Stéphane: 448, 462; Accardo, Anthony: 361, 445, 464, 465, 469; Collin, Marie Marthe: 301, 302, 330, 331, 352, 353, 434, 435, 438, 439, 446, 472; Gorde, Monique: 282, 356, 357, 436; Gregory, Lane: 16, 228, 229, 234, 252, 254, 255, 333, 334, 349, 355, 376; Courtesy ©Hergé-Casterman: 417; Kieffer, Christa: 16, 325 Metivet, Henry: 298, 299, 300, 316; Miller, Lyle: 32, 374, 375; Miyamoto, Masami: 381, 410, 456; Nicholson, Norman: 337, 398, 399; Spellman, Susan: 274, 275, 378, 379, 404; Taber, Ed: 240, 256, 265, 281, 289, 294, 308, 310, 341, 343, 364, 379, 389, 414, 451, 466, 477, 482; Thewlis, Diana: 12, 231, 232, 233, 278, 279, 402, 403; Watorek, Kena: 250, 251, 258, 262, 276, 460, 461.

Realia

Realia courtesy of the following: A.N. Rafting, Le Grand Liou: 238; Air Afrique: 26; Banque Industrielle et Mobilière Privée: 481; Banque Nationale de Paris: 463; Caisse d'Épargne Écureuil: 480; Cartotec, illustration Yannick Intesse: 295; Collections de la Comédie-Française: 401; Crédit Agricole: 480; Christian Dior: 269; © Éditions Les Quatre Zéphires: 13; Elle Magazine: 252, 318; L'Équipe: 354; Espace Soleil: 236; France Télécom: 449; Galeries Lafayette, illustration Mats Gutafson: 259; Hachette-Gautier Languereau, illustration M. Boutet de Monvel: 14; © Hallmark Cards: 384; Hergé-Casterman: 417; Laboratoire Conseil Oberlin: 385, 386; Ligue Française Pour Les Auberges de la Jeunesse: 453; Locapark: 303; Michelin Red Guide France, 1992 Edition, Pneu Michelin, Services de Tourisme: 455; Monoprix: 263; Pariscope Magazine, Backdraft, © by Universal City Studios, Inc. courtesy of MCA Publishing Rights, a Division of MCA Inc.: 412; La Pomme de Pin: 9; La Poste: 463, 476; La Redoute Catalogue: 359; Rev'Vacances: 424; SNCF: 27; Société IAG: 456; © Télérama: 342; Théâtres Privés Paris: 401; Vélo Sprint 2000 Magazine: 336.

Fabric designs by *Les Olivades*.

Maps

Eureka Cartography, Berkeley, CA.

Acknowledgments

We wish to express our deep appreciation to the numerous individuals throughout the United States and France who have advised us in the development of these teaching materials. Special thanks are extended to the people whose names appear here.

Baud Family
Nice, France

Esther Bennett
Notre Dame High School
Sherman Oaks, California

Brillié Family
Paris, France

Kathryn Bryers
French Teacher
Berlin, Connecticut

Donnatella Carta
French Teacher
Berkeley Public High School
Berkeley, California

G. Gail Castaldo
The Pingry School
Martinsville, New Jersey

Myriam Chapman
Bank Street School for Children
New York, New York

Susan Coleman
Northridge, California

Veronica Dewey
Brother Rice High School
Birmingham, Michigan

École Sainte-Anne
Paris, France

Lyne Flaherty
Hingham High School
Hingham, Massachusetts

Julie High
North Monterey County School District
Moss Landing, California

Marie-Jo Hofmann
Poudre School District
Fort Collins, Colorado

Marcia Brown Karper
Fayetteville-Manlius Central Schools
Manlius, New York

Jacques Lefèbvre
Lycée du Parc Impérial
Nice, France

Annette Lowry
Ft. Worth Independent School District
Ft. Worth, Texas

Fabienne Raab
Paris, France

Sally Schneider
Plano Independent School District
Plano, Texas

Alex P. Sena
Horace Mann Junior High School
Colorado Springs, Colorado

Robbie Trombetta
Culver City, California

Alain Weber
Headmaster
French American International School
San Francisco, California

Faith Weldon
Schalmont Central School District
Schenectady, New York

Bennett Williams
Department Head/French Teacher
Berkeley Public High School
Berkeley, California

TABLE DES MATIÈRES

PART B

RÉVISION

CHAPITRE 9

LES SPORTS ET LES ACTIVITÉS D'ÉTÉ

CHAPITRE 10

LES BOUTIQUES ET LES VÊTEMENTS

CHAPITRE 11

LA ROUTINE ET LA FORME PHYSIQUE

CHAPITRE 14

L'HIVER ET LES SPORTS D'HIVER

CHAPITRE 15

LA SANTÉ ET LA MÉDECINE

CHAPITRE 18

L'ARGENT ET LA BANQUE

APPENDICES

RÉVISION
A

LES COPAINS ET
LES COURS

Une Française

Voici Nathalie.
Elle est française.
Nathalie est de Paris, la capitale.
Nathalie est très intelligente.
Elle est élève au lycée.
Elle va au lycée Henri IV.

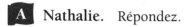 **A Nathalie.** Répondez.

1. Qui est la fille?
2. Elle est de quelle nationalité?
3. Elle est de quelle ville?
4. Nathalie est intelligente ou pas?
5. Elle va à quel lycée?

Deux Français

ÉRIC: Salut, Paul.
PAUL: Salut, Éric. Ça va?
ÉRIC: Oui, ça va bien, et toi?
PAUL: Pas mal.
ÉRIC: Où vas-tu maintenant?
PAUL: Je vais au cours de français.
ÉRIC: Qui est le prof?
PAUL: M. Guillemette. Il est très chouette.

B Salut, Paul! Répondez d'après la conversation.

1. Éric va bien ou pas?
2. Où est-ce que Paul va maintenant?
3. Qui est le professeur de français?
4. Comment est-il?

C **Les deux copains.** Répondez d'après la photo.

1. Qui sont les deux garçons?
2. Où sont-ils maintenant?
3. D'où sont les deux garçons?
4. Ils sont de quelle nationalité?
5. Comment sont les deux garçons?

Peter et Steve sont de New York.

D **Personnellement.** Donnez des réponses personnelles.

1. Salut!
2. Comment ça va?
3. Qui est ton (ta) prof de français?
4. Comment est-il (elle)?
5. Comment est le cours de français?

STRUCTURE

Les articles définis et indéfinis

1. In French, you use the definite articles *le, la, l'* to express "the." Note that these articles change to *les* in the plural. Remember that before a vowel or a silent *h*, *le* and *la* change to *l'* and there is a liaison between *les* and the following word.

SINGULIER	PLURIEL
le garçon	les garçons
la fille	les filles
l'ami	les‿amis
l'école	les‿écoles

Qui est le garçon? C'est Paul Gallimard.
Qui est la fille? C'est sa cousine.

2. In French, you use the indefinite articles *un, une* to express "a" or "an." Note that these articles change to *des* in the plural.

SINGULIER	PLURIEL
un garçon	des garçons
un immeuble	des immeubles
une fille	des filles
une école	des‿écoles

François est un ami sympathique.
Carole est une amie sincère.
François et Carole sont des amis très chouettes.

A **La fille est à l'école.** Complétez avec «le», «la», «l'» ou «les».

Qui est ⎯⎯ fille là-bas? C'est Pauline. Pauline est ⎯⎯ amie de Guy Laserre.
₁ ₂

Pauline et Guy sont élèves dans ⎯⎯ même lycée à Paris. ⎯⎯ professeur de
₃ ₄

français est M. Ettori. ⎯⎯ classe de français est assez grande. Il y a vingt-huit
₅

élèves dans ⎯⎯ classe. Mais ⎯⎯ professeur de français est très content. ⎯⎯
₆ ₇ ₈

élèves sont très intelligents. Et ⎯⎯ cours de français est très intéressant.
₉

B **Un garçon et une fille.** Complétez avec «un», «une» ou «des».

1. Patrick est ___ beau garçon.
2. Et Corinne est ___ jolie fille.
3. Patrick est ___ ami sincère.
4. Et Corinne est ___ amie sincère aussi.
5. Corinne et Patrick sont élèves dans ___ lycée excellent à Paris.
6. Ils ont ___ cours et ___ professeurs très intéressants.
7. Corinne habite dans ___ bel appartement à Paris.
8. L'appartement de la famille de Patrick est dans ___ très joli immeuble dans ___ très beau quartier de Paris.
9. La famille de Patrick a ___ voisins très sympathiques.
10. Les voisins ont ___ belle maison en Bretagne.

L'accord des adjectifs

1. Adjectives agree with the nouns they describe. If the noun is feminine, the adjective must be in the feminine form. If the noun is plural, the adjective must be in the plural form. Review the following.

	FÉMININ	MASCULIN
SINGULIER	une fille intelligente une amie sincère	un garçon intelligent un ami sincère
PLURIEL	des filles intelligentes des amies sincères	des garçons intelligents des amis sincères

2. Note that adjectives that end in a consonant in the masculine form (*intelligent*) change pronunciation in the feminine form. Adjectives that end in *-e* (*sincère*) do not change pronunciation.

C **Qui est-ce?**

Décrivez un ami.

D **Les amies.**

Décrivez les filles.

Les verbes *être* et *aller*

1. Review the forms of the irregular verbs *être,* "to be," and *aller,* "to go."

ÊTRE	ALLER
je suis	je vais
tu es	tu vas
il	il
elle } est	elle } va
on	on
nous sommes	nous allons
vous êtes	vous allez
ils	ils
elles } sont	elles } vont

2. Note that to make a sentence negative, you put *ne... pas* (or *n'... pas*) around the verb.

Je suis française.	**Je *ne* suis *pas* américaine.**
Jeanne est élève dans un lycée français.	**Elle *n'*est *pas* élève dans une école américaine.**

3. Remember that you also use *aller* to express how someone feels.

Comment vas-tu?
Comment allez-vous? } **Je vais bien, merci.**

E **Charles est de New York.** Répétez la conversation.

ANNICK: Bonjour, Charles. Ça va?
CHARLES: Oui, ça va bien, et toi?
ANNICK: Bien, merci. Tu es français, Charles, n'est-ce pas?
CHARLES: Mais non, je ne suis pas français. Je suis américain.
ANNICK: Sans blague! Tu es de quelle ville?
CHARLES: Je suis de New York.
ANNICK: Tu vas à l'université à New York?
CHARLES: Non, non. Je ne vais pas à l'université. Je vais à l'école secondaire.

Répondez d'après la conversation.

1. Charles est français?
2. Il est de quelle nationalité?
3. Il est de quelle ville?
4. Il va à l'université?
5. Où est-ce qu'il va à l'école?

F **Moi!** Donnez des réponses personnelles.

1. Qui es-tu?
2. D'où es-tu?
3. Tu es de quelle nationalité?
4. Tu vas à quelle école?
5. Tu vas à l'école avec des copains?
6. Tes copains et toi, vous allez à l'école à pied ou en bus?
7. Où est l'école?
8. Comment sont les professeurs?

G **Au restaurant.** Complétez avec «être» ou «aller».

1. Ce soir la famille de Françoise Carron ___ au restaurant.
2. C'___ un petit restaurant. Il ___ vraiment très bon.
3. Tous les serveurs ___ vietnamiens.
4. La cuisine vietnamienne ___ délicieuse.
5. Le copain de Françoise y ___ aussi.
6. Françoise et son copain ___ commander un plat végétarien.
7. Ta famille et toi, vous ___ dîner au restaurant ce soir ou vous ___ dîner chez vous?
8. Au restaurant, qui ___ demander l'addition?
9. Qui ___ payer?
10. Vous ___ laisser un pourboire?

Les contractions avec *à* et *de*

1. The preposition *à* can mean "to," "in," or "at." It remains unchanged when followed by the articles *la* and *l'*, but it contracts with *le* to form one word, *au*, and with *les* to form one word, *aux*. Note the liaison with *aux* and a word that begins with a vowel or silent *h*. The *x* is pronounced like a *z*. Review the following.

à + la = à la	**Je vais *à la* boulangerie.**
à + l' = à l'	**Je vais *à l'*école.**
à + le = au	**Je vais *au* restaurant.**
à + les = aux	**Je parle *aux* élèves.**

2. The preposition *de*, meaning "of" or "from," also contracts with *le* and *les* to form one word, *du* or *des*. Note that *de* is also a part of many longer prepositions such as *près de*, *loin de*, etc.

de + la = de la	**Il habite près *de la* cathédrale.**
de + l' = de l'	**Il habite près *de l'*école.**
de + le = du	**Elle habite loin *du* parc.**
de + les = des	**Elle habite loin *des* magasins.**

H **On y va ou pas?** Complétez avec «à».

Aujourd'hui on ne va pas ___ parc, on ne va pas ___ restaurant, on ne va pas
                        1   2
___ maison, on ne va pas ___ pâtisserie. Où est-ce qu'on va alors? On va ___
 3   4   5
école. On va ___ cours de français. On va parler ___ professeur et ___ élèves.
             6   7   8

I **Où habites-tu?** Donnez des réponses personnelles.

1. Tu habites près ou loin de l'aéroport?
2. Tu vas souvent à l'aéroport?
3. Tu habites près ou loin de la gare?
4. Tu vas souvent à la gare?
5. Tu habites près ou loin de l'école?
6. Tu quittes l'école à quelle heure?
7. Tu habites près ou loin des magasins?
8. Tu vas souvent au magasin?

Activités de communication

A **Des copains.** Imagine you are walking down the street in Aix-en-Provence and run into one of your French friends (your partner). Talk to your friend using the following cues.

1. Greet each other.
2. Ask each other how things are going.
3. Say goodbye.

B **L'ami(e) idéal(e).** Make a list of some personality traits you look for in a friend. Then ask your partner if he or she likes the same things in a friend.

> Élève 1: Pour moi, l'ami(e) idéal(e) est très sympathique. Tu es d'accord?
> Élève 2: Oui, je suis d'accord. Pour moi, l'ami(e) idéal(e) est aussi très patient(e).

C **Au restaurant.** Working with a partner, prepare a conversation between a waiter or waitress and a customer in a restaurant. The following are some words and expressions you may want to use.

la carte	saignant
le service	à point
un hamburger	bien cuit
une pizza	l'addition
un coca	

La carte pomme de pain :

Les sandwichs

LE LYONNAIS ROSETTE DE LYON 450 CALORIES

LE COMTE COMTÉ DU JURA 430 CALORIES

LE PARISIEN JAMBON AU TORCHON 333 CALORIES

LE SAVOYARD JAMBON CRU 347 CALORIES

LE SPECIAL JAMBON/CRUDITÉS 400 CALORIES

LE PROVENÇAL OEUFS/CRUDITÉS 400 CALORIES

LE CORDON BLEU JAMBON AU TORCHON - COMTÉ 530 CALORIES

LE VILLAGEOIS VOLAILLE/CRUDITÉS 360 CALORIES

LE NIÇOIS THON/CRUDITÉS 420 CALORIES

- bière de luxe pression
- bordeaux A.O.C.
- cidre normand
- boisson à l'orange
- coca-cola
- chocolat - café - thé

- eau minérale
- la salade fraîcheur
- la salade pomme de pain
- la quiche lorraine
- le feuilleté volaille

- le croissant
- le pain au chocolat
- le chausson aux
- la tarte aux pommes
- les glaces et sorbets

RÉVISION

B

DES ACTIVITÉS AMUSANTES

MANDARINE
RHUM RAISIN
PECHE

LAIT FRAPPE
(MILK SHAKE) 25

SUPPL' CHANTILLY...... 10

PATISSERIES   19

VOIR

MOTS ET CONVERSATION

La fête de Caroline

Caroline donne une fête.
Elle invite des copains.

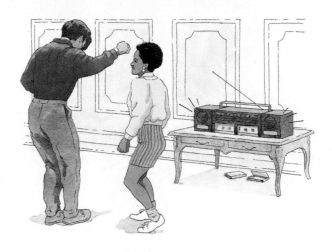

Les copains arrivent chez Caroline à
   sept heures.
Ils parlent à Caroline.

Pendant la fête, les copains dansent.
Ils écoutent des cassettes.

A   Chez Caroline.   Répondez.

1. Caroline donne une fête?
2. Elle invite des copains?
3. Les copains arrivent chez Caroline à sept heures?
4. Ils parlent à Caroline? Ils parlent français ou anglais?
5. Pendant la fête, les copains dansent?
6. Ils écoutent des cassettes?

B   Qui?   Répondez.

1. Qui donne la fête?
2. Qui arrive chez Caroline?
3. Quand est-ce qu'ils arrivent?
4. Qui parle?
5. À qui est-ce qu'ils parlent?
6. Qui écoute des cassettes?
7. Qui danse?

C La maison de Caroline.   Lisez le paragraphe.

La maison de Caroline est jolie.
Au rez-de-chaussée il y a quatre pièces.
Au premier étage il y a les chambres à coucher.
Caroline a une très jolie chambre à coucher.
Elle fait ses devoirs dans sa chambre à coucher.

D Comment est sa maison?   Décrivez la maison de Caroline.

E Qu'est-ce que les amis de Caroline font?   Choisissez la bonne réponse.

1. Les amis écoutent des cassettes?
   a. Oui, ils détestent la musique.
   b. Oui, ils adorent le rock.
   c. Oui, ils vont au théâtre.

2. Quand est-ce qu'ils dansent?
   a. Le samedi soir à la fête.
   b. Quand je vais à l'école.
   c. Quand nous réservons une table au restaurant.

3. Ils parlent français à Caroline?
   a. Oui, je téléphone à mon amie.
   b. Oui, ils sont français.
   c. Oui, nous parlons français.

4. La maison de Caroline est grande?
   a. Oui, il y a deux étages.
   b. Oui, il y a trois pièces.
   c. Oui, il y a deux immeubles.

STRUCTURE

Les verbes réguliers en *-er*

The infinitive of many regular French verbs ends in *-er*. Review the following present tense forms of regular *-er* verbs. Note that before a verb beginning with a vowel or silent *h, je* becomes *j'* and there is liaison between *nous, vous, ils,* or *elles* and the following word.

INFINITIVE	PARLER	AIMER	
STEM	**parl-**	**aim-**	ENDINGS
	je parle	j' aime	-e
	tu parles	tu aimes	-es
	il elle } parle on	il elle } aime on	-e
	nous parlons	nous aimons	-ons
	vous parlez	vous aimez	-ez
	ils elles } parlent	ils aiment elles aiment	-ent

A **Moi!** Donnez des réponses personnelles.

1. Tu habites quelle ville?
2. Tu habites une petite ville ou une grande ville?
3. Tu arrives à l'école à quelle heure le matin?
4. Tu parles à tes copains?
5. Tes copains et toi, vous étudiez le français?
6. Vous aimez le cours de français?
7. Vous chantez en français?

Le Pont d'Avignon

B **Une fête.** Donnez des réponses personnelles.

1. Tu aimes donner des fêtes?
2. Tu donnes des fêtes?
3. Qui invites-tu?
4. Tu téléphones à tes copains?
5. Ils acceptent toujours ton invitation?
6. Quel soir est-ce que tu donnes la fête?
7. Tes amis arrivent à quelle heure?
8. Tes copains et toi, vous dansez pendant la fête?

C **On dîne au restaurant.** Complétez.

1. Ce soir Angélique ne ___ pas le dîner. (préparer)
2. Elle ___ d'aller dîner au restaurant. (décider)
3. Elle ___ à sa copine. (téléphoner)
4. Elle ___ sa copine au restaurant. (inviter)
5. Elles ___ dans un restaurant italien. (aller)
6. Les deux amies ___ au restaurant à sept heures. (arriver)
7. Le serveur ___ à leur table. (arriver)
8. Les deux amies ___ une pizza. (commander)
9. Angélique ___ l'addition. (demander)
10. Tu ___ la pizza? (aimer)
11. Quand tes copains et toi ___ dans un restaurant italien, qu'est-ce que vous ___? (aller, commander)

L'infinitif

1. The infinitive form follows verbs such as *aimer, détester, adorer,* and *préférer.*

> **J'aime danser mais je déteste chanter.**
> **Je n'aime pas du tout chanter.**

2. You also use the infinitive after the verb *aller* to tell what you or others are going to do.

> **Ce soir je vais regarder la télé.**
> **Demain nous allons donner une fête.**

D **Mes préférences.** Donnez des réponses personnelles.

1. Tu aimes manger?
2. Tu préfères manger dans un restaurant italien ou dans un restaurant chinois?
3. Tu vas dîner au restaurant ce soir?

4. Tu aimes donner des fêtes?
5. Tu vas inviter tes amis à la fête?
6. Tu préfères donner des fêtes ou aller à des fêtes?

E **Pas maintenant.** Répondez d'après le modèle.

> **Tu regardes la télé maintenant?**
> *Non, mais je vais regarder la télé ce soir.*

1. Tu écoutes la radio maintenant?
2. Tu travailles maintenant?

3. Ton copain téléphone maintenant?
4. Ton copain arrive maintenant?

F **Qu'est-ce qu'ils aiment faire?** Répondez d'après les dessins.

1.

2.

3.

4.

5.

Les verbes *avoir* et *faire*

1. Review the forms of the irregular verbs *avoir*, "to have," and *faire*, "to do," "to make."

AVOIR	FAIRE
j' ai	je fais
tu as	tu fais
il	il
elle }a	elle }fait
on	on
nous avons	nous faisons
vous avez	vous faites
ils ont	ils
elles ont	elles }font

2. You use the verb *avoir* to express age.

   Tu as quel âge? Moi, j'ai quatorze ans.

3. The verb *faire* is used in many expressions.

   faire du français   faire la cuisine
   faire de la gymnastique   faire un pique-nique
   faire les courses

4. Remember that in negative sentences *un*, *une*, and *des* change to *de* (*d'*).

J'ai un frère.	**Je *n'*ai *pas de* sœur.**
Elle fait du français.	**Elle *ne* fait *pas d'*espagnol.**
Tu as des livres.	**Tu *n'*as *pas de* cahiers.**

G **Les Dejarnac.**   Complétez avec «avoir».

1. La famille Dejarnac ____ une maison dans la banlieue parisienne.
2. La maison des Dejarnac ____ sept pièces.
3. M. et Mme Dejarnac ____ deux enfants.
4. Pierre ____ cinq ans et Michèle ____ douze ans.
5. Les Dejarnac ____ un chien?
6. Vous ____ un chien?
7. Non, nous n'____ pas de chien mais nous ____ un chat.

H **Moi!**   Donnez des réponses personnelles.

1. Tu as une grande ou une petite famille?
2. Tu as combien de frères?
3. Tu as combien de sœurs?
4. Ta famille et toi, vous avez un chat ou un chien?
5. Tu as une voiture?

I **On fait les courses.**   Répétez la conversation.

CHRISTINE: Salut, Michèle. Comment vas-tu?
MICHÈLE: Bien, merci. Et toi?
CHRISTINE: Pas mal. Où vas-tu maintenant?
MICHÈLE: Je vais faire les courses.
CHRISTINE: Tu fais les courses où?
MICHÈLE: Au marché de la rue Mouffetard. Et aujourd'hui j'ai beaucoup de choses à acheter.

Répondez d'après la conversation.

1. Michèle va bien?
2. Est-ce qu'elle va faire les courses?
3. Elle va au marché de la rue Mouffetard?
4. Elle a beaucoup de choses à acheter?

Le partitif

1. In French, you use the definite article when talking about a specific item.

   La salade est sur *la* table dans *la* cuisine.

2. You also use the definite article when talking about a noun in the general sense.

   Moi, j'aime beaucoup *le* chocolat.

3. However, when you refer to only a part or a certain quantity of something, the partitive construction is used. The partitive is expressed in French by *de* + the definite article.

de + le = du	J'ai *du* pain.
de + la = de la	J'ai *de la* crème.
de + l' = de l'	J'ai *de l'*argent.
de + les = des	J'ai *des* gâteaux.

4. When the partitive follows a verb in the negative, all forms change to *de* or *d'*.

J'ai du pain.	Je n'ai pas *de* pain.
J'ai de la viande.	Je n'ai pas *de* viande.
J'ai de l'argent.	Je n'ai pas *d'*argent.
J'ai des fruits.	Je n'ai pas *de* fruits.

J Qu'est-ce qu'on peut acheter à l'épicerie? Répondez.

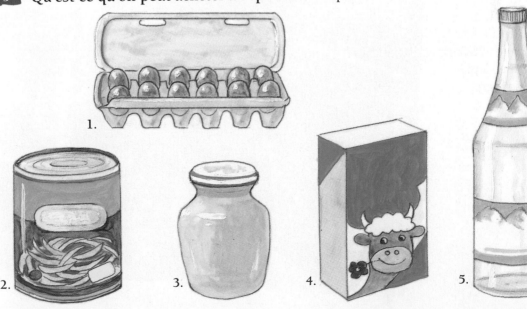

1.

2.   3.   4.   5.

K **Pas aujourd'hui.** Répondez d'après le modèle.

> l'eau minérale
>
> *J'aime l'eau minérale.*
> *J'achète souvent de l'eau minérale.*
> *Mais aujourd'hui je n'achète pas d'eau minérale.*

1. le poisson
2. la viande
3. le bœuf
4. les fruits
5. le pain français
6. les pâtisseries

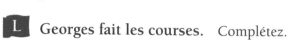

L **Georges fait les courses.** Complétez.

Georges fait les courses. Il va à la boulangerie où il achète ___ pain. Georges
achète ___ pain tous les jours. Mais il n'achete pas toujours ___ viande.
Aujourd'hui il n'achète pas ___ viande. Il ne va pas à la boucherie. Il achète
___ poisson. Pour acheter ___ poisson il va à la poissonnerie. Ensuite il va à
l'épicerie du coin où il achète ___ eau minérale et ___ boîtes de conserve. Il
n'achète pas ___ lait aujourd'hui.

M **Mes possessions.** Donnez des réponses personnelles.

1. Tu as un crayon?
2. Tu as un stylo?
3. Tu as un cahier?
4. Tu as un sac à dos?
5. Tu as un chat?
6. Tu as un ordinateur?
7. Tu as une sœur?
8. Tu as un frère?

Les adjectifs possessifs

1. Like all other French adjectives, the possessive adjectives must agree with the noun they modify. Remember that *son, sa,* and *ses* can mean either "his" or "her." The agreement is with the item owned, not the owner.

> la voiture de Marc $\longrightarrow$ sa voiture
> le livre de Marie $\longrightarrow$ son livre

MASCULIN SINGULIER	FÉMININ SINGULIER	PLURIEL
mon père	ma mère	mes parents
ton père	ta mère	tes parents
son père	sa mère	ses parents

2. Remember that the masculine singular form is used before feminine singular nouns that begin with a vowel and that there is a liaison.

> mon amie   ton amie   son amie

3. The adjectives *notre, votre,* and *leur* have only two forms, singular and plural.

MASCULIN SINGULIER	FÉMININ SINGULIER	PLURIEL
notre cousin	notre cousine	nos cousin(e)s
votre cousin	votre cousine	vos cousin(e)s
leur cousin	leur cousine	leurs cousin(e)s

N **Moi!**   Donnez des réponses personnelles.

1. Tu as des oncles et des tantes?
2. Tu as une grande ou une petite famille?
   Tu as combien de cousins?
3. Tes parents ont une voiture?
4. Leur voiture est dans le garage le soir?
5. Ta mère travaille?
6. Ton père travaille?
7. Où est votre maison ou appartement?
8. Votre maison ou appartement a combien de pièces?

Activités de communication

A **La chambre d'Alain.** Look at the picture of Alain Legrand's room. Based on what you see, ask your partner questions about Alain, his possessions, his likes and dislikes.

B **J'aime....** Work with a partner. Find out what food he or she likes or doesn't like to eat. Then tell the class your common likes and dislikes.

> Élève 1: Robert, tu aimes les haricots verts?
> Élève 2: Oui, j'aime les haricots verts. (Non, je déteste les haricots verts.) Et toi?
> Élève 1: Moi, j'aime les haricots verts aussi.
> Élève 1: (*à la classe*): Robert et moi, nous aimons les haricots verts. (Robert et moi, nous détestons les haricots verts./ Moi, j'aime les haricots verts, mais Robert déteste les haricots verts.)

C **Ma famille.** Imagine that you are a new student at your school. Describe your family to a classmate by answering the following questions that he or she asks you.

> Où est-ce que tu habites?
> Comment est ta maison ou ton appartement?
> Il y a combien de personnes dans ta famille?
> Tu as combien de frères et combien de sœurs?
> Tu as quel âge?
> Tu vas à quelle école?
> Tu aimes quels cours?
> Tu n'aimes pas quels cours?
> Qu'est-ce que tu fais après les cours?

D **Ma maison et ma chambre.** Write a short paragraph describing your house or apartment and your room.

E **Aujourd'hui.** Work with a partner. Find out the following information from him or her.

1. what day it is
2. what the date is today
3. what time it is
4. what time his or her English class is
5. what time he or she is leaving school today

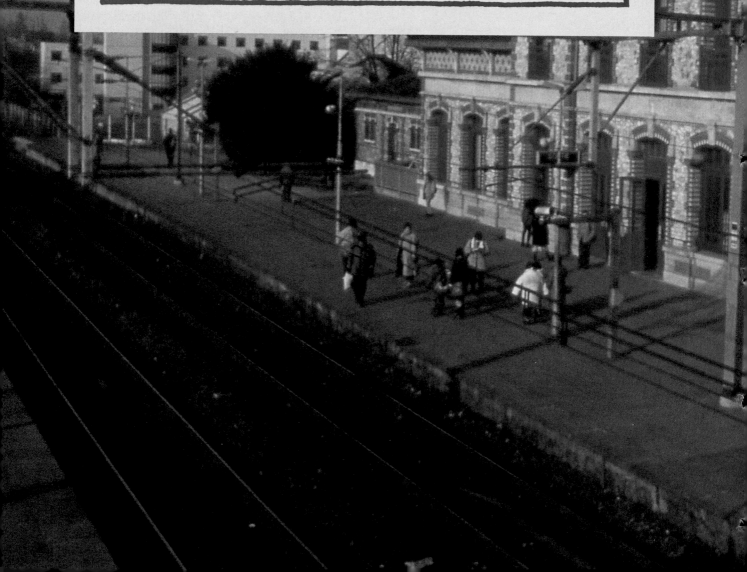

RÉVISION

C

ON VOYAGE

MOTS ET CONVERSATION

À l'aéroport

AHMED: Salut, Thérèse. Qu'est-ce que tu fais ici à l'aéroport?

THÉRÈSE: Je vais au Sénégal.

AHMED: Pas possible! Moi aussi, je pars pour Dakar. Tu as ta carte d'embarquement?

THÉRÈSE: Bien sûr.

AHMED: Tu as quelle place?

THÉRÈSE: 22A. On annonce le départ d'un avion. C'est quel numéro de vol?

AHMED: Le 214. C'est notre vol. L'avion part de quelle porte?

THÉRÈSE: De la porte vingt-cinq.

A **On part pour Dakar.** Répondez d'après la conversation.

1. Où est Thérèse?
2. Où va-t-elle?
3. Qui parle à Thérèse à l'aéroport?
4. Ahmed part pour quelle ville?
5. Et Thérèse part pour quel pays?
6. Elle a sa carte d'embarquement?
7. Thérèse a quelle place?
8. Qu'est-ce qu'ils entendent?
9. Quel est le numéro de leur vol?
10. Leur avion part de quelle porte?

À la gare

Alain est dans la gare à Deauville. Il a de la chance. Il n'y a pas de queue devant le guichet. Il va au guichet. Il achète un billet aller-retour en deuxième pour Paris. Il composte le billet et va sur le quai où il attend le train. Le train part exactement à 14h10. Alain monte dans une voiture non fumeurs.

B **Un voyage en train.** Répondez par «oui» ou «non».

1. Alain est dans la salle d'attente de la gare?
2. Il est dans la gare à Paris?
3. Il y a une queue devant le guichet?
4. Alain achète un aller simple?
5. Il voyage en première classe?
6. Alain va sur le quai?
7. Le train part en retard?
8. Alain choisit une voiture fumeurs?

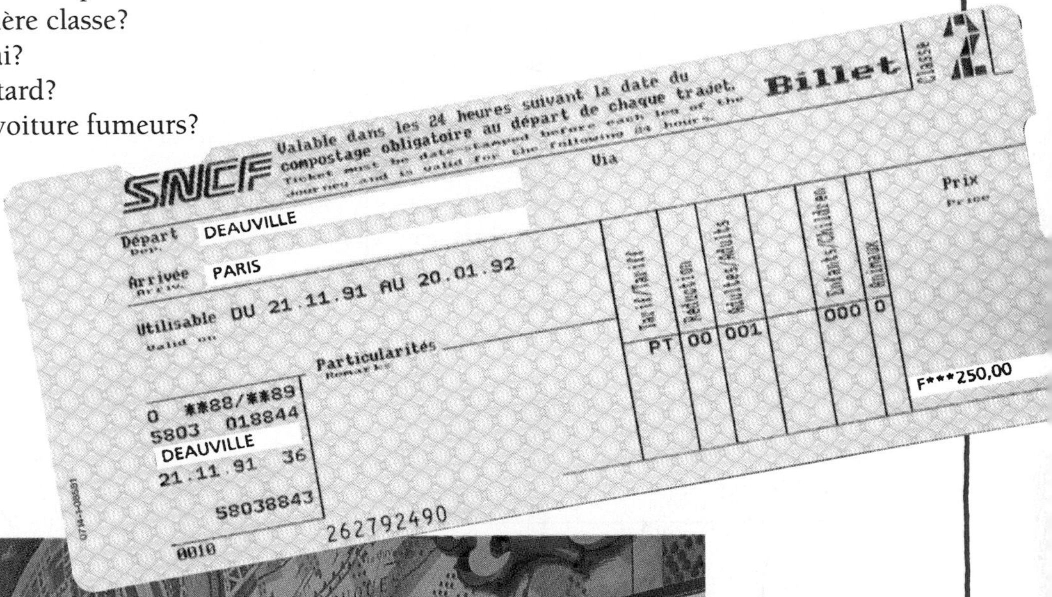

SNCF

Valable dans les 24 heures suivant la date du compostage obligatoire au départ de chaque trajet. Ticket must be date-stamped before each leg of the journey and is valid for the following 24 hours.

Billet Classe 2

Départ	DEAUVILLE		Via							Prix Price
Arrivée	PARIS									
Utilisable	DU 21.11.91 AU 20.01.92			Tarif/Tariff	Réduction	Adultes/Adults		Enfants/Children	Animaux	
				PT	00	001		000	0	

Particularités Remarks

```
0  **88/**89
5803   018844
DEAUVILLE
21.11.91   36
     58038843
0010        262792490
```

F***250,00

Les verbes en *-ir* et *-re*

Review the following forms of regular *-ir* and *-re* verbs in French.

INFINITIVE	FINIR	
STEM	**fin-**	ENDINGS
	je finis	-is
	tu finis	-is
	il elle }finit on	-it
	nous finissons	-issons
	vous finissez	-issez
	ils }finissent elles	-issent

INFINITIVE	ATTENDRE	
STEM	**attend-**	ENDINGS
	j' attends	-s
	tu attends	-s
	il elle }attend on	-
	nous attendons	-ons
	vous attendez	-ez
	ils attendent elles attendent	-ent

A **Un voyage en avion.** Répondez.

1. Quand tu voyages, tu choisis un vol Air France?
2. Tu choisis une place côté fenêtre ou côté couloir?
3. Beaucoup de passagers choisissent des places côté couloir?
4. Vous réussissez à avoir toujours les places que vous désirez?
5. Votre avion atterrit généralement à l'heure?

B **Un voyage en train.** Complétez.

1. On ___ les billets au guichet. (vendre)
2. On ___ des magazines et des journaux au kiosque. (vendre)
3. Les passagers ___ le train. (attendre)
4. Nous aussi, nous ___ . (attendre)
5. Vous ___ le train dans la salle d'attente. (attendre)
6. J'___ l'annonce du départ de notre train. (entendre)
7. Marie aussi ___ l'annonce au haut-parleur. (entendre)

Les verbes *partir, sortir, servir* et *dormir*

Study the following irregular verbs which also end in *-ir* in the infinitive.

PARTIR	SORTIR	SERVIR	DORMIR
je **pars**	je **sors**	je **sers**	je **dors**
tu **pars**	tu **sors**	tu **sers**	tu **dors**
il elle on **part**	il elle on **sort**	il elle on **sert**	il elle on **dort**
nous **partons**	nous **sortons**	nous **servons**	nous **dormons**
vous **partez**	vous **sortez**	vous **servez**	vous **dormez**
ils elles **partent**	ils elles **sortent**	ils elles **servent**	ils elles **dorment**

C **En voiture!** Répondez d'après les indications.

1. Le train part de quelle voie? (numéro deux)
2. Il part à quelle heure? (18h16)
3. On sert des repas dans le train? (oui)
4. Qui sert les repas? (les serveurs)
5. Les passagers dorment? (oui, dans une voiture-lit)
6. Le contrôleur arrive. Tu sors ton billet? (oui)

D **Carole fait un voyage.** Complétez.

Carole est à la Gare du Nord. Où est-ce qu'on ___ (vendre) les billets? Ah,
                                          1
voilà le guichet. Carole achète son billet. Elle ___ (sortir) de l'argent de son
                                                   2
sac à dos et paie. Son train ___ (partir) de la voie numéro quatre. Tous les
                              3
trains ___ (partir) à l'heure. Beaucoup de passagers ___ (dormir) dans le train.
       4   5
Mais Carole ne ___ (dormir) pas. Elle aime bien voyager en train.
               6

Les adjectifs *ce, quel* et *tout*

Review the forms of the adjectives *ce* (this, that), *quel* (which) and *tout* (the whole, all, every). Remember that you use the definite article with *tout*.

ce train	cette voiture	ces billets	ces places
quel train	quelle voiture	quels billets	quelles places
tout le train	toute la voiture	tous les billets	toutes les places

E **Tous les élèves aiment ce professeur.** Complétez d'après les indications.

1. ___ les élèves aiment ___ cours. (tout, ce)
2. ___ professeur est très intéressant. (ce)
3. Mais tu parles de ___ cours et de ___ professeur? (quel, quel)
4. De ___ cours? Du cours d'histoire! Et de ___ professeur? De Madame Rambouillet, bien sûr. (quel, quel)
5. Le cours d'histoire est dans ___ salle de classe? (quel)

F **Quel train va à Avignon?** Complétez avec «tout», «ce» ou «quel».

1. Est-ce que ___ les trains vont à Avignon?
2. Non, ___ les trains qui partent de ___ gare ne vont pas nécessairement à Avignon. Mais le prochain train qui part de ___ quai va à Avignon.
3. Il va partir de ___ quai à ___ heure? Il va partir à dix heures.
4. Il est nécessaire de payer un supplément pour ___ train? Non.
5. ___ voitures sont non fumeurs?
6. ___ voitures sont non fumeurs.

Le Palais des Papes à Avignon

Les verbes *pouvoir* et *vouloir*

1. Review the forms of the verbs *pouvoir*, "to be able," "can," and *vouloir*, "to want."

POUVOIR	VOULOIR
je peux	je veux
tu peux	tu veux
il elle }peut on	il elle }veut on
nous pouvons	nous voulons
vous pouvez	vous voulez
ils elles }peuvent	ils elles }veulent

2. These verbs are frequently followed by the infinitive.

> **Je peux sortir et je veux sortir.**
> **Tu veux sortir avec moi?**
> **Elle ne veut pas sortir avec Gilles.**

G **Un petit voyage à Nice.** Répondez par «oui».

1. Marie-Claire veut aller à Nice?
2. Elle peut partir demain?
3. Son frère veut aller à Nice aussi?
4. Ils peuvent faire le voyage ensemble?
5. Ils veulent aller à Nice en train?
6. Ils peuvent aller à Nice en train? En avion?
7. Ils veulent regarder la mer Méditerranée?
8. Tu veux regarder la mer Méditerranée?
9. Tu peux regarder la mer Méditerranée?

Vues de la côte et de la mer Méditerranée

Activités de communication

A **On fait les courses.** You and two classmates are planning a picnic in Évian-les-Bains, a town on Lake Geneva. First, make a list of what you need. Then take turns asking one another where you would buy these items.

> **du pain**
> Élève 1: Où est-ce qu'on achète du pain?
> Élève 2: On achète du pain à la boulangerie.

B **En avion.** Make a list of words associated with airline travel. Write a short paragraph using these words to describe a plane trip you plan to make (or would like to make).

C **À la gare.** Working with a partner, prepare a conversation between a passenger who wants to buy a ticket and a ticket agent in a train station. You may want to use some of the following words and expressions.

un aller-retour	en première/en deuxième
un aller simple	à quelle heure
un billet	le quai
combien	la voie

D **La gare.** Describe the illustration in your own words.

E **Des photos.** Make up as many questions as you can about each photo, then ask your partner your questions. You may take turns asking the questions and responding.

LES SPORTS ET LES ACTIVITÉS D'ÉTÉ

OBJECTIFS

In this chapter you will learn to do the following:

1. talk about summer leisure activities
2. tell what one must do
3. describe summer weather
4. describe people's activities
5. emphasize and clarify whom you are talking about
6. describe people and things
7. tell some differences between French and American vacation habits

VOCABULAIRE

MOTS 1

EN ÉTÉ

la mer

une station balnéaire
au bord de la mer

une vague

le sable

la plage

des lunettes de soleil

un maillot (de bain)

À la plage il faut faire attention.
Il faut mettre de la crème solaire.
André met de la crème solaire.
Il prend un bain de soleil.
Il bronze.

Christine met des lunettes de soleil.
Mais elle attrape un coup de soleil.
Pourquoi? Parce qu'elle ne fait pas attention.
Elle ne met pas de crème solaire.

Note: The impersonal expression *il faut,* "one must," is used often in French. It is followed by the infinitive.

faire de la planche à voile

faire de la plongée sous-marine

faire du ski nautique

faire du surf

faire une promenade

aller à la pêche

plonger

nager

une piscine

un moniteur

Robert aime nager.
Il nage dans la piscine.
Et Caroline plonge dans la piscine.

Laure prend des leçons de natation.
Elle apprend à nager.
Elle comprend les instructions du moniteur.

Exercices

A **Tu aimes les activités d'été?** Donnez des réponses personnelles.

1. Tu aimes nager quand il y a de grandes vagues?
2. Tu aimes plonger dans une piscine?
3. Tu aimes faire de la planche à voile?
4. Tu aimes faire de la plongée sous-marine?
5. Tu aimes faire du ski nautique?
6. Tu aimes faire du surf?
7. Tu aimes aller à la pêche?
8. Tu aimes prendre des bains de soleil sur le sable?
9. Tu aimes faire des promenades sur la plage?

B **Qu'est-ce qu'on fait en été?** Donnez des réponses personnelles.

1. En été, tu aimes aller à la plage?
2. Tu vas à quelle station balnéaire?
3. Tu préfères nager dans la mer ou dans une piscine?
4. Quand tu vas à la plage, tu mets un beau maillot?
5. À ton avis, est-ce qu'il faut mettre de la crème solaire?
6. Est-ce que tu mets de la crème solaire?
7. Tu bronzes facilement ou tu attrapes des coups de soleil?
8. Tu mets des lunettes de soleil quand tu vas à la plage?

C **Qu'est-ce qu'elle apprend à faire?** Répondez d'après la photo.

1. Jeanne apprend à nager?
2. Elle prend des leçons de natation?
3. Elle apprend à nager dans la mer ou dans une piscine?
4. Elle comprend bien les instructions de la monitrice?

NATATION – SKI NAUTIQUE

POUR ÉVITER DE MULTIPLES DANGERS:
courants, trous d'eau, épaves, vents, marées, barres, sables mouvants, tourbillons, etc.

CHOISISSEZ UNE PLAGE SURVEILLÉE.

Baignade interdite

Baignade dangereuse

Baignade autorisée

LA BAIGNADE

La natation est un **sport**; n'allez pas au-delà de vos possibilités.

L'hydrocution est un **accident** qui survient le plus souvent après:
- un repas copieux
- un bain de soleil prolongé

VOCABULAIRE

MOTS 2

LE TENNIS

une balle

une raquette

un court de tennis

une jupette

un tee-shirt

un filet

un short

les limites

des chaussures de tennis (f.)

hors des limites

On joue au tennis.
C'est un match de tennis.
Un des joueurs sert.

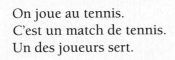

L'autre joueur renvoie la balle.
Il frappe fort.
Le score est quinze à zéro.

une partie en simple
un match entre deux joueurs

une partie en double
un match entre quatre joueurs

gagner le match

Note: The verb *jouer* takes the preposition *à* when followed by a sport.

On joue au tennis. On joue au volley. On joue au foot.

LE TEMPS EN ÉTÉ

Quel temps fait-il?

Il fait du soleil. Il fait beau.

Il fait chaud.

Il fait mauvais.

Il y a des nuages. Il pleut.

Il fait du vent.

Il fait froid.

Exercices

A **Un match de tennis.** Donnez des réponses personnelles.

1. Tu aimes le tennis?
2. Tu joues au tennis?
3. Si tu ne joues pas au tennis, tu veux apprendre à jouer au tennis?
4. Tu as une raquette?
5. Il y a un court de tennis près de ta maison ou ton appartement?
6. Ton école a des courts de tennis?

B **Le tennis.** Complétez.

1. Quand un garçon ou un homme joue au tennis, il met un ___, un ___ et des ___.
2. Quand une fille ou une femme joue au tennis, elle met un ___, une ___ et des ___.
3. ___ est un match entre deux joueurs.
4. ___ est un match entre quatre personnes.
5. Quand on joue au tennis, on a une ___ et des ___.
6. 15-"love" est un ___ de quinze à zéro.
7. On ___ ou ___ la balle avec la raquette.
8. Un joueur sert, mais la balle va dans le ___. Quand il sert encore la balle est ___! Il n'a pas de chance!
9. Un des joueurs ___ très fort. Il ___ le match.

C **Le temps.** Répondez.

1. En été, il fait beau ou il fait mauvais dans ta ville?
2. Il fait du soleil?
3. Il pleut souvent?
4. Il fait du vent à la plage?
5. Quel temps fait-il aujourd'hui?

D **Quel temps fait-il?** Répondez d'après les dessins.

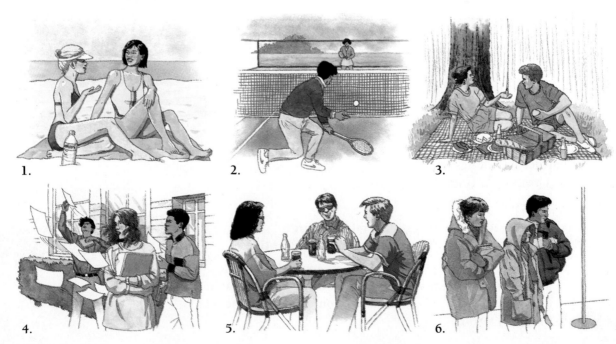

1.

2.

3.

4.

5.

6.

Activités de communication

Mots 1 et 2

A **À la plage.** Describe three different types of weather at the beach. Your partner will tell you what kind of activity he or she likes (or doesn't like) to do on that kind of day at the beach.

> Élève 1: Il fait du vent.
> Élève 2: Quand il fait du vent, j'aime faire de la planche à voile.

B **Les vacances parfaites.** Working with a partner, plan a summer vacation at the beach. Say where you would like to go and why, and what you like to do there. Report to the class.

> Élève 1: Je voudrais aller à Hawaii parce qu'il fait toujours du soleil là-bas. J'aime nager. Et toi?
> Élève 2: Moi aussi, j'aime Hawaii. Je voudrais faire de la plongée sous-marine et du surf.
> Élève 1 (*à la classe*): Nous voulons aller à Hawaii. Moi, j'aime nager et mon ami(e) veut faire de la plongée sous-marine et du surf.

C **Un match de tennis entre Guy et Nadine.** Write a short paragraph describing the tennis match and the players in the illustration below. Tell what the players are wearing, how they play, what the score is, and who wins.

D **Il faut...** Choose three places or situations from the list below. Ask your partner two things that one must do (or must not do) for each place or situation proposed. Then reverse roles.

> à l'école
>
> Élève 1: À l'école, qu'est-ce qu'il faut faire?
> Élève 2: À l'école, il faut étudier et faire attention.

à la plage   au cours de français
après un dîner au restaurant   pour gagner un match
avant un examen   pour organiser une fête
avant un voyage

STRUCTURE

Les verbes *prendre, apprendre* et *comprendre* au présent

Describing People's Activities

1. The verb *prendre*, "to take," is irregular. Study the following forms.

PRENDRE			
je	prends	nous	prenons
tu	prends	vous	prenez
il		ils	
elle	prend	elles	prennent
on			

> **Je prends mes livres quand je quitte la classe.**
> **Vous prenez l'avion pour aller à Boston mais Julie et Marc prennent le train.**

Note that the singular forms of *prendre* are the same as those of any regular *-re* verb, but the plural forms are irregular.

2. The verb *prendre* has a number of additional meanings. Here are a few of them.

a. Used with food or beverages, *prendre* means either "to eat" or "to drink."

> **Au restaurant Marie-Lise prend toujours du poulet.**
> **Quand les enfants ont soif ils prennent de l'eau.**

b. *Prendre le petit déjeuner* means "to eat breakfast." Note, however, that you do not use *prendre* with other meals in French. "To eat lunch" is *déjeuner* and "to eat dinner" is *dîner*.

> **Gérard prend son petit déjeuner à la maison mais il déjeune à la cafétéria.**

c. *Prendre les billets* means "to buy tickets."

> **Je prends mon billet au guichet et j'attends le train.**

3. Two other verbs that are conjugated like *prendre* are *apprendre*, "to learn," and *comprendre*, "to understand." You use the preposition *à* after *apprendre* when it is followed by an infinitive.

> **Ma sœur et mon frère apprennent à jouer au tennis.**
> **Vous comprenez le français, n'est-ce pas?**

Exercices

A   **On prend un bain de soleil.**   Répondez.

1. On prend un bain de soleil à la plage?
2. On prend un bain de soleil quand il y a des nuages?
3. On met de la crème solaire quand on prend un bain de soleil?
4. On bronze quand on prend un bain de soleil?

B   **Moi, en été.**   Donnez des réponses personnelles.

1. En été, tu prends des bains de soleil sur le sable?
2. Tu bronzes ou tu attrapes des coups de soleil?
3. Tu préfères nager dans une piscine, dans la mer ou dans un lac?
4. Tu prends des leçons de surf?
5. Tu apprends à faire de la planche à voile?
6. Tu apprends à faire du ski nautique?
7. Tu comprends le moniteur?

C   **Qu'est-ce que tu prends?**   Posez des questions à un copain ou à une copine d'après le modèle.

> le train
> Élève 1: Tu prends le train?
> Élève 2: Non, je ne prends pas le train. (Oui, je prends le train.)

1. ton billet au guichet à la gare
2. le bus pour aller à l'école
3. l'avion pour aller à New York
4. l'avion pour aller en France

D   **Le petit déjeuner.**   Répondez en utilisant «nous».

1. Vous prenez le petit déjeuner à la maison?
2. Vous prenez le petit déjeuner à quelle heure?
3. Vous prenez le petit déjeuner quand vous êtes en retard?
4. Vous prenez le petit déjeuner dans la cuisine ou dans la salle à manger?
5. Vous prenez du lait au petit déjeuner?

E   **Qu'est-ce qu'ils prennent?**   Changez d'après le modèle.

> **Il prend un coca. (citron pressé)**
> *Il prend un coca et ses copains prennent un citron pressé.*

1. Il prend un crème. (un express)
2. Il prend une salade. (une soupe à l'oignon)
3. Il prend un sandwich au pâté. (un croque-monsieur)
4. Il prend une glace au chocolat. (une glace à la vanille)
5. Il prend de l'eau minérale. (du thé)

F **Au cours de français.** Répondez.

1. Au cours de français, les élèves apprennent beaucoup de mots?
2. Ils apprennent le vocabulaire?
3. Ils apprennent des règles de grammaire?
4. Ils apprennent la civilisation française?
5. Et toi, tu apprends à parler français?
6. Tes copains et toi, vous comprenez bien quand le professeur parle français?

Les pronoms accentués

Emphasizing and Clarifying Whom You Are Talking About

1. Compare the subject pronouns below with the corresponding stress pronouns.

SUBJECT PRONOUNS	STRESS PRONOUNS
je	moi
tu	toi
il	lui
elle	elle
nous	nous
vous	vous
ils	eux
elles	elles

Une belle plage de sable à Antibes

2. You use stress pronouns in several ways in French.

   a. to reinforce or stress the subject

   > Moi, je vais au bord de la mer en été.
   > Lui, il reste à la maison.

   b. after a preposition such as *avec, pour, chez,* etc.

   > David veut jouer avec nous.
   > Les filles rentrent chez elles après la fête.

   c. alone or in a phrase without a verb

   > Qui fait du ski nautique? Moi!
   > Et eux? Est-ce qu'ils prennent des leçons?

   d. before and after *et* or *ou*

   > Marie et moi, nous allons à la plage.
   > Qui va faire les courses ce soir? Lui ou elle?

e. after *c'est* or *ce n'est pas*

> **C'est toi, Yvonne?**
> **Oui, c'est moi.**
> **C'est Jean-Luc?**
> **Non, ce n'est pas lui.**

f. With *-même(s)* to express "myself," "herself," and so forth.

> **Je vais faire les valises moi-même.**
> **Ils font la cuisine eux-mêmes.**

Exercices

A   Moi, toi et les autres.   Complétez.

DAVID: ___, j'adore nager.

CÉLINE: Et ton frère? Il aime nager?

DAVID: ___ ? Il aime faire du ski nautique.

CÉLINE: Et ta sœur, ___, elle aime faire du ski nautique aussi?

DAVID: Non, mais ___, elle aime faire de la planche à voile.

CÉLINE: Sans blague! Ma copine et ___, nous aimons faire de la planche à voile aussi.

DAVID: ___ aussi, j'aime faire de la planche à voile. Mais mes copains, ___, ils n'aiment pas ça.

B   Tu aimes les sports d'été?   Répondez d'après le modèle.

> **Tu aimes nager?**
> *Moi? Oui, j'adore nager.*

1. Tu aimes aller au bord de la mer?
2. Et ton frère, il aime faire du ski nautique?
3. Et tes sœurs, elles aiment faire de la plongée sous-marine?
4. Et vous, vous aimez nager?
5. Et tes copains, ils aiment faire du surf?

C   Une fête.   Complétez.

1. Tu vas donner une fête pour Jean?
   Oui, je vais donner une fête pour ___.
2. Qui va organiser la fête? Toi? Oui, c'est ___.
3. Et qui va faire les courses? Ta mère?
   Pas ___! Moi, je vais aller au marché ___-même!
4. Jean va arriver chez toi avec ses copains?
   Oui, il va arriver chez ___ avec ___.

Les adjectifs avec une double consonne

Describing People and Things

1. Note that certain adjectives double their final consonant in the feminine forms. Study the following.

	FÉMININ	MASCULIN
SINGULIER	une compagnie aérienne une voiture européenne	un vol aérien un café européen
PLURIEL	des compagnies aériennes des voitures européennes	des vols aériens des cafés européens

2. Here are some other adjectives that follow the same pattern.

   canadien(ne)   italien(ne)   parisien(ne)

3. The adjective *bon*, which precedes the noun, also doubles its final consonant. Study these forms.

   C'est une très bonne idée.   Robert est un très bon élève.
   Il a de bonnes notes.   Et il a de bons profs.

4. The adjective *gentil*, "nice," also doubles its final consonant.

   une fille gentille   un garçon gentil

Exercices

A D'après vous.   Répondez.

1. C'est une bonne idée de voyager avec une bonne compagnie aérienne canadienne?
2. C'est une bonne idée de passer une bonne journée sur une belle plage?
3. Est-ce que la compagnie aérienne italienne sert des spécialités italiennes pendant ses vols?
4. Est-ce que les femmes parisiennes font leurs courses dans les beaux magasins parisiens?

B Une compagnie canadienne.   Complétez.

La compagnie ____ (aérien) ____ (canadien) offre des vols vers des
        1   2
destinations ____ (européen). Le service est très ____ (bon). À bord les
             3   4
stewards sont très ____ (gentil) et les hôtesses de l'air aussi sont très ____
                    5   6
(gentil). Il est agréable d'avoir une ____ (bon) place dans un avion ____
                                       7   8
(canadien) et de faire un ____ (bon) voyage ____ (européen).
                          9   10

CONVERSATION

Scènes de la vie   *Une belle journée d'été*

NATHALIE: Il fait terriblement chaud!
FRANÇOISE: C'est vrai, c'est horrible!
NATHALIE: Tu veux aller à la plage?
FRANÇOISE: D'accord. Je vais chercher mon maillot de bain.

NATHALIE: Tu as de la crème solaire?
FRANÇOISE: Oui. Pourquoi? Tu vas prendre un bain de soleil?
NATHALIE: Mais bien sûr!

FRANÇOISE: Pas moi.
NATHALIE: Pas toi? Qu'est-ce que tu vas faire alors?
FRANÇOISE: Je vais nager et faire du ski nautique.

 La plage.   Répondez d'après la conversation.

1. Il fait chaud?
2. Nathalie veut aller à la plage?
3. Qu'est-ce que Françoise va chercher?
4. Qui n'a pas de crème solaire?

5. Qui va prendre un bain de soleil?
6. Elle aime bronzer?
7. Et Françoise, qu'est-ce qu'elle va faire?

Prononciation   *Les sons /y/ et /y/ + voyelle*

The sound /y/ occurs in three positions: final, between two vowel sounds, and in combination with another vowel sound. Repeat the following.

fille	soleil	gentille
maillot	travailler	billet
canadien	aérien	vieux

Now repeat the following sentences.

J'ai un vieux maillot.
On ne travaille pas bien au soleil.
C'est un avion canadien.

un vieux soleil en maillot

Activités de communication

A **Qu'est-ce que vous prenez?** Divide into small groups and choose a leader. The leader will ask the others the following questions, take notes, then report to the class.

1. Qu'est-ce que tu prends quand tu as très soif?
2. Qu'est-ce que tu prends comme boisson au déjeuner?
3. Qu'est-ce que tu prends quand tu as très, très faim?
4. Qu'est-ce que tu prends quand tu es invité(e) au restaurant?

> **À la classe: Dans mon groupe, trois personnes prennent de l'eau quand elles ont très soif. Les deux autres prennent du coca.**

B **Moi, je veux apprendre à...** Ask your partner what he or she would like to learn to do and why. Then reverse roles.

> **Élève 1: Qu'est-ce que tu veux apprendre à faire?**
> **Élève 2: Moi, je veux apprendre à bien parler français.**
> **Élève 1: Pourquoi?**
> **Élève 2: Parce que je voudrais aller en France.**

C **En été.** Tell your partner some things you do in the summer, then find out what your partner likes to do.

> **Élève 1: En été je vais à la plage, je fais du surf et de la planche à voile. Et toi, qu'est-ce que tu aimes faire en été?**
> **Élève 2: Moi, j'aime aller à la plage aussi, mais je ne fais pas de surf. J'aime nager et j'aime faire des voyages avec ma famille.**

LES VACANCES D'ÉTÉ

C'est le premier août. Tout le monde prend la route pour aller au bord de la mer. Les vacances d'été commencent. En France le mois d'août, c'est le mois des vacances. On ne travaille pas. On passe le mois entier au bord de la mer ou à la montagne.

Qu'elles sont belles[1], les plages en France! Il y a des stations balnéaires le long des côtes[2]: sur la Manche au nord, sur l'Océan Atlantique à l'ouest, et sur la Côte d'Azur au sud, au bord de la mer Méditerranée.

Qu'est-ce qu'on fait au bord de la mer? On va à la plage, bien sûr. À la plage on prend des bains de soleil. Tout le monde veut rentrer chez soi[3] bien bronzé. Les

Une belle plage bretonne

gens[4] sportifs nagent ou font de la planche à voile. Moi, je fais du ski nautique. Qu'est-ce que tu fais en été?

Vers deux heures on a faim. Après une belle journée à la plage on a une faim de loup. L'air de la mer donne faim. On fait un pique-nique sur la plage ou on va dans un petit restaurant en plein air[5] où on commande des fruits de mer[6].

[1] Qu'elles sont belles   *How beautiful they are*
[2] le long des côtes   *along the coasts*
[3] chez soi   *home*
[4] les gens   *people*
[5] en plein air   *outdoor*
[6] des fruits de mer   *seafood*

Étude de mots

A **Quel est le mot?** Trouvez une expression équivalente.

1. sportif
2. une faim de loup
3. le mois entier
4. en plein air
5. partout
6. commencer

a. dans toutes les régions
b. tout le mois
c. très faim
d. qui aime les sports
e. à l'extérieur, dehors
f. le contraire de *finir*

B **Des faits.** Complétez les phrases d'après la lecture.

1. Le ___ d'août a trente et un jours.
2. Le mois d'août est le mois des ___ parce que les gens ne travaillent pas.
3. Le long des ___ de la France, il y a de très ___ plages.
4. Les Pyrénées et les Alpes sont des ___.
5. L'Océan Atlantique est à l'___ de la France.

Compréhension

A **Au bord de la mer.** Répondez d'après la lecture.

1. Quelle est la date?
2. Tout le monde prend la route pour aller où?
3. On passe combien de temps au bord de la mer?
4. Il y a des plages partout en France?
5. Qu'est-ce qu'on fait à la plage?
6. Que font les gens sportifs?
7. Tout le monde veut rentrer chez soi comment?
8. Quelle est l'heure du déjeuner?
9. Où est-ce qu'on va manger?
10. Qu'est-ce qu'on commande au bord de la mer?

B **Les vacances.** Trouvez les renseignements suivants dans la lecture.

1. Quel est le mois des vacances, le mois où très peu de gens travaillent?
2. Où est-ce que les Français aiment passer leurs vacances?
3. Les Français passent combien de temps au bord de la mer ou à la montagne?

DÉCOUVERTE CULTURELLE

*L*es Français sont très travailleurs. Mais les vacances sont très importantes pour eux. Le Français typique a à peu près cinq semaines de vacances par an. Le mois favori pour les vacances d'été, c'est le mois d'août. Le premier août il y a des bouchons et des embouteillages[1] partout. Tout le monde est pressé[2] d'arriver au bord de la mer pour commencer les vacances.

Tes parents ont combien de semaines de vacances? Ta famille et toi, où passez-vous les vacances? Quand est-ce que vous y allez? Vous y passez combien de temps?

[1] des bouchons et des embouteillages *traffic jams*
[2] est pressé *is in a hurry*

RÉALITÉS

Voici Yannick Noah **1**. C'est un champion de tennis célèbre. Tu voudrais jouer contre lui?

C'est une colonie de vacances en montagne **2**. Les enfants jouent avec les monitrices. Tout le monde adore l'été. C'est la belle saison.

Voici la plage de Nice, une ville sur la Côte d'Azur **3**. Sur la plage à Nice, il y a du sable ou des galets?

Voici Audierne, un joli port de pêche en Bretagne **4**. Il y a beaucoup de bateaux dans le port?

La jeune femme fait une promenade en vélo en montagne **5**. C'est un vélo tout terrain (VTT).

CULMINATION

Activités de communication orale

A **Une nouvelle amie.** You have just met a French student on the beach in Saint-Tropez. You want to find out more about him or her. Ask the French student (your partner) for the following information. Then reverse roles.

1. if he or she likes the beach
2. what sports he or she likes to play at the beach
3. where he or she has lunch and at what time
4. if he or she would like to have lunch with you tomorrow

B **Tu veux jouer au tennis avec moi?** During your lunch together, your new French friend (your partner) asks you the following questions. Answer, then reverse roles.

1. if you play tennis (or would like to learn to play)
2. if you have a racket
3. if you want to play tennis (or want to learn to play tennis) with him or her tomorrow

C **Une belle journée.** Work with a partner or in small groups and describe a day at the beach. Each person will say one sentence to make a continuing story. Be sure to include the following information.

1. what the weather is like
2. what beach you are going to
3. what time you leave the house
4. how you get to the beach
5. whom you go with
6. what you do there
7. what you eat and drink there
8. what time you leave the beach

Activité de communication écrite

Une carte postale. You are spending two weeks at the beach resort of your choice. Write a postcard to a friend about your vacation. Be sure to include the following information.

1. where you are and what the place is like
2. what the weather is like
3. what your daily activities are
4. a new sport you are learning and what you think of the instructor
5. when you are going to return home

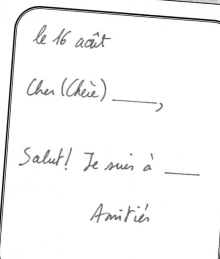

le 16 août

Cher (Chère) _____,

Salut! Je suis à _____

Amitiés

Réintroduction et recombinaison

On prend le train. Complétez.

1. Jacques ___ le train. (prendre)
2. Jacques et ses copains ___ le train. (prendre)
3. Ils ___ au bord de la mer. (aller)
4. Ils ___ le train dans la salle d'attente. (attendre)
5. Jacques ___ au guichet. (aller)
6. Au guichet il ___ les billets pour tous ses copains. (prendre)
7. Les copains ___ l'annonce du départ du train. (entendre)
8. Ils ___ l'annonce. (comprendre)
9. Ils ___ sur le quai. (aller)
10. Ils ___ dans le train. (monter)
11. Ils ___ à la prochaine gare. (descendre)
12. Ils ___ à Deauville à quatorze heures dix-huit. (arriver)

La plage de Deauville en Normandie

Vocabulaire

NOMS
l'été (m.)
la station balnéaire
le bord de la mer
la plage
le sable
la mer
la vague
la crème solaire
les lunettes de soleil (f.)
le maillot (de bain)
la natation
la piscine
la leçon
le moniteur

le tennis
le court de tennis
la balle
le filet
la raquette
le match
le joueur
la partie (en simple, en double)
les limites (f.)
le score
les chaussures de tennis (f.)
le tee-shirt
le short

la jupette

ADJECTIFS
aérien(ne)
bon(ne)
canadien(ne)
européen(ne)
gentil(le)
italien(ne)
parisien(ne)

VERBES
bronzer
frapper
gagner
jouer à
nager
plonger
renvoyer
apprendre (à)
comprendre
prendre

AUTRES MOTS ET EXPRESSIONS
faire de la planche à voile
faire de la plongée sous-marine
faire du ski nautique
faire du surf
faire une promenade
aller à la pêche

attraper un coup de soleil
prendre le petit déjeuner
prendre un bain de soleil
prendre un billet
Il faut + infinitif
entre
fort
hors des limites

pourquoi
parce que

Quel temps fait-il?
Il fait beau.
Il fait chaud.
Il fait du soleil.
Il fait froid.
Il fait mauvais.
Il fait du vent.
Il pleut.
Il y a des nuages.

LES BOUTIQUES ET LES VÊTEMENTS

OBJECTIFS

In this chapter you will learn to do the following:

1. identify and describe articles of clothing
2. state color and size preferences
3. shop for clothing
4. express opinions and make observations
5. describe people and things using certain adjectives
6. compare people and things
7. talk about differences in clothes shopping in France and the U.S.

249

VOCABULAIRE

MOTS 1

LES VÊTEMENTS POUR HOMMES

une veste

une chemise

un pantalon

une cravate

un complet

LES VÊTEMENTS POUR FEMMES

une jupe

un chemisier

un collant

un tailleur

une robe habillée

une robe sport

un blouson

un pull

une chaussette

un jean

une paire de chaussures

Marc porte un sweat-shirt.

LAURENT

la boutique d'un grand couturier

AU GRAND MAGASIN

une cliente

des soldes

un vendeur

une vendeuse

~~250F~~
SOLDES
180F

un client

un rayon prêt-à-porter

Lise voit beaucoup de chemisiers.
Elle voit les chemisiers au rayon prêt-à-porter.
Elle va faire ses achats au rayon prêt-à-porter.

le prix

1000F
plus cher

100F
moins cher

25F
bon marché

240F
cher

Mme Laval paie à la caisse.
Elle dépense* de l'argent.

* dépenser: employer de l'argent pour faire
des achats

Exercices

A **Albert et Christine.** Répondez d'après les dessins.

1. Qu'est-ce qu'Albert va mettre?

2. Qu'est-ce que Christine porte?

B **Qu'est-ce qu'on met?** Répondez.

1. Ce soir M. Ben-Azar va aller dans un restaurant élégant. Qu'est-ce qu'il va porter?
2. Qu'est-ce que sa femme va mettre?
3. Qu'est-ce que tu portes à l'école?
4. Qu'est-ce que tu portes quand il n'y a pas de cours?
5. Qu'est-ce que tu mets quand il fait froid?
6. Qu'est-ce qu'une femme met quand elle va au travail?
7. Qu'est-ce qu'un homme met quand il va au travail?

REVUE DE DÉTAILS

NEWS MODE

REPÉRÉ AUX QUATRE COINS DE LA MODE, TOUT CE QUI NOUS PLAÎT. DE LA TÊTE AUX PIEDS.

STRETCH (1) Robe en panne de velours (Capucine Puerari, 1 360 F, 5 tailles, 8 coloris, rens. 45 49 26 90).
SOIR CHIC (2) Veste croisée, en drap de laine, sur jupe en taffetas de soie (Corinne Sarrut, 1 900 F, 3 tailles, 5 coloris (veste) et 900 F, du 36 au 42, en noir ou bronze (jupe), rens. 42 61 71 60). Gilet en satin (Chacok).
INTÉRIEUR (3) Robe de chambre en soie (Claudie Pierlot, 800 F, 2 tailles, 3 coloris, rens. 42 36 69 93).

COL HIRONDELLE Très 70, des chemises bicolores en coton (Agnès B., 490 F, 3 tailles, 3 coloris, rens. 45 08 56 56).

C **Une boutique ou un grand magasin?** Répondez.

1. On vend beaucoup de marchandises différentes dans la boutique d'un grand couturier ou dans un grand magasin?
2. Il y a beaucoup de rayons dans une boutique ou dans un grand magasin?
3. Qui vend des marchandises dans les boutiques et les grands magasins?
4. Et qui fait des achats?
5. Où est-ce qu'on paie dans les boutiques et les grands magasins?
6. Est-ce que les femmes riches achètent leurs vêtements au rayon prêt-à-porter ou chez les grands couturiers?
7. Est-ce qu'on peut acheter des vêtements sport et habillés dans un grand magasin?
8. Est-ce que les gens riches dépensent beaucoup d'argent pour leurs vêtements?

D **On va acheter des vêtements.** Complétez.

1. Il y a beaucoup de réductions pendant les ___. Les prix sont plus bas, moins élevés.
2. Je préfère faire mes achats quand il y a des ___ parce que je ___ moins d'argent.
3. Le jean est une sorte de ___ sport, pas habillé.
4. Quel est le ___ de ce blouson? 800 francs?
5. Oh là là! Ce blouson n'est pas bon marché! Il est très ___.

VOCABULAIRE

MOTS 2

un cadeau

une manche longue

un chemisier à manches longues

une manche courte

Martine voit des chemisiers.
Elle trouve les chemisiers merveilleux,
vraiment fantastiques!
Elle pense, «Tiens! Je vais acheter un cadeau».

Elle est très contente (heureuse).
Pourquoi? Parce qu'elle voit que les
chemisiers sont en solde.

De quelle couleur est le chemisier?
Il est vert.

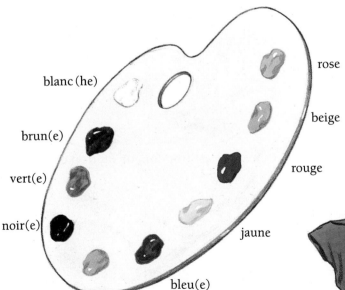

blanc (he)

rose

beige

brun(e)

vert(e)

rouge

noir(e)

jaune

gris(e)

bleu(e)

Note: The colors below are invariable.
They do not change to agree with the
noun they describe.

bleu marine   marron   orange

des chaussures marron

À mon avis cette couleur est plus jolie que l'autre.
Je trouve que cette couleur est plus jolie que l'autre.
Et je crois que Catherine préfère cette couleur aussi.

une robe orange

un pantalon
bleu marine

Exercices

A **Qu'est-ce que Martine voit?** Répondez.

1. Qu'est-ce que Martine veut acheter?
2. Elle aime les chemisiers?
3. Elle trouve que les chemisiers sont merveilleux, vraiment fantastiques?
4. Est-ce que Martine voit que les chemisiers sont en solde?

B **De quelle couleur...?** Donnez des réponses personnelles.

1. De quelle couleur est ton blouson favori?
2. De quelle couleur est ton jean favori?
3. De quelle couleur est ta chemise favorite ou ton chemisier favori?
4. Qu'est-ce que tu portes aujourd'hui? De quelle couleur sont tes vêtements?

C **De petits problèmes.** Répondez d'après les dessins.

1. Ces chaussures sont trop larges ou trop étroites?

2. Cette jupe est trop longue ou trop courte?

3. Cette chemise a des manches longues ou courtes?

4. Ce pantalon est serré ou large?

D **Mes préférences.** Donnez des réponses personnelles.

1. Tu préfères des vêtements sport ou habillés?
2. Tu préfères des chaussures à talons bas ou hauts? Tu fais quelle pointure?
3. Tu préfères une chemise ou un chemisier à manches longues ou courtes?
4. Tu préfères tes vêtements un peu serrés ou larges?
5. Tu préfères un pantalon plus large? Tu voudrais la taille au-dessus?
6. Tu préfères un pantalon plus serré? Tu voudrais la taille au-dessous?
7. Tu préfères faire des achats quand il y a des soldes ou pas?
8. Tu aimes dépenser beaucoup d'argent pour tes vêtements?
9. Tu aimes acheter des cadeaux pour tes copains ou tes copines? Qu'est-ce que tu achètes?

Activités de communication
Mots 1 et 2

A **Qui est-ce?** Describe what someone in the class is wearing. Your partner will guess who it is.

B **Une paire de chaussures.** You are in a shoe store in Montreal. Your partner will play the role of the salesperson.

1. Greet each other.
2. Tell the salesperson what you want.
3. The salesperson asks about the size and color you prefer. Answer.
4. The salesperson shows you a pair of shoes and asks how you like them.
5. The shoes don't fit. Ask for a larger (smaller) size.
6. The salesperson brings the correct size. Find out the price and if they're on sale.

C **Qui porte...?** Suggest three articles of clothing to your partner. He or she will say who wears each item (men, women, or both) and when or where the person wears it. Then reverse roles.

> Élève 1: un blouson
> Élève 2: Les hommes et les femmes portent un blouson quand il fait froid.

D **Les grands couturiers.** You and your classmates have been asked to create the most colorful outfit imaginable for a famous person. The first student will propose one item of clothing in any color. The next student will repeat that item and add another. Everyone will take a turn.

> Élève 1: Pour Tom Cruise, je choisis une chemise rouge...
> Élève 2: Pour Tom Cruise, je choisis une chemise rouge avec une cravate verte...

Les verbes *croire* et *voir* au présent

Expressing Opinions and Making Observations

1. Study the following forms of the irregular verbs *croire*, "to think," "to believe," and *voir*, "to see."

CROIRE	VOIR
je crois	je vois
tu crois	tu vois
il	il
elle } croit	elle } voit
on	on
nous croyons	nous voyons
vous croyez	vous voyez
ils	ils
elles } croient	elles } voient

2. The verbs *croire* and *voir* are often followed by a clause. The clause is introduced by *que*, which is shortened to *qu'* before a vowel or a silent *h*. In French you must use *que* even though its equivalent, "that," is often omitted in English.

   Je crois que c'est une bonne idée.
   Je vois qu'elle aime cette boutique.

Exercices

A Qu'est-ce qu'elle voit?
Qu'est-ce qu'Annick voit dans la vitrine de la boutique?

B **La fête.** Répondez d'après le modèle.

> **Il va faire beau demain soir?**
> *Oui, je crois. Toi, tu ne crois pas?*

1. Il faut porter une robe habillée à la fête?
2. David va inviter Sylvie à la fête?
3. La fête va être amusante?
4. On va servir un gâteau énorme?
5. L'appartement de David est assez grand pour la fête?

C **Tu vois des films?** Donnez des réponses personnelles.

1. Tu vois beaucoup de films?
2. Tu vois des films au cinéma ou à la télé?
3. En général, tu vois des films d'horreur, des films d'aventures ou des films d'amour?
4. Tes parents voient souvent des films?
5. Tu vois tes copains pendant le week-end? Qu'est-ce que tu fais avec eux?

D **Les croyances.** Répondez par «oui».

> **Tes copains et toi, vous croyez que le tennis est un sport merveilleux?**
> **Oui, nous croyons que le tennis est un sport merveilleux.**

1. Vous croyez que Paris est une belle ville?
2. Vos parents croient que vous êtes intelligents?
3. Votre professeur de français croit que vous travaillez bien?
4. Vos amis croient que vous êtes sympathiques?
5. Vous croyez que les jeans sont chic?
6. Vos grands-parents croient que vous êtes adorables?

E **Des opinions différentes!** Complétez avec «croire».

1. Moi, je ___ que la cousine de Sandra est française mais mes copains ___ qu'elle est italienne.
2. Le professeur ___ que l'examen va être facile mais les élèves ___ que l'examen va être difficile.
3. Tu ___ que les chats sont plus intelligents que les chiens mais ton frère ___ que les chiens sont plus intelligents que les chats.
4. Hélène ___ que Paris est près de Nice mais nous ___ que c'est assez loin de Nice.
5. Tu ___ qu'il va pleuvoir mais je ___ qu'il va faire beau.

GALERIES Lafayette

Le Grand Magasin Capitale de la Mode.

D'autres adjectifs irréguliers   *Describing People and Things*

1. In spoken French the feminine forms of the adjective end in a consonant sound. This consonant sound is dropped in the masculine forms. Here are some irregular adjectives that follow this pattern. Note their spelling changes.

FÉMININ PLURIEL	FÉMININ SINGULIER	MASCULIN PLURIEL	MASCULIN SINGULIER
sérieuses	sérieuse	sérieux	sérieux
délicieuses	délicieuse	délicieux	délicieux
heureuses	heureuse	heureux	heureux
merveilleuses	merveilleuse	merveilleux	merveilleux
basses	basse	bas	bas
favorites	favorite	favoris	favori
longues	longue	longs	long
premières	première	premiers	premier
dernières	dernière	derniers	dernier
entières	entière	entiers	entier
chères*	chère	chers	cher

* All forms of *cher* are pronounced the same way.

2. Here are two adjectives whose endings are pronounced in both the feminine and masculine forms. Note that the feminine ending has a softer sound than the masculine one.

sportives	sportive	sportifs	sportif
actives	active	actifs	actif

Exercices

A La prononciation.   Prononcez.

1. active / actif
2. favorite / favori
3. longue / long
4. basse / bas
5. merveilleuse / merveilleux
6. délicieuse / délicieux
7. généreuse / généreux
8. première / premier

B Nathalie et son frère.   Répondez par «oui».

1. Nathalie est sportive?
2. Son frère est sportif?
3. Nathalie est active?
4. Et lui, il est actif?
5. Le rouge est la couleur favorite de Nathalie?
6. La planche à voile est son sport favori?
7. Nathalie est sérieuse?
8. Et son frère est un garçon sérieux?
9. Elle est souvent heureuse?
10. Et lui, il est souvent heureux?

C **La famille Beauchamp.** Complétez.

La famille Beauchamp est très ___ (sportif). Les parents sont très ___ (actif)
                                    1   2
et les deux enfants, Véronique et Nicole, sont ___ (actif) aussi. Aujourd'hui,
                                               3
les deux filles sont très ___ (heureux) parce qu'elles partent pour Biarritz, leur
                          4
station balnéaire ___ (favori), où chaque année la famille passe des vacances
                  5
___ (merveilleux). À Biarritz, les filles et les parents vont pratiquer leurs
 6
sports ___ (favori), la planche à voile et la natation. Après de ___ (long)
       7   8
journées à la plage, tout le monde est content de manger des fruits de mer ___
                                                                           9
(délicieux) à la terrasse d'un restaurant.

Le comparatif des adjectifs   *Comparing People and Things*

1. You use the comparative to compare two or more people or things. The
   following words are used to express comparisons.

(+)	*plus...que*
(−)	*moins...que*
(=)	*aussi...que*

Study the following sentences.

> Cette vendeuse est plus sympathique que
>   l'autre vendeuse.
> Ce blouson est moins cher que la veste.
> Les chaussures américaines sont aussi chères
>   que les chaussures françaises.

2. Note the liaison after *plus* and *moins* when they are
   followed by a vowel.

   > plus intéressant
   > moins élégant

3. If you are comparing people, you use the stress pronouns after *que.*

Il est plus jeune que son ami.	Il est plus jeune que *lui.*
Elle est plus âgée que ses amis.	Elle est plus âgée qu'*eux.*

4. Note that the adjective *bon* has an irregular form in the comparative,
   meilleur.

   > Ils trouvent que le pain français est meilleur que le pain américain.
   > La robe rose est meilleur marché que la robe blanche.

Exercices

A **Plus ou moins que l'autre.** Répondez d'après les dessins. Suivez le modèle.

Le blouson rouge est plus grand que le blouson noir?
Oui, le blouson rouge est plus grand que le blouson noir.

1. Le blouson rouge est plus cher que le blouson noir?
2. Le blouson rouge est moins joli que le blouson noir?

3. La jupe bleue est moins chère que la jupe grise?
4. La jupe grise est plus courte que la jupe bleue?

5. La robe jaune est aussi élégante que la robe verte?
6. La robe jaune est moins habillée que la robe verte?

B **Non, pas plus.** Répondez d'après le modèle.

Cette chemise est plus chère que l'autre?
Non, elle n'est pas plus chère. Mais elle est aussi chère que l'autre.

1. Cette cravate est plus chère que l'autre?
2. Cette robe est plus habillée que l'autre?
3. Ce pull est plus cher que l'autre?
4. Ce chemisier est plus serré que l'autre?
5. Ces chaussures sont plus larges que les autres?
6. Ces manches sont plus courtes que les autres?

C **À mon avis.** Donnez des réponses personnelles.

1. Le cours de français est plus difficile ou plus facile que le cours de maths?
2. Le professeur de français est plus sévère, moins sévère ou aussi sévère que les autres professeurs?
3. Le football américain est plus intéressant ou moins intéressant que le basket-ball?
4. Une Volkswagen est moins chère ou plus chère qu'une Porsche?
5. Le coca est meilleur que le lait ou le lait est meilleur que le coca?
6. Les fruits et les légumes sont meilleurs pour la santé (*health*) que les pâtisseries?

Le superlatif

1. You use the superlative to single out one item from the group and compare it to all the others. You form the superlative in French by using *le, la,* or *les* and *plus* or *moins* with the adjective.

> **Cette robe est *la plus jolie* de la boutique.**
> **Cette robe est *la moins chère* de la boutique.**

2. Note that the superlative is followed by *de* + a noun.

> **Robert est le plus intelligent de la classe.**
> **Carole est la meilleure en maths du lycée.**
> **Les frères Dumas sont les plus amusants de tous les élèves.**

Exercices

A **La plus chère et la plus grande.** Répondez d'après l'indication.

1. Quelle boutique est la plus chère de toute la ville? (cette boutique)
2. Quelle ville est la plus grande de tout le pays? (Paris)
3. Quel magasin est le plus grand du centre commercial? (Monoprix)
4. Quel marché est le moins cher de tous les marchés? (le Village Suisse)
5. Quel couturier est le plus célèbre? (Yves Saint-Laurent)

B **Ma famille.** Donnez des réponses personnelles.

1. Qui est le plus jeune ou la plus jeune de ta famille?
2. Qui est le plus âgé ou la plus âgée de ta famille?
3. Qui est le plus amusant ou la plus amusante de ta famille?
4. Qui est le plus intelligent ou la plus intelligente de ta famille?
5. Qui est le plus beau ou la plus belle de ta famille?
6. Qui est le plus timide ou la plus timide de ta famille?
7. Qui est le plus sportif ou la plus sportive de ta famille?
8. Qui est le plus heureux ou la plus heureuse de ta famille?

CONVERSATION

Scènes de la vie *Un petit cadeau pour Papa*

LA VENDEUSE: Vous désirez, Mademoiselle?
SANDRINE: Je voudrais un petit cadeau pour mon père.
LA VENDEUSE: Pour la Fête des Pères?
SANDRINE: Non, c'est pour son anniversaire.

LA VENDEUSE: Une chemise, peut-être?
SANDRINE: Oui. Pourquoi pas?
LA VENDEUSE: Il fait quelle taille, votre père?
SANDRINE: Il fait du quarante, je crois. Oui, c'est ça, quarante.

LA VENDEUSE: Vous préférez quelle couleur?
SANDRINE: Bleu marine ou blanc. Il aime le look conservateur.
LA VENDEUSE: Bien, Mademoiselle. Et vous avez de la chance. Toutes les chemises sont en solde aujourd'hui.

Un cadeau d'anniversaire. Répondez d'après la conversation.

1. Sandrine est dans un grand magasin?
2. Elle est au rayon chemises ou complets?
3. Elle est au rayon hommes ou femmes?
4. Elle veut acheter un cadeau?
5. C'est pour qui, le cadeau?
6. Qu'est-ce que la vendeuse propose?
7. Le père de Sandrine fait quelle taille?
8. Sandrine préfère quelle couleur?
9. Les chemises sont en solde?
10. La chemise va être plus chère ou moins chère?

Prononciation   *Les sons /sh/ et /zh/*

It is important to make a distinction between the sound /sh/ as in *chat* and /zh/ as in *joli*. Put your fingers on your throat. When you say the sound /zh/ as in *joli* you should feel a vibration, but not when you say /sh/ as in *chat*. Repeat the following words with the sounds /sh/ and /zh/.

a*ch*eter	lar*ge*
*ch*aussure	*j*upe
*ch*emise	oran*ge*
a*ch*ats	bei*ge*
*sh*ort	*j*eune

*chemise oran*ge

Now repeat the following sentences that combine both sounds.

J'achète toujours des chaussures bon marché.
Je cherche un joli tee-shirt jaune et un short orange.

Activités de communication

A   **Une boutique chic.**   You are in a boutique on the chic Rue du Faubourg Saint-Honoré in Paris. A classmate will play the role of the salesperson.

1. Greet each other.
2. The salesperson asks if he or she can help you. Say what you would like with as much detail as possible.
3. The salesperson asks your size.
4. The salesperson shows you the item of clothing and asks if you like it.
5. Ask the price and tell the salesperson whether or not you want to buy the item.

B   **Comparaisons.**   Work in small groups. Using the adjectives below on the right, think of as many comparisons as possible for each pair on the left. Report to the class.

les chiens et les chats
Les chiens sonts plus intelligents que les chats (moins calmes, aussi beaux, etc.).

l'anglais et les maths	âgé	intelligent
ton père et ta mère	meilleur	sympathique
les avions et les trains	difficile	patient
une Rolls-Royce et une Toyota	rapide	actif
ton école et une autre école	cher	sportif
les filles et les garçons	heureux	facile

LECTURE ET CULTURE

LES ACHATS

Si la France est un pays de gastronomie, c'est aussi un pays de haute couture. Les noms des grands couturiers sont célèbres dans le monde entier—Yves Saint-Laurent, Dior, Courrèges, Cardin, Givenchy, Lacroix. Ces couturiers dictent la mode non seulement à Paris, mais à Tokyo, New York et Rio. À Paris on vend les vêtements et accessoires de ces couturiers dans des boutiques Place Vendôme, rue du Faubourg Saint-Honoré ou rue François Ier.

Mais attention[1]! La plupart des Français ne font pas leurs achats chez les grands couturiers. Il y a des grands magasins de toutes les catégories, des plus luxueuses aux plus modestes—les Galeries Lafayette, la Samaritaine, Monoprix, Prisunic, etc. Dans les grands magasins on peut aller d'un rayon à l'autre et acheter toutes sortes de choses dans le même magasin. Beaucoup de gens profitent des soldes quand on vend les marchandises avec d'importantes réductions.

À Paris les jeunes—garçons et filles—achètent leurs vêtements dans les mêmes boutiques unisexe du Quartier Latin. Dans ces boutiques on trouve du prêt-à-porter original et à la mode[2]. Mais si on a très peu d'argent à dépenser on peut aller aux Puces[3] ou au Village Suisse. Nicole adore aller aux Puces ou au Village Suisse où elle trouve presque[4] toujours un chemisier ou un accessoire avec la griffe[5] célèbre d'un grand couturier—et à un prix très bas.

[1] Attention! *Careful! Watch out!*
[2] à la mode *in style*
[3] aux Puces *to the flea market*
[4] presque *almost*
[5] la griffe *label*

Étude de mots

 Cherchez les mots. Choisissez la définition.

1. le créateur de modèles
2. fameux
3. en vogue, populaire
4. fantastique
5. les produits commerciaux
6. profiter
7. presque toujours

a. à la mode
b. le couturier
c. célèbre
d. les marchandises
e. fréquemment
f. bénéficier
g. merveilleux

Compréhension

A **Boutiques et magasins.** Complétez.

1. La France est un pays de gastronomie et de ___.
2. Deux ___ célèbres sont Pierre Cardin et Yves Saint-Laurent.
3. Les vêtements faits par un couturier portent la ___ du couturier.
4. Les Galeries Lafayette et La Samaritaine sont des ___, pas des boutiques.
5. Les clients dans un grand magasin peuvent aller d'un ___ à l'autre et ils peuvent acheter toutes sortes de choses dans le même magasin.
6. Pendant les ___ il y a d'importantes réductions.
7. Une boutique ___ vend des vêtements pour garçons et filles.

B **Le shopping.** Répondez.

1. On vend les vêtements et les accessoires des grands couturiers au Prisunic?
2. Il y a beaucoup de différents grands magasins en France?
3. Tous les grands magasins sont plus ou moins de la même catégorie?
4. Pendant les soldes, tout est plus cher ou meilleur marché?
5. Qu'est-ce qu'une boutique unisexe?
6. Qui aime les boutiques unisexe?
7. Les marchandises sont chères aux Puces?

C **Les achats.** Trouvez les renseignements suivants dans la lecture.

1. trois couturiers français
2. deux grands magasins français
3. deux marchés parisiens qui ont des prix très bas

DÉCOUVERTE CULTURELLE

En France et en Europe en général les pointures et les tailles ne sont pas les mêmes qu'aux États-Unis. Voici les tailles des vêtements et les pointures des chaussures.

Si vous voulez acheter des chaussures en France, vous demandez quelle pointure? Si vous voulez acheter une chemise ou un chemisier, vous demandez quelle taille?

FEMMES				
CHAUSSURES				
États-Unis	5½–6	6½–7	7½–8	8½–9
France	37–38	38–39	39–40	40–41
ROBES, TAILLEURS, PULLS, CHEMISIERS				
États-Unis	32	34	36	38	40
France	38	40	42	44	46

HOMMES				
CHEMISES				
États-Unis	14½	15	15½	16	16½
France	37	38	39	40	41
CHAUSSURES				
États-Unis	6½–7	7½–8	8½–9	9½–10
France	40–41	41–42	42–43	43–44

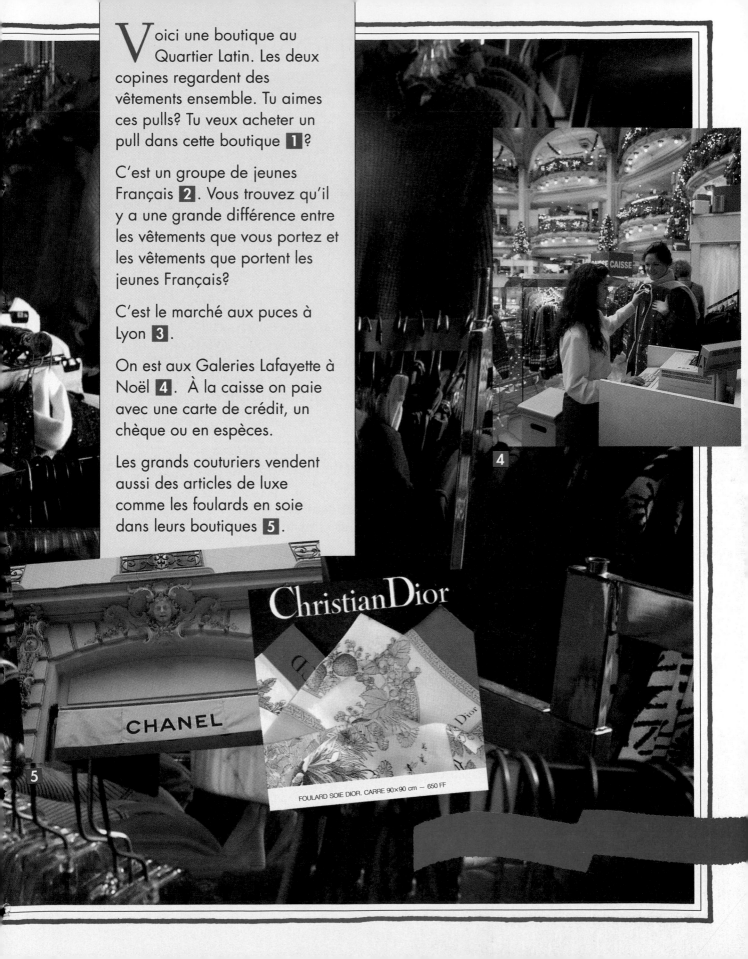

Voici une boutique au Quartier Latin. Les deux copines regardent des vêtements ensemble. Tu aimes ces pulls? Tu veux acheter un pull dans cette boutique **1**?

C'est un groupe de jeunes Français **2**. Vous trouvez qu'il y a une grande différence entre les vêtements que vous portez et les vêtements que portent les jeunes Français?

C'est le marché aux puces à Lyon **3**.

On est aux Galeries Lafayette à Noël **4**. À la caisse on paie avec une carte de crédit, un chèque ou en espèces.

Les grands couturiers vendent aussi des articles de luxe comme les foulards en soie dans leurs boutiques **5**.

ChristianDior

CHANEL

FOULARD SOIE DIOR. CARRE 90×90 cm — 650 FF

CULMINATION

Activités de communication orale

A **Un sondage: le shopping.** Divide into groups and choose a leader. The leader will ask the others in the group the following questions about their shopping habits, take notes, and report to the class.

1. Quel est ton magasin favori? Pourquoi?
2. Tu préfères les grands magasins ou les boutiques?
3. Quand tu achètes des vêtements, tu préfères y aller seul(e) ou avec un(e) ami(e)?

B **Jeu de mémoire.** Study the clothing of all the students in one row for several minutes. One student will turn his or her back to the class and answer classmates' questions about what the people in the row are wearing. (*Qui porte un tee-shirt rouge? un jean noir? etc.*) If the student can't answer, the people in the row may help out by giving hints such as *La personne est blonde* or *Elle est assise derrière Suzanne.*

C **Les élèves.** Find out your partner's opinions of the students in your school. Ask him or her who is the nicest, the funniest, the most intelligent, the best-looking, and the most popular. Then reverse roles.

> Élève 1: À ton avis, qui est le (la) plus sympathique de l'école?
> Élève 2: À mon avis, Robert Mercier est le plus sympathique de l'école.

Activités de communication écrite

A **Le catalogue.** Write five descriptions for a clothing catalogue. Describe the items using the vocabulary in this chapter. Tell what sizes the items come in, what colors, what occasions they could be worn for, and the prices.

> Voici une belle robe longue, très habillée, rouge et noire, parfaite pour les fêtes. Tailles: 36 à 42. Prix: 1.200F

B **Le look de ton école.** Write a note to your French friend describing *le look* at your school. Tell what boys and girls usually wear to school and what types of clothing and colors are "in" (*à la mode*).

Réintroduction et recombinaison

A Des préférences. Complétez.

1. ___, je préfère un look sportif.
2. Mais ___, il préfère un look conservateur.
3. Les autres, ___, ils font toujours leurs achats dans les boutiques chères.
4. Et ___? Où est-ce que tu fais tes achats?

B En été. Donnez des réponses personnelles.

1. Quand est-ce que tu mets un maillot?
2. Qu'est-ce que tu portes quand il fait chaud?
3. Tu vas dans quelle sorte de magasin pour acheter un maillot?
4. Tu voudrais un maillot de quelle couleur?
5. Est-ce qu'on met des lunettes de soleil quand il pleut?
6. Qu'est-ce qu'une femme porte quand elle joue au tennis?

Vocabulaire

NOMS

les vêtements (m.)
le blouson
la chaussette
la chaussure
la paire
le talon
le jean
le pantalon
le pull
le sweat-shirt
le chemisier
la manche
le collant
la jupe
la robe
le tailleur
la chemise
le complet
la cravate
la veste
le cadeau
la couleur
la taille
   au-dessus
   en dessous

la pointure
le grand magasin
la boutique
le rayon (prêt-à-porter)
le client
la cliente
le vendeur
la vendeuse
le prix
les soldes (f.)
le grand couturier

ADJECTIFS

bon marché
cher, chère
bas(se)
haut(e)
long(ue)
court(e)
étroit(e)
serré(e)
large
habillé(e)
sport
sportif, sportive
actif, active
favori(te)

heureux, heureuse
merveilleux,
   merveilleuse
sérieux, sérieuse
délicieux, délicieuse
dernier, dernière
entier, entière
meilleur(e)
beige
bleu(e)
bleu marine
blanc, blanche
brun(e)
gris(e)
jaune
marron
noir(e)
orange
rose
rouge
vert(e)

VERBES

croire
dépenser
penser
porter
voir

AUTRES MOTS ET EXPRESSIONS

à mon avis
beaucoup de
faire des achats
trop
vraiment

{ 11 }

LA ROUTINE ET LA FORME PHYSIQUE

OBJECTIFS

In this chapter you will learn to do the following:

1. describe your personal grooming habits and your daily routine
2. find out and tell someone's name
3. tell some things people do to stay fit
4. tell what people do for themselves and others
5. ask "who" and "whom"
6. talk about what people do to stay fit in France and the U.S.

VOCABULAIRE

MOTS 1

LA ROUTINE

les cheveux (m.)

la figure

les dents (f.)

la main

se réveiller

se lever

se laver

se laver
les cheveux

se brosser les dents

se raser

se peigner

se maquiller

s'habiller

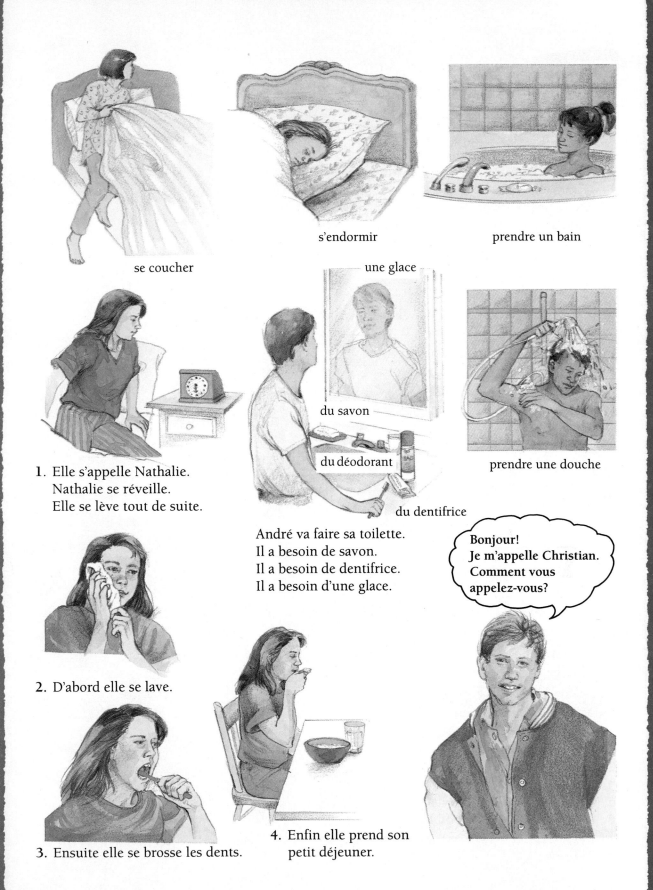

se coucher

s'endormir

prendre un bain

une glace

du savon

du déodorant

du dentifrice

prendre une douche

1. Elle s'appelle Nathalie.
   Nathalie se réveille.
   Elle se lève tout de suite.

André va faire sa toilette.
Il a besoin de savon.
Il a besoin de dentifrice.
Il a besoin d'une glace.

Bonjour!
Je m'appelle Christian.
Comment vous
appelez-vous?

2. D'abord elle se lave.

3. Ensuite elle se brosse les dents.

4. Enfin elle prend son
   petit déjeuner.

Exercices

A **La routine de Nathalie.**   Répondez.

1. Le matin Nathalie se réveille à six heures et demie?
2. Elle se lève tout de suite?
3. D'abord elle va dans la salle de bains pour faire sa toilette?
4. Ensuite elle se lave les mains et la figure avec du savon?
5. Elle se brosse les dents avec du dentifrice et une brosse à dents?
6. À ton avis, elle prend une douche ou un bain?
7. À ton avis, elle se maquille? Elle se peigne? Elle se regarde dans la glace? Elle s'habille?
8. Elle prend son petit déjeuner?

B **La routine de Gérard.**   Répondez d'après les dessins.

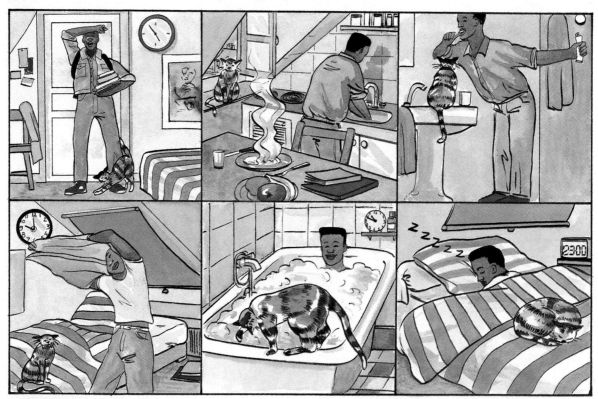

1. Gérard rentre chez lui vers cinq heures?
2. Il se lave les mains avant le dîner?
3. Il dîne dans la cuisine ou dans la salle à manger?
4. Il se brosse les dents après le dîner?
5. À dix heures il se déshabille?
6. Il prend un bain le soir ou le matin?
7. Quand il se couche, il s'endort tout de suite?

C Dans quelle pièce? Complétez.

1. On se brosse les dents dans ___.
2. On s'endort dans ___.
3. On prend une douche dans ___.
4. On se regarde dans la glace dans ___.
5. On se couche dans ___.
6. On prend son petit déjeuner dans ___.
7. La douche est dans ___.
8. Le lit est dans ___.

D Il a besoin de... Choisissez la bonne réponse.

1. Il va se brosser les dents. Il a besoin de ___.
   a. crème   b. dentifrice

2. Il va prendre une douche. Il a besoin de ___.
   a. savon   b. dentifrice

3. Il va se raser. Il a besoin d'un ___.
   a. peigne   b. rasoir

4. Il veut se peigner. Il a besoin d'un ___.
   a. peigne   b. rasoir

5. Il veut se laver les cheveux. Il a besoin de ___.
   a. déodorant   b. shampooing

6 F 90 Bain crème, parfums au choix, 1 litre

20 F 00 Lot de 3 brosses à dents GIBBS Intégral

35 F 00 1 brosse + 1 froufrou + 1 peigne + 1 miroir, coloris divers

4 F 90 Gel douche, parfums au choix, 300 ml (le litre : 16,34 F)

VOCABULAIRE

MOTS 2

LA FORME PHYSIQUE

grossir

maigrir

un gymnase

faire de la
gymnastique

un club de forme

faire de l'exercice

faire de l'aérobic

pratiquer un sport

mettre un
survêtement

Robert veut se mettre en forme.
Pour se mettre en forme il se
  promène.
Il se promène dans le parc.

Robert veut rester en forme.
C'est toujours le problème.
Pour rester en forme il fait de
  l'exercice.

Il fait du jogging.

Les copains s'amusent.
Ils s'amusent bien.

Exercices

A **Pour rester en forme.** C'est bon ou mauvais pour la santé (*health*)?

> **manger beaucoup de chocolat**
> *Manger beaucoup de chocolat, c'est mauvais pour la santé.*

1. bien manger
2. manger beaucoup de pâtisseries
3. prendre du lait
4. prendre du coca au petit déjeuner
5. ne pas faire d'exercice
6. faire de l'aérobic
7. prendre des vitamines
8. fumer
9. pratiquer un sport
10. grossir
11. se promener tous les jours
12. se mettre en forme

B **En forme.** Donnez des réponses personnelles.

1. Tu aimes être en forme?
2. Tu fais de l'exercice pour rester en forme?
3. Tu fais du jogging? Tu mets un survêtement?
4. Tu pratiques un sport?
5. Tu pratiques quel sport?
6. Tu es membre d'un club de forme?
7. Tu fais de la gymnastique à l'école ou au gymnase?
8. Tu grossis quand tu manges beaucoup?
9. Rester en forme, c'est un problème pour toi?

C **Quel est le mot?** Choisissez.

1. Il prend des kilos. Il ___.
   a. grossit   b. maigrit
2. Il perd des kilos. Il ___.
   a. grossit   b. maigrit
3. Il va faire du jogging. Il met ___.
   a. une chemise   b. un survêtement
4. Il va faire du jogging. Il met ___.
   a. un complet   b. des tennis
5. Il va au parc. Il va ___.
   a. se promener   b. se raser
6. Il va ___ avec ses copains dans le parc.
   a. s'amuser   b. se réveiller

Activités de communication

Mots 1 et 2

A **La routine.** Tell your French Canadian friend (your partner) about a member of your family. Give the following information. Then reverse roles.

1. his or her name
2. what time he or she gets up
3. some of his or her grooming habits
4. what he or she does to stay in shape
5. what sports he or she participates in

B **Les sportifs.** Work with a partner. Ask him or her the following questions, then reverse roles.

1. Qu'est-ce que tu fais pour rester en forme?
2. Où...?
3. Avec qui...?
4. Quand...?

C **Qu'est-ce que je veux faire? Devine!** Tell your partner an item that you need. Your partner will guess what you want to do, choosing from the list below.

Élève 1: J'ai besoin d'une raquette.
Élève 2: Tu veux jouer au tennis.

aller à la plage	faire un voyage
dîner dans un restaurant élégant	jouer au tennis
faire du jogging	manger
faire les courses	prendre un bain de soleil
faire les devoirs de...	préparer le dîner

D **Madame Nette.** Madame Nette is a very organized woman whose daily routine is always the same. You and your classmates will take turns describing Madame Nette's day from morning to night. The first student will suggest her first activity of the day. The next student will repeat that activity and add another.

Élève 1: Madame Nette se réveille à six heures.
Élève 2: Madame Nette se réveille à six heures.
   Elle se lève tout de suite.

Les verbes réfléchis

Telling What People Do for Themselves

1. Compare the following pairs of sentences.

Chantal lave le bébé.

Chantal se lave.

Chantal regarde le bébé.

Chantal se regarde.

Chantal couche le bébé.

Chantal se couche.

In the sentences on the left Chantal performs the action and the baby receives it. In the sentences on the right Chantal herself is the receiver of the action. In these sentences Chantal both performs and receives the action of the verb. For this reason the pronoun *se* must be used. *Se* refers to Chantal and is called a reflexive pronoun. It indicates that the action of the verb is reflected back to the subject.

2. Each subject pronoun has its corresponding reflexive pronoun. Study the following.

SE LAVER	S'HABILLER
je me lave	je m' habille
tu te laves	tu t' habilles
il se lave	il s' habille
elle se lave	elle s' habille
on se lave	on s' habille
nous nous lavons	nous nous habillons
vous vous lavez	vous vous habillez
ils se lavent	ils s' habillent
elles se lavent	elles s' habillent

Note that *me, te,* and *se* become *m', t',* and *s'* before a vowel or silent *h*.

3. In the negative form of a reflexive verb, *ne* is placed before the reflexive pronoun. *Pas* follows the verb.

Je me réveille mais je *ne* me lève *pas* tout de suite.
On *ne* se brosse *pas* les dents avant le dîner.
Je me couche mais je *ne* m'endors *pas* tout de suite.
Nous *ne* nous rasons *pas* tous les jours.

Exercices

A **La routine de Charles.** Répétez la conversation.

ROGER: Tu te lèves à quelle heure, Charles?
CHARLES: À quelle heure est-ce que je me lève ou je me réveille?
ROGER: Tu te lèves.
CHARLES: Je me lève à six heures et demie.
ROGER: Et tu quittes la maison à quelle heure?
CHARLES: À sept heures. Je me lave, je me brosse les dents, je me rase et je prends mon petit déjeuner en une demi-heure.
ROGER: Et tu t'habilles aussi?
CHARLES: Bien sûr que je m'habille!

Répondez d'après la conversation.

1. Charles se lève à quelle heure?
2. Il se lave?
3. Il se brosse les dents dans la salle de bains?
4. Il se rase?
5. Il quitte la maison à quelle heure?

B **Jacqueline et Véronique.** Changez *Jacqueline* en *Jacqueline et Véronique.*

1. Jacqueline se réveille à sept heures.
2. Jacqueline se lève tout de suite.
3. Jacqueline se brosse les dents.
4. Jacqueline se lave les mains et la figure.
5. Jacqueline se brosse les cheveux.
6. Jacqueline se maquille.

C **Je fais ma toilette.** Donnez des réponses personnelles.

1. Tu te lèves à quelle heure?
2. Tu vas dans la salle de bains?
3. Tu fais ta toilette?
4. Tu te laves les mains et la figure?
5. Tu prends une douche ou un bain?
6. Tu te laves les cheveux avec du shampooing?
7. Tu te brosses les dents?
8. Tu te peignes?
9. Tu t'habilles vite (rapidement)?

D **Marc répond.** Complétez.

1. Marc, tu ___? (se raser)
2. Oui, je ___. (se raser)
3. Tu ___ tous les jours? (se raser)
4. Oui, malheureusement il faut ___ tous les jours. (se raser)
5. Tu ___ les cheveux ou tu ___? (se brosser, se peigner)
6. Moi, je ___. Je ne ___ pas les cheveux. (se peigner, se brosser)
7. Tu ___ avant ou après le petit déjeuner? (s'habiller)
8. Je ___ avant le petit déjeuner. (s'habiller)

Verbes avec changements d'orthographe

Verbs with Spelling Changes

1. The verbs *se promener* and *se lever*, like *acheter,* take an *accent grave* in all forms except the infinitive, *nous,* and *vous.*

SE PROMENER	
je me promène	nous nous promenons
tu te promènes	vous vous promenez
il/elle/on se promène	ils/elles se promènent

SE LEVER	
je me lève	nous nous levons
tu te lèves	vous vous levez
il/elle/on se lève	ils/elles se lèvent

2. The verb *s'appeler* doubles the *l* in all forms except the infinitive, *nous*, and *vous*.

S'APPELER	
je m'appelle	nous nous appelons
tu t'appelles	vous vous appelez
il/elle/on s'appelle	ils/elles s'appellent

3. Verbs that end in *-ger* such as *manger*, *nager*, and *voyager* add an *e* in the *nous* form in order to maintain the soft consonant sound.

    nous mangeons   **nous nageons**   **nous voyageons**

4. Verbs that end in *-cer*, such as *commencer*, take a cedilla on the *c* in the *nous* form in order to maintain the soft consonant sound.

    nous commençons

Exercices

A **Moi et toi.**   Mettez au pluriel.

> **Je me lève à sept heures et tu te lèves à neuf heures.**
> *Nous nous levons à sept heures et vous vous levez à neuf heures.*

1. Je me lève à 8 heures.
2. Je vais au magasin où j'achète un short.
3. Je me promène dans le parc.
4. Ensuite je nage dans la piscine.
5. Je commence à avoir faim.
6. Je rentre chez moi et je mange une pomme.
7. Et toi, tu te lèves à quelle heure?
8. Qu'est-ce que tu achètes au magasin?
9. Tu te promènes dans le parc aussi?
10. Ensuite tu nages dans la piscine?

B **Je m'appelle...**   Complétez avec «s'appeler».

1. Bonjour, je ___ ...
2. Mon frère ___ ...
3. Et ma sœur ___ ...
4. Mon père ___ ...
5. Ma mère ___ ...
6. Mes meilleurs amis ___ ...
7. Et comment _____-vous?
8. Nous ___ Dupont.

Le pronom interrogatif *qui*   *Asking "Who" or "Whom"*

1. You have been using the pronoun *qui* to form a question.

> **Qui est là?**
> **Qui parle?**
> **Qui se lève?**

2. You can also use *qui* as the object of the verb or as the object of a preposition. In this case *qui* means "whom."

> **Tu vois qui?**
> **Vous invitez qui?**
>
> **Vous parlez à qui?**
> **Vous allez au cinéma avec qui?**

3. Note that in the above questions *qui* is at the end of the sentence. In informal French, people put the question word at the end of the sentence and raise the tone of their voice. However, in formal or written French, the pronoun *qui* is placed at the beginning of the question and the subject and verb are inverted. Observe the following differences.

INFORMAL	FORMAL / WRITTEN
Tu vois qui?	**Qui vois-tu?**
Vous invitez qui?	**Qui invitez-vous?**
Vous parlez à qui?	**À qui parlez-vous?**
Vous allez au cinéma avec qui?	**Avec qui allez-vous au cinéma?**

Exercices

A **Pardon? Qui ça?** Posez des questions d'après le modèle.

> **Marie parle.**
> *Pardon? Qui parle?*

1. Son frère arrive.
2. Sa mère va à la porte.
3. Sa mère est très contente.
4. Le frère de Marie s'appelle David.
5. David a un cadeau.

B **Qui?** Posez des questions d'après le modèle.

> **Je regarde Suzanne.**
> *Tu regardes qui?*

1. Je téléphone à Robert.
2. Je parle à Robert.
3. J'invite Alice.
4. Je vois mon ami.
5. Je danse avec Isabelle.

C **Parlons bien.** Récrivez les questions d'après le modèle.

> **Vous ressemblez à qui?**
> *À qui ressemblez-vous?*

1. Vous téléphonez à qui?
2. Vous parlez à qui?
3. Vous invitez qui à la fête?
4. Vous achetez un cadeau pour qui?
5. Vous allez au restaurant avec qui?
6. Vous êtes derrière qui dans la queue?

CONVERSATION

Scènes de la vie   *Qui est en forme?*

ANDRÉ: Tu te lèves à quelle heure, Richard?
RICHARD: Moi, je me lève à sept heures. Mais je me réveille à six heures et demie.

ANDRÉ: Ah, tu aimes rester un peu au lit.
RICHARD: Oui, mais je peux faire ma toilette, m'habiller et être prêt à quitter la maison en cinq minutes.

ANDRÉ: Tu vas faire du jogging cet après-midi?
RICHARD: Bien sûr. Il faut rester en forme.
ANDRÉ: Rester en forme? Il faut d'abord se mettre en forme!

 La forme.   Répondez d'après la conversation.

1. André parle à qui?
2. Richard se réveille à quelle heure?
3. Mais il reste au lit jusqu'à quelle heure?
4. Il aime rester au lit?
5. Qu'est-ce qu'il peut vite faire?
6. Richard va faire du jogging cet après-midi?
7. Qui veut rester en forme?
8. Qui veut se mettre en forme?
9. Alors, qui est en meilleure forme en ce moment?

Prononciation   *Les sons /s/ et /z/*

It is important to make a distinction between the sounds /s/ and /z/. You would not want to confuse *poisson* with *poison*! Repeat the following words with the sound /s/ as in *assez* and /z/ as in *raser*.

assez	dessert	cassette	boisson	classe
raser	désert	magasin	prise	valise

Now repeat the following sentences. Pay attention to which sounds occur.

Ils s'appellent Dumas.	Ils appellent leur chien.
Elles s'habillent vite.	Elles habillent les bébés.
Ils sont sympathiques.	Ils ont faim.

poisson / poison

Activités de communication

A   L'horaire du matin.   Find out the following information from your partner about his or her morning routine. Then reverse roles.

1. when your partner wakes up
2. if he or she gets up right away
3. what your partner does next
4. if your partner has breakfast
5. what time he or she leaves home

B   L'horaire du soir.   Now find out the following information about your partner's evening routine. Then reverse roles.

1. what time your partner returns home
2. when he or she does homework
3. when he or she has dinner
4. when your partner goes to bed
5. if he or she falls asleep right away

C   La révolte du samedi et du dimanche.   Nobody wants to do the same things on the weekend that he or she does during the week. Working in small groups, make a list of weekend activities that are different from your weekday ones. Report to the class.

Le samedi et le dimanche, nous ne nous levons pas à sept heures.
Nous ne prenons pas notre petit déjeuner à huit heures.
Nous nous promenons dans le parc...

LA FORME PHYSIQUE

Dans beaucoup de pays, la forme physique et la santé sont en ce moment une obsession. La forme physique et la santé intéressent bien sûr les Français mais peut-être pas au même point ou degré qu'aux États-Unis.

Que font les Français pour rester en forme? Les Français estiment qu'il faut faire de l'exercice. On voit des gens qui font du jogging dans les parcs et le long des fleuves[1]. Il y a maintenant de plus en plus de clubs de forme avec tout l'équipement nécessaire pour se mettre en forme. Il y a des classes pour faire de l'aérobic et pour les jeunes il y a des soirées aérobic. Dans les villes, il y a de plus en plus de piscines couvertes[2] pour faire de la natation toute l'année. Le cyclisme est très populaire en France. Le cyclisme est sans aucun doute[3] une excellente forme d'exercice. Le Tour de France est une course[4] cycliste internationale qui a lieu[5] en juillet. Et le tennis? Le tennis est un autre sport qui a de plus en plus de «disciples» en France. On parle toujours des marathons qui ont lieu dans les grandes villes des États-Unis. Il y a aussi un très grand marathon à Paris au mois d'octobre. Beaucoup de coureurs[6] participent au marathon de Paris.

[1] fleuves *rivers*
[2] piscines couvertes *indoor pools*
[3] sans aucun doute *without a doubt*
[4] course *race*
[5] a lieu *takes place*
[6] coureurs *runners*

Étude de mots

A **Le français, c'est facile.** Trouvez quatre mots apparentés dans la lecture.

B **Les noms et les verbes.** Trouvez le verbe qui correspond au nom.

1. l'équipement
2. une obsession
3. la participation
4. l'intérêt
5. le coureur, la course

a. intéresser
b. participer
c. obséder
d. équiper
e. courir

Compréhension

A **Oui ou non?** Corrigez les phrases fausses.

1. La forme physique intéresse beaucoup plus les Français que les Américains.
2. Les Français ne font pas d'exercice.
3. Il y a des clubs de forme en France.
4. L'aérobic n'est pas du tout populaire en France.
5. Le cyclisme n'est pas populaire chez les Français.
6. Le Tour de France est une course cycliste internationale qui a lieu en France.
7. Le marathon de Paris est une autre course cycliste.
8. Très peu de gens font du tennis en France.

B **La forme physique en France.** Répondez.

1. Qu'est-ce que les Français font pour rester en forme?
2. Qu'est-ce qu'il y a dans les clubs de forme?
3. Où peut-on nager toute l'année?
4. Quel sport a de plus en plus de «disciples»?
5. Il y a un grand marathon dans quelle ville?
6. Le marathon de Paris a lieu quand?
7. Le Tour de France a lieu quand?

C **L'essentiel.** Quelle est l'idée principale de cette lecture?

DÉCOUVERTE CULTURELLE

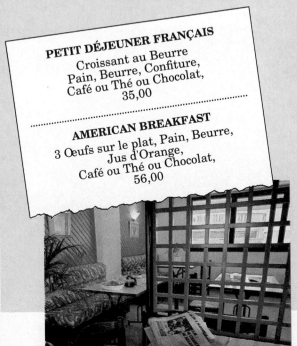

PETIT DÉJEUNER FRANÇAIS
Croissant au Beurre
Pain, Beurre, Confiture,
Café ou Thé ou Chocolat,
35,00

AMERICAN BREAKFAST
3 Œufs sur le plat, Pain, Beurre,
Jus d'Orange,
Café ou Thé ou Chocolat,
56,00

*A*vant de quitter la maison, André prend son petit déjeuner. Mais qu'est-ce qu'un petit déjeuner typiquement français? C'est du pain, des croissants ou des brioches avec une tasse de café au lait pour les adultes et une tasse de chocolat chaud pour les enfants. Mais des œufs, du bacon, des pommes de terre, absolument pas! Même les céréales ne sont pas très populaires chez les Français.

Comparez les deux petits déjeuners sur la carte d'un café parisien. Qui prend des œufs sur le plat, les Français ou les Américains? Qui prend des croissants?

RÉALITÉS

Cette nageuse française nage la brasse papillon **1**. Elle porte un bonnet de bain et des lunettes. À ton avis, c'est une nageuse sérieuse?

Voici des cyclistes dans le Tour de France **2**. Ils traversent tout le pays—la campagne et les villes.

Voici un groupe de jeunes gens **3**. Ils s'amusent bien. Ils font de l'aérobic.

Ces deux hommes sont au gymnase **4**. Ils jouent au racquetball. Le racquetball ressemble à quels autres sports? Est-ce que le racquetball est un sport populaire aux États-Unis?

Voici des coureurs dans le marathon de Paris **5**. Il y a beaucoup de jeunes filles et de femmes qui participent au marathon de Paris?

4

5

CULMINATION

Activités de communication orale

A **Qui est devant qui?** One student will turn his or her back to the class and answer questions from the others about where students are seated. Use the words below in your questions.

à côté de   à gauche de   derrière   à droite de   devant

Élève 1: **Isabelle est devant qui?**
Élève 2: **Elle est devant Paul.**

B **Une interview.** An exchange student from France (your partner) has arrived at your school. You are interviewing him or her for the school newspaper. Ask the student for the following information.

1. what his or her name is
2. where he or she is from
3. what he or she does with classmates after school
4. what his or her friends' names are
5. what clothes he or she likes to wear
6. what he or she does to stay in shape
7. what he or she likes to eat

Activités de communication écrite

A **Qu'est-ce qu'un petit déjeuner typiquement français?** You are living with a French family for the summer. Write a note to one of your friends describing a typical French breakfast. Tell him or her if you like it or not.

En France au petit déjeuner, on prend...

B **Monsieur Dodu veut se mettre en forme.**
Monsieur Dodu would like to lose some weight and get in shape. As his personal trainer, write out a daily routine for him. Indicate when he gets up, when he exercises, and what type of exercise he does. Also plan his meals and indicate what time the meals are.

La routine de M. Dodu
6h	Il se réveille et il se lève tout de suite.
6h15 à 7h	Il fait de l'exercice avec moi.
7h à 7h05	Il prend une douche froide.

Réintroduction et recombinaison

A **À votre tour.** Répondez.

1. Quand tu t'habilles le matin, qu'est-ce que tu mets?
2. Qu'est-ce que tu prends au petit déjeuner?
3. Tu vas à l'école comment? En bus, en voiture ou à pied?
4. Tu fais des achats après les cours?
5. Tu aimes faire des achats dans un grand magasin ou dans une boutique?
6. Tu achètes des cadeaux pour tes copains?
7. De quelle couleur est ton pantalon ou ton tee-shirt favori?
8. Pour les chaussures tu fais quelle pointure?
9. Tu demandes la pointure au-dessus ou au-dessous quand les chaussures sont trop larges?

B **L'anniversaire de mon frère.** Complétez.

Je ____ (aller) aux Galeries Lafayette. Je ____ (vouloir) acheter
   1   2
un cadeau pour mon frère. C'est son anniversaire. Qu'est-ce
que je ____ (pouvoir) acheter? Qu'est-ce qu'il ____ (aimer)?
        3   4
Je ____ (aller) au rayon articles de sport. Je ____ (voir) une
    5   6
raquette de tennis. Voilà! C'est une bonne idée. Mon frère
____ (aimer) bien le tennis. Ses copains et lui ____ (jouer)
 7   8
souvent au tennis mais mon frère ____ (avoir) une vieille
                                    9
raquette. J'____ (acheter) la raquette et je ____ (payer) à
      10   11
la caisse.

J'AIME PAS LE SPORT !
J'AIME PAS ME FATIGUER !
J'AIME RIEN !

Vocabulaire

NOMS

les cheveux (m.)
les dents (f.)
la figure
la main

le dentifrice
le savon
le déodorant
la glace

le club de forme
le gymnase
le parc
le survêtement

le lit

le problème

VERBES

s'amuser
s'appeler
se réveiller
se lever
se brosser
se laver
se peigner
s'habiller
se maquiller
se raser
se promener
se coucher

s'endormir
maigrir
grossir

ADVERBES

d'abord
enfin
ensuite
tout de suite

**AUTRES MOTS
ET EXPRESSIONS**

avoir besoin de
faire de l'exercice
faire de l'aérobic

faire de la gymnastique
faire du jogging
pratiquer un sport
se mettre en forme
rester en forme
faire sa toilette
prendre un bain
   (une douche)

CHAPITRE 12

LA VOITURE ET LA ROUTE

OBJECTIFS

In this chapter you will learn to do the following:

1. talk about cars and good driving habits
2. buy gas and have your car serviced
3. express "nothing," "no one," and "never"
4. describe people's activities using certain irregular verbs
5. ask questions formally and informally
6. compare driving in France and in the U.S.

VOCABULAIRE

MOTS 1

LA VOITURE

les deux roues

une moto

un vélomoteur

une voiture de sport

un break

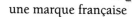
PEUGEOT
une marque française

une décapotable

un conducteur

une clé

mettre le contact

accélérer

une conductrice

rouler vite

La conductrice freine.

La voiture s'arrête.

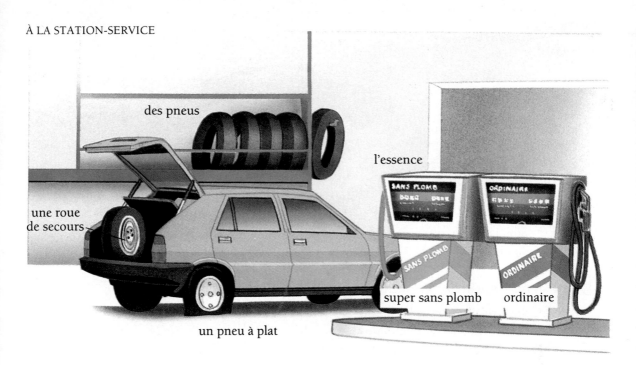

des pneus

l'essence

une roue de secours

super sans plomb   ordinaire

un pneu à plat

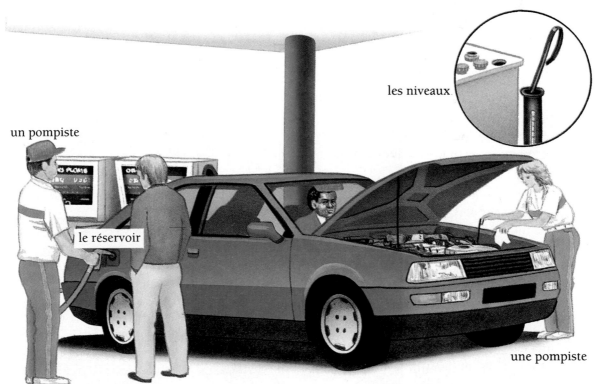

les niveaux

un pompiste

le réservoir

une pompiste

Le pompiste fait le plein.
Il met trente litres de super sans plomb dans le réservoir.
Quelqu'un parle au pompiste.
Une autre pompiste vérifie les niveaux.

Exercices

A Qu'est-ce que c'est?
Répondez d'après les dessins.

1.

2.

3.

4.

1. C'est une voiture de sport ou un break?
2. C'est un vélomoteur ou une moto?
3. La moto a deux roues ou quatre roues?
4. La décapotable, c'est la voiture de sport ou le break?

B Tu as une voiture? Donnez des réponses personnelles.

1. Tu as une voiture? Tu as quelle marque de voiture?
2. Tu veux une voiture? De quelle marque?
3. Tu préfères les breaks ou les voitures de sport?
4. Tu aimes les décapotables?
5. Tu préfères les voitures ou les motos?
6. Ta mère roule vite? Et ton père?

C Les voitures. Choisissez la bonne réponse.

1. À la station-service le pompiste fait le plein. Il met de l'essence dans ___.
   a. le radiateur   **b.** le réservoir

2. Il vérifie les niveaux. Il met de l'eau dans ___.
   a. le moteur   **b.** le radiateur

3. Il met de l'air dans ___.
   a. les roues   **b.** les pneus

4. Le conducteur veut rouler plus vite. Il ___.
   a. freine   **b.** accélère

5. La conductrice veut s'arrêter. Elle ___.
   a. freine   **b.** accélère

6. Quand quelqu'un a un pneu à plat, il ou elle a besoin d'___.
   a. une roue de secours   **b.** une clé

7. Pour mettre le contact, on a besoin d'___.
   a. une clé   **b.** un réservoir

8. En général, dans les voitures de sport on met de l'essence ___.
   a. super   **b.** ordinaire

9. Aux États-Unis les nouvelles voitures consomment de l'essence ___.
   a. avec plomb   **b.** sans plomb

VOCABULAIRE

MOTS 2

l'auto-école (f.)

un permis de conduire

prendre des leçons de conduite

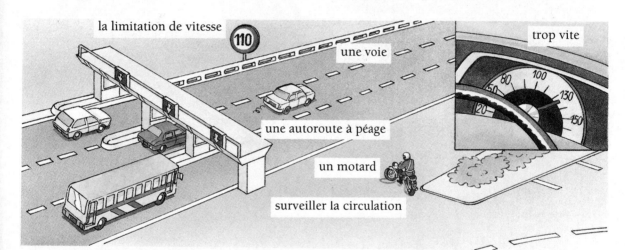

la limitation de vitesse

une voie

trop vite

une autoroute à péage

un motard

surveiller la circulation

un croisement

un carrefour

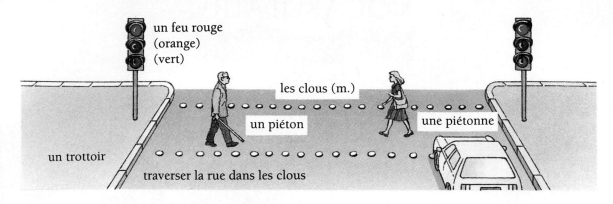

un feu rouge (orange) (vert)

les clous (m.)

un piéton

une piétonne

un trottoir

traverser la rue dans les clous

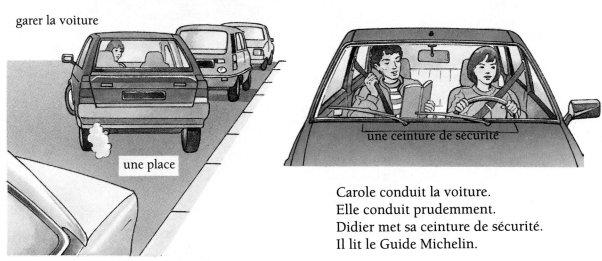

garer la voiture

une place

une ceinture de sécurité

Carole conduit la voiture.
Elle conduit prudemment.
Didier met sa ceinture de sécurité.
Il lit le Guide Michelin.

Il est interdit de stationner ici.

une contractuelle

ZUT!

une contravention

Camille lit la contravention.
Elle est fâchée.
Elle dit «Zut!»

La contractuelle écrit une contravention.
La contractuelle ne dit rien.
Elle ne parle à personne.

Exercices

A **En voiture.** Répondez par «oui» ou «non».

1. Il faut payer quand on roule sur une autoroute à péage?
2. Les autoroutes ont souvent quatre ou six voies?
3. À un carrefour il faut faire attention aux piétons?
4. Il faut mettre sa ceinture de sécurité quand on conduit?
5. On peut conduire sans avoir de permis de conduire?
6. Il faut conduire prudemment à un croisement?
7. Il faut respecter la limitation de vitesse?
8. Il faut rouler vite quand le feu est rouge?
9. Il faut s'arrêter quand le feu est vert?
10. Il faut accélérer pour s'arrêter?
11. Il est interdit de stationner sur le trottoir?

B **À vous de choisir.** Choisissez la bonne réponse.

1. Les ___ traversent la rue dans les clous quand le feu est vert.
   a. motards   **b.** piétons
2. Les motards surveillent ___.
   a. la circulation   **b.** le stationnement
3. Les contractuelles surveillent ___.
   a. le stationnement   **b.** la circulation
4. Les motards donnent des contraventions aux ___ qui roulent trop vite.
   a. conducteurs   **b.** contractuelles
5. Quand on veut garer sa voiture, on cherche ___.
   a. une place   **b.** le trottoir

C **Tu conduis ou pas?** Donnez des réponses personnelles.

1. Tu as ton permis de conduire?
2. Tu vas passer ton permis de conduire?
3. Tu as quel âge maintenant?
4. On passe le permis de conduire à quel âge?
5. Tu vas prendre des leçons de conduite?
6. Tu vas prendre des leçons de conduite à l'école ou à une auto-école?

D **Que font-ils?** Complétez en utilisant «conduit», «lit», «dit» ou «écrit».

1. Carole ___ la voiture.
2. Didier ne ___ pas la voiture.
3. Didier ___ le Guide Michelin.
4. Carole ne ___ pas le guide parce qu'elle ___.
5. La contractuelle ___ une contravention.
6. Carole est fâchée. Elle ___ «Zut!»
7. La contractuelle ne ___ rien. Elle ne parle à personne.

FIN DE STATIONNEMENT AUTORISE
DATE   HEURE
277 17:49
04/10/91   08,00
PRIX 1
LOCAPARK - LOCAPARK - LOCAP
PLACER CE TICKET DERRIERE VOTRE PARE-BRISE LISIBLE DE L'EXTERIEUR

Activités de communication

Mots 1 et 2

A **C'est une bonne idée?** Ask a classmate if it's a good idea to do the following things when driving.

> conduire sans avoir de permis de conduire
>
> Élève 1: **C'est une bonne idée de conduire sans avoir de permis de conduire?**
>
> Élève 2: **Non, ce n'est pas une bonne idée de conduire sans avoir de permis de conduire.**

1. traverser la rue quand le feu est rouge
2. rouler avec un pneu à plat
3. rouler sans avoir beaucoup d'essence dans le réservoir
4. se maquiller quand on conduit
5. lire le Guide Michelin quand on conduit

B **Le permis de conduire.** A French student visiting the U.S. (your partner) asks you for the following information. Answer, then reverse roles.

1. if you have a driver's license
2. if you are going to take driver's ed at school
3. if you have a car (or want a car)
4. what make of car you have or want

C **Tu as de bons réflexes?** Work with a partner and write down several situations one might encounter while driving. Your partner will tell how he or she would react by saying: *je freine, je m'arrête,* or *j'accélère.* Reverse roles.

> Élève 1: **Il y a un animal devant toi sur la route.**
>
> Élève 2: **Je freine.**

D **Il ou elle conduit bien ou mal?** Your driver's ed instructor at school (your partner) wants to test your knowledge of good driving habits. Using suggestions from the list below, he or she will describe three or four drivers. You must decide if the person described drives well or not. Reverse roles.

> s'arrêter au feu rouge
>
> Élève 1: **Elle s'arrête au feu rouge.**
>
> Élève 2: **Elle conduit bien.**

1. rouler trop vite
2. s'arrêter au feu rouge
3. freiner au feu orange
4. garer la voiture dans une zone de stationnement interdit
5. accélérer quand il ou elle voit un piéton dans les clous

RÉPUBLIQUE FRANÇAISE

F

PERMIS DE CONDUIRE

Korekort
Führerschein
Αδεια δδητηδεωξ
Driving licence
Ceadunas Tiomana
Patente di guida
Rijbewijs

Modèle des
COMMUNAUTÉS EUROPÉENNES

STRUCTURE

Les verbes *conduire, lire, écrire et dire* au présent

Describing People's Activities

1. Study the following forms of the verbs *conduire*, "to drive," *lire*, "to read," *écrire*, "to write," and *dire*, "to say." Note how similar they are to one another in the present tense.

2. Note the irregular verb form of *dire: vous dites*.

CONDUIRE	LIRE	ÉCRIRE	DIRE
je conduis	je lis	j' écris	je dis
tu conduis	tu lis	tu écris	tu dis
il elle } conduit on	il elle } lit on	il elle } écrit on	il elle } dit on
nous conduisons	nous lisons	nous écrivons	nous disons
vous conduisez	vous lisez	vous écrivez	vous dites
ils elles } conduisent	ils elles } lisent	ils écrivent elles écrivent	ils elles } disent

Exercices

A   Didier va à Bourges.   Répondez par «oui».

1. Didier va à Bourges?
2. Didier conduit prudemment?
3. Avant le voyage Didier lit le Guide Michelin?
4. Didier dit que Bourges est loin?
5. Didier écrit une lettre à son copain Guillaume?
6. Dans sa lettre il dit que Bourges est une jolie ville?
7. Guillaume lit la lettre de Didier?

B   Je lis et j'écris.   Donnez des réponses personnelles.

1. Tu aimes lire?
2. Tu lis beaucoup?
3. Tu lis le journal tous les jours?
4. Tu lis des magazines?
5. Tu lis quels magazines?
6. Tu écris des lettres à tes amis?
7. Tu écris à tes grands-parents ou tu téléphones à tes grands-parents?

C **Une question, mon ami.** Posez des questions à un copain ou une copine d'après le modèle.

> écrire beaucoup de lettres
> Élève 1: Tu écris beaucoup de lettres?
> Élève 2: Oui, j'écris beaucoup de lettres. (Non, je n'écris pas beaucoup de lettres).

1. écrire des poèmes
2. écrire des compositions au cours d'anglais
3. lire le journal
4. lire des magazines
5. conduire une nouvelle voiture
6. dire que les voitures de sport sont chouettes

D **Ses amis et lui.** Complétez.

1. Lui, il dit des choses stupides, des bêtises, et ses amis ___ des bêtises aussi.
2. Lui, il conduit une vieille voiture et ses amis ___ de vieilles voitures aussi.
3. Lui, il conduit prudemment et ses amis ___ prudemment aussi.
4. Lui, il écrit une lettre et ses amis ___ une lettre aussi.
5. Lui, il lit un magazine et ses amis ___ un magazine aussi.

E **Oui ou non?** Répondez en utilisant «nous».

1. Vous dites des bêtises?
2. Vous dites des choses sérieuses?
3. Vous dites des choses intéressantes?
4. Vous dites des choses amusantes?
5. Vous conduisez beaucoup?
6. Vous lisez beaucoup?
7. Vous écrivez souvent à vos amis?

F **Qui dit ça?** Complétez avec «dire».

1. On ___ que les autoroutes sont bonnes en France.
2. Je ___ que les autoroutes françaises sont bonnes mais je ___ aussi qu'il y a trop de circulation.
3. Jean ___ que la plupart des autoroutes sont à péage.
4. Tu ___ qu'il faut payer sur les autoroutes à péage?
5. Paul et Monique, qu'est-ce que vous ___? Vous ___ qu'il faut payer sur les autoroutes américaines aussi? Vous ___ que la plupart des autoroutes aux États-Unis sont à péage?
6. Nos amis américains ___ qu'il y a beaucoup d'autoroutes à huit voies, c'est-à-dire quatre voies dans chaque sens (direction).

ZONE D'ENLÈVEMENT DES VÉHICULES EN INFRACTION

Les mots négatifs

Expressing "Nothing," "No one," and "Never"

1. You have already learned the negative expression *ne... pas.* Study the following negative expressions that function the same way as *ne... pas.*

AFFIRMATIF	NÉGATIF
Il dit quelque chose.	Il ne dit rien.
Il écrit quelque chose.	Il n'écrit rien.
Il voit quelqu'un.	Il ne voit personne.
Il parle à quelqu'un.	Il ne parle à personne.
Il voyage toujours.	Il ne voyage jamais.
Il lit souvent.	Il ne lit jamais.
Il écrit quelquefois.	Il n'écrit jamais.

2. As with *ne... pas,* when *ne... jamais* is followed by *un, une, des,* or *de la, de l',* *du,* and *des,* these words change to *de.*

Il fait souvent une promenade.   Il ne fait jamais de promenade.
Elle fait toujours du sport.   Elle ne fait jamais de sport.

Exercices

A **Non, au contraire.**   Répondez par «non».

Il voit quelque chose?
Non, il ne voit rien.

1. Il dit quelque chose?
2. Il écrit quelque chose?
3. Il entend quelque chose?
4. Il lit quelque chose?
5. Il vend quelque chose?
6. Il regarde quelque chose?
7. Il voit quelqu'un?
8. Il regarde quelqu'un?
9. Il parle à quelqu'un?
10. Il écrit à quelqu'un?

B **Elle ne voyage jamais.**   Répondez d'après le modèle.

Pascale adore nager.
Tu crois? Elle dit ça, mais elle ne nage jamais.

1. Pascale adore conduire.
2. Pascale adore lire.
3. Pascale adore voyager.
4. Pascale adore faire du sport.
5. Pascale adore jouer au tennis.
6. Pascale adore faire du ski nautique.

Les questions et les mots interrogatifs

Asking Questions Formally and Informally

1. Review the following ways in which questions can be formed in French.

> **Vous parlez français?**
> **Est-ce que vous parlez français?**
> **Parlez-vous français?**

2. Review the following question words you have already learned.

à quelle heure	**comment**	**où**	**quand**
combien de	**pourquoi**	**qui**	

3. Note that you can use these question words in three ways.

   a. In informal, spoken French the question word is often placed at the end of the sentence.

   > **Tu vas où?**
   > **Tu vas au cinéma avec qui?**
   > **Vous allez arriver au cinéma à quelle heure?**

   b. The question word can also be used with *est-ce que*.

   > **Où est-ce que tu vas?**
   > **Avec qui est-ce que tu vas au cinéma?**
   > **Quand est-ce que vous allez arriver au cinéma?**

   c. In more formal conversation and in written French the subject and verb are inverted after a question word.

   > **Où vas-tu?**
   > **Avec qui vas-tu au cinéma?**
   > **Quand allez-vous arriver au cinéma?**

4. With a noun subject, both the noun and *il(s)* and *elle(s)* are used in the inverted question form.

   > **Où *les copains* dînent-*ils*?**
   > **Comment *Marie* conduit-*elle*?**
   > **Combien de roues *les motos* ont-*elles*?**
   > **Pourquoi *Jean* vend-*il** la voiture?**

   * The final **d** is pronounced as a /t/.

5. In the inverted question form you insert a *t* between *il*, *elle*, or *on* and any verb that does not end in a *t* or a *d*.

   > **Où Béatrice déjeune-t-elle?**
   > **Comment va-t-on rue Racine?**
   > **Pourquoi gare-t-elle sa voiture sur le trottoir?**

Exercices

A **Tu vas où?** Transposez les questions d'après le modèle.

> **Arlette, où vas-tu?**
> *Tu vas où, Arlette?*

1. Où vas-tu?
2. Comment vas-tu au restaurant?
3. À quelle heure arrives-tu au restaurant?
4. Avec qui dînes-tu?
5. Où es-tu maintenant?

B **Où allez-vous?** Transposez les questions d'après le modèle.

> **Où est-ce que vous allez?**
> *Où allez-vous?*

1. Où est-ce que vous allez dîner?
2. Comment est-ce que vous allez au restaurant?
3. Est-ce que vous conduisez?
4. Est-ce que vous prenez l'autoroute à péage?
5. Avec qui est-ce que vous allez au restaurant?
6. Est-ce que vous parlez français au serveur?

C **Encore des questions!** Écrivez des questions d'après le modèle.

> **Marie lit la carte.**
> *Marie lit-elle la carte?*

1. Marie va au restaurant.
2. Marie conduit.
3. Marie gare sa voiture devant le restaurant.
4. Marie regarde la carte.
5. Marie parle au serveur.
6. Marie commande un sandwich au jambon.
7. Le serveur sert le sandwich.
8. Marie mange le sandwich.
9. Le sandwich est bon.
10. Marie paie.
11. Marie laisse un pourboire pour le serveur.

D **À qui Jean parle-t-il?** Écrivez des questions d'après le modèle.

> **Jean parle à sa copine. (à qui)**
> *À qui Jean parle-t-il?*

1. Jean parle à sa copine au téléphone. (à qui)
2. Il invite sa copine au cinéma. (qui)
3. Ils vont aller au cinéma ce soir. (quand)
4. Jean arrive chez sa copine à sept heures. (à quelle heure)
5. Ils voient le film «Extraterrestre». (quel film)
6. Après le cinéma ils vont au café. (quand)

CONVERSATION

Scènes de la vie   *Tu as ton permis de conduire?*

FRANCINE: Tu as ton permis de conduire?
PHILIPPE: Non, je n'ai pas mon permis. J'ai seulement quinze ans.

FRANCINE: Mais tu conduis, n'est-ce pas?
PHILIPPE: Tu veux rigoler! Je ne conduis jamais!

FRANCINE: C'est bizarre. Je suis sûre que...
PHILIPPE: Ah... je comprends! Tu vois mon frère Alain qui conduit et tu crois que c'est moi.

 Qui conduit?   Répondez d'après la conversation.

1. Philippe a son permis de conduire?
2. Pourquoi pas?
3. Francine croit que Philippe conduit?
4. Le frère de Philippe conduit?
5. Francine voit qui?
6. Elle croit que c'est qui?

Prononciation   *Le son /wa/*

Repeat the following words with the sound /wa/ as in *moi*:

toi	voie	réservoir
croisement	trottoir	pouvoir

Now repeat the following sentences:

Tu ne vois pas le croisement devant toi!
Il va pouvoir partir à trois heures.
Moi, je ne crois pas Antoine!

trottoir

Activités de communication

A **Une enquête.** Copy the chart on the right. Interview your partner and find out how often he or she does some of the following activities. Fill in the chart with his or her answers. Reverse roles and report to the class.

Activité	souvent	quelquefois	jamais
Jouer au tennis			X

> Élève 1: Tu joues au tennis?
> Élève 2: Non, je ne joue jamais au tennis.
> Élève 1 (*à la classe*): Patrick ne joue jamais au tennis.

acheter des cadeaux	écrire des lettres	lire le journal
aller au bord de la mer	faire de la planche à voile	manger des fruits de mer
chanter sous la douche	faire des voyages	prendre des bains de soleil
conduire	faire du jogging	regarder la télé
écouter du jazz	faire les courses	

B **Qu'est-ce qu'on lit, écrit et dit?** Choose from the list below and tell your partner what some of the following people read, write, and say. Then reverse roles.

le professeur	ton frère ou ta sœur	tes amis et toi
tes parents	les élèves	

LIRE	ÉCRIRE	DIRE
des journaux	des compositions	des choses amusantes
des livres	des exercices au tableau	des choses brillantes
des magazines	des lettres à tes grands-parents	des choses importantes
la page des sports	des mots (*notes*) aux amis	des choses stupides

C **Qu'est-ce que tu aimes lire?** Using the list below, find out what your partner likes to read. Take notes and report to the class.

la littérature classique	les poèmes	les biographies
la science-fiction	les magazines	le journal

> Élève 1: Est-ce que tu aimes lire la littérature classique?
> Élève 2: Oui, j'aime lire la littérature classique et...
> Élève 1 (*à la classe*): Stacy aime lire la littérature classique et...

D **Qu'est-ce que tu dis?** Write down several statements that would make your classmates respond with one of the expressions below. Your teacher will collect the papers and call on students to respond.

Absolument pas!	C'est un miracle!	Quelle surprise!
C'est chouette, ça!	Jamais!	Tu veux rigoler!
C'est impossible!	Quelle chance!	Zut!

> Suzanne a un «A» à l'examen de français!
> Je dis, «C'est chouette, ça!» (Je dis, «C'est impossible!»)

LECTURE ET CULTURE

ON VA CONDUIRE EN FRANCE?

En France presque[1] tout le monde a une voiture. Les Français conduisent quelles marques de voiture? Il y a deux marques françaises qui sont très populaires, Renault et Peugeot. On voit aussi beaucoup de voitures japonaises sur les autoroutes françaises, mais très peu de voitures américaines.

Les autoroutes en France sont très bonnes. Elles ont trois ou quatre voies dans chaque sens (direction). La plupart des autoroutes sont à péage. Il y a aussi des routes nationales qui sont des routes à grande circulation. Les routes départementales sont plus pittoresques mais il faut faire attention aux croisements, qui peuvent être dangereux.

Si vous conduisez en France, il faut respecter la limitation de vitesse sur les routes et dans les agglomérations[2]. Les motards surveillent la circulation. Si vous roulez trop vite, vous allez avoir une contravention.

Et le stationnement! Il n'y a jamais assez de[3] parkings ou de places pour garer les voitures. Si vous garez votre voiture là où le stationnement est interdit, vous allez trouver une contravention sur le parebrise[4] à votre retour[5]. Les contractuelles sont très vigilantes et très strictes.

[1] presque *almost*
[2] les agglomérations *populated areas*
[3] assez de *enough*
[4] le parebrise *windshield*
[5] à votre retour *upon your return*

Étude de mots

A **Le français, c'est facile.** Trouvez cinq mots apparentés dans la lecture.

B **Synonymes.** Trouvez les expressions équivalentes.

1. vite
2. la direction
3. surveiller
4. l'agglomération
5. garer

a. rapidement
b. une zone développée
c. stationner
d. le sens
e. contrôler, observer attentivement

Compréhension

A **Sur la route en France.** Corrigez les phrases.

1. Il y a plus de voitures américaines que de voitures japonaises en France.
2. Il n'y a pas de voitures françaises. L'industrie automobile n'existe pas en France.
3. Beaucoup d'autoroutes en France ne sont pas bonnes.
4. On ne paie jamais sur les autoroutes à péage françaises.
5. La plus grande route c'est la route départementale.
6. Il y a des croisements dangereux sur les autoroutes.
7. Il n'y a pas de limitation de vitesse dans les agglomérations.
8. Les conducteurs aiment avoir des contraventions.

B **En route.** Répondez.

1. Les grandes autoroutes en France ont combien de voies dans chaque sens?
2. Qu'est-ce qu'il faut payer sur la plupart des autoroutes?
3. Il y a une limitation de vitesse sur les routes en France?
4. Qui surveille les autoroutes?
5. Il y a toujours assez de places pour stationner?
6. Qui a la responsabilité de surveiller le stationnement?
7. Quelles sont deux marques françaises de voiture?

DÉCOUVERTE CULTURELLE

Voici un vélomoteur. Il faut avoir plus de seize ans et un permis spécial pour conduire un vélomoteur.

Le rêve[1] de beaucoup de jeunes, c'est une moto. On peut conduire une moto à partir de seize ans[2] avec un permis spécial moto. Et le casque[3] est obligatoire! Si vous êtes en France, vous pouvez conduire une moto? Pourquoi?

Et pour conduire une voiture il faut avoir dix-huit ans en France. Là où vous habitez, il faut avoir quel âge pour obtenir un permis de conduire?

[1] le rêve *the dream*
[2] à partir de seize ans *from age 16 on*
[3] le casque *the helmet*

RÉALITÉS

MOUGINS

GRASSE

A 8

APPEL

PIETONS

L'agent de police est dans les villes **1**. Les agents de police règlent la circulation.

Voici trois panneaux routiers **2**. Quel panneau indique une autoroute à péage, à ton avis?

Pour traverser la rue, les piétons appuient sur le bouton **3**.

Voici des gendarmes français **4**. Eux, ils sont toujours sur la route, souvent à moto. Ils portent toujours un casque s'ils sont à moto.

Voici quelques signaux importants qu'il faut comprendre pour conduire en France **5**. Quelle est la limitation de vitesse sur cette route?

CULMINATION

Activités de communication orale

A À la station-service.

1. Make up as many questions about this illustration as you can.
2. Work with a classmate and have him or her answer your questions.

B **La route.** Work with a partner. Write down as many questions as possible that a French person might ask about driving in the U.S. Refer to the list below for some ideas. Then ask your partner your questions.

> **beaucoup de circulation**
>
> Est-ce qu'il y a beaucoup de circulation?
> Où est-ce qu'il y a beaucoup de circulation?
> Il y a beaucoup de circulation à quelle heure?, etc.

des autoroutes à péage
la limitation de vitesse
assez de parkings dans la ville
des vélomoteurs
beaucoup de stations-service
de l'essence sans plomb
des motards
des contraventions

mettre une ceinture de sécurité
prendre des leçons de conduite

Activités de communication écrite

A **Mon permis de conduire.** Write a letter to a French friend telling your age, where you live, and whether or not you have a driver's license. Tell some things you have to do to get a license. Find out some things your friend must do in France to get a driver's license.

B **Zut!** Write a short dialogue between a driver and a *contractuelle* who is giving him or her a ticket.

Réintroduction et recombinaison

A **Personnellement.** Donnez des réponses personnelles.

1. Comment t'appelles-tu?
2. Tu es d'où?
3. Tu es de quelle nationalité?
4. Tu vas à quelle école?
5. Qui est ton professeur de français?
6. Qu'est-ce que tu fais au cours de français?
7. Tu aimes être en forme?
8. Qu'est-ce que tu fais pour rester en forme?

B **Jamais!** Répondez en utilisant «ne... jamais».

1. Tes parents se lèvent à midi en semaine?
2. Les élèves se couchent à six heures du soir?
3. Le professeur s'endort en classe?
4. Les garçons se rasent en classe?
5. Les élèves se regardent dans une glace pendant un examen?

Vocabulaire

NOMS

la voiture
la voiture de sport
le break
la décapotable
la marque
les deux roues (f.)
la moto
le vélomoteur
la roue de secours
le pneu (à plat)
le réservoir
la clé
la ceinture de sécurité
le conducteur
la conductrice
l'auto-école (f.)
la leçon de conduite

le permis de conduire
le guide

la route
l'autoroute à péage (f.)
la voie
la limitation de vitesse
le motard
la circulation
le croisement
le carrefour
le trottoir
le piéton
la piétonne
les clous (m.)
le feu
le stationnement
la place
la contractuelle
la contravention

la station-service
le (la) pompiste
l'essence (f.)
  super
  ordinaire
  sans plomb
les niveaux (m.)

VERBES

rouler
accélérer
freiner
s'arrêter
traverser
surveiller
conduire
dire
écrire
lire

AUTRES MOTS ET EXPRESSIONS

garer la voiture
faire le plein
vérifier les niveaux
mettre le contact
quelqu'un
ne... jamais
ne... personne
ne... rien

fâché(e)
il est interdit
prudemment
sans
trop
vite
Zut!

RÉVISION

CHAPITRES 9-12

Conversation *Stéphanie en robe!*

ANTOINE: Qu'est-ce que je vois! Stéphanie en robe!
STÉPHANIE: Euh...tu crois que la robe bleue est plus jolie que la robe rose?
ANTOINE: Mais non. Tu es très jolie en rose.
STÉPHANIE: Je préfère vraiment les pantalons!
ANTOINE: Tu sors avec qui?
STÉPHANIE: Avec Jérôme. On va au restaurant.
ANTOINE: Ah oui, avec lui, c'est toujours les restaurants chic.
STÉPHANIE: Oui, mais on s'amuse bien ensemble.
ANTOINE: Tu pars à quelle heure?
STÉPHANIE: Dans cinq minutes. Je me peigne, je me maquille et je pars.

Stéphanie et son frère. Répondez.

1. Qu'est-ce qu'Antoine voit?
2. De quelle couleur est la robe de Stéphanie?
3. D'après Antoine, la robe bleue est plus jolie que la robe rose?
4. Qu'est-ce que Stéphanie préfère, les robes ou les pantalons?
5. À ton avis, est-ce qu'Antoine aime Jérôme?
6. Est-ce que Stéphanie aime sortir avec Jérôme? Pourquoi?
7. Est-ce que Stéphanie va partir dans quelques minutes?
8. Qu'est-ce qu'elle va faire avant de partir?

Structure

Les verbes réfléchis

Review the present tense forms of reflexive verbs.

1. Remember that in reflexive constructions, the subject and the reflexive pronoun refer to the same person.

SE LEVER	
je me lève	*nous nous* levons
tu te lèves	*vous vous* levez
il/elle/on se lève	*ils/elles se* lèvent

2. Review the placement of *ne...pas, ne...plus, ne...jamais.*

> **Vous *ne* vous levez *pas*?**
> **Il *ne* s'endort *jamais* tout de suite.**

A **On sort.** Complétez.

Ma sœur et moi, nous ____ (s'amuser) bien quand nous sortons. Mais elle ____
1   2
(se préparer) pendant des heures, et moi, je ____ (se laver) et je ____
                                                                3   4
(s'habiller) en deux minutes. D'abord, elle, elle ____ (se brosser) les dents
                                                                                          5
pendant cinq minutes! Puis elle ____ (s'habiller), mais elle ____ (se changer)
                                                        6   7
trois fois *(times)* avant de se décider. Puis, elle ____ (se maquiller) pendant une
                                                                                  8
demi-heure. Enfin, elle ____ (se peigner). Pendant ce temps, moi, je lis un
                                          9
livre. Quelquefois, je ____ (s'endormir)!
                              10

Les verbes *prendre*, *croire*, *voir*, *lire*, *dire*, *écrire* et *conduire*

Review the following forms of some irregular verbs you have learned.

PRENDRE	je prends, tu prends, il / elle / on prend nous prenons, vous prenez, ils / elles prennent
COMPRENDRE	je comprends, tu comprends, il / elle / on comprend nous comprenons, vous comprenez, ils / elles comprennent
CROIRE	je crois, tu crois, il / elle / on croit nous croyons, vous croyez, ils / elles croient
VOIR	je vois, tu vois, il / elle / on voit nous voyons, vous voyez, ils / elles voient
LIRE	je lis, tu lis, il / elle / on lit nous lisons, vous lisez, ils / elles lisent
DIRE	je dis, tu dis, il / elle / on dit nous disons, vous dites, ils / elles disent
ÉCRIRE	j'écris, tu écris, il / elle / on écrit nous écrivons, vous écrivez, ils / elles écrivent
CONDUIRE	je conduis, tu conduis, il / elle / on conduit nous conduisons, vous conduisez, ils / elles conduisent

B **Qu'est-ce qu'on fait?** Remplacez les mots en italique et faites les changements nécessaires.

1. *Vous* écrivez beaucoup? (elles)
2. *Moi, je* lis beaucoup. (elles)
3. *Ils* écrivent souvent à leurs parents? (tu)
4. *Ils* voient leurs parents toutes les semaines. (je)
5. *Amélie* conduit bien? (tes frères)
6. Non, *elle* apprend à conduire. (ils)
7. *Tu* dis déjà «au revoir»? (vous)
8. Oui, *je* prends l'avion dans une heure. (nous)
9. *Tu* conduis beaucoup? (elles)
10. Non, *je* vois mal. (elles)
11. *Robert* lit le journal tous les matins? (ils)
12. *Je* crois qu'*il* lit le journal. (nous, ils)

Les pronoms accentués

1. Review the stress pronouns and the corresponding subject pronouns.

SUBJECT PRONOUNS	STRESS PRONOUNS
je	moi
tu	toi
il	lui
elle	elle
nous	nous
vous	vous
ils	eux
elles	elles

2. Remember that you use stress pronouns

   a. to emphasize the subject.
   b. after a preposition.
   c. when there is no verb in the sentence.
   d. after *c'est* or *ce sont*.
   e. after *que* in comparisons.

Moi, j'ai faim!
C'est pour moi?
Qui? Moi?
C'est lui qui n'écrit jamais.
Anne est plus grande que toi.

C **En vacances.** Répondez d'après le modèle.

> **Sa mère joue au tennis. Et son père?**
> *Lui aussi, il joue au tennis.*

1. Son frère fait de la plongée sous-marine. Et ses cousins?
2. Je fais de la planche à voile. Et toi?
3. Nous bronzons facilement. Et vous deux?
4. Il plonge bien. Et ses sœurs?
5. Vous sortez ce soir. Et nous?
6. Tu vas au restaurant. Et moi?
7. Ils aiment les fruits de mer. Et elle?
8. J'aime le soleil. Et vous?

Le comparatif et le superlatif

1. You use the comparative to compare two people or two items.

   Nathalie est plus (moins, aussi) sportive que son frère.

2. You use the superlative to single out one person or one item from the group and compare it to all the others.

   Nathalie est la plus (la moins) sportive de la famille.
   Serge est le plus (le moins) sportif de la famille.
   Ils sont les plus (les moins) sportifs de la famille.

3. Remember that the adjective *bon* has an irregular form in the comparative and the superlative: *meilleur(e)*.

   Mon idée est meilleure que ton idée.
   Jean-Claude est le meilleur de la classe.

D **Bernard et moi.**   Répondez d'après le modèle.

   Élève 1: Bernard est très sérieux.
   Élève 2: Il est plus sérieux que moi?
   Élève 1: Non, mais il est aussi sérieux que toi.

1. Bernard est très timide.
2. Bernard est très sportif.
3. Bernard est très généreux.
4. Bernard est très actif.
5. Bernard est très nerveux.
6. Bernard est très grand.
7. Bernard est très patient.
8. Bernard est très intelligent.

E **Nathalie et moi.**   Changez Bernard en Nathalie dans l'Exercice D.

F **Les élèves de Mme Leblond.**   Répondez d'après le modèle.

   Véronique est très amusante.
   Véronique est la plus amusante de la classe.

1. Alain est très timide.
2. Catherine et Émilie sont très intelligentes.
3. Louise est très jolie.
4. Les frères Gautier sont très désagréables.
5. Les sœurs Duhamel sont très gentilles.
6. Olivier est très aimable.
7. Valérie est très réservée.
8. Martine est très bonne.

Activité de communication

Au Club Med.   Imagine that you are a group leader (*un gentil organisateur* or *un G.O.*) at Club Med. Tell about your daily routine: what time you get up, what you wear, what sports you play, what you eat, and what you do at night.

ÉCOLOGIE: LA POLLUTION DE L'EAU

Avant la lecture

1. Is water scarce or abundant where you live? Think about the role that water plays in your town. Are there any regulations concerning the watering of lawns, the washing of cars, the amount of certain substances that can be present in the town water?

2. Here are four titles. Scan the text and see if you can match these titles with the four paragraphs in the text.

> **La répartition de l'eau**
> **Sauvons l'eau!**
> **La circulation de l'eau**
> **Les différents genres de pollution**

Lecture

Le Gange déborde et cause des inondations.

La sécheresse dans le désert

L'eau, tu es
la plus grande richesse
qui soit° au monde,   *exists*
et tu es la plus délicate,
toi, si pure
au ventre° de la terre.   *in the depths of*

Antoine de Saint-Exupéry

Nous "sommes" de l'eau. Notre corps est composé de 65% d'eau. On trouve l'eau partout: 96% dans les mers et les océans, 3% dans les glaciers et 1% qui prend part au «cycle de l'eau».

L'eau des lacs et des mers s'évapore. Ensuite elle retombe en pluie et s'infiltre dans le sol. Du sol, elle est absorbée par les arbres où elle arrive dans les feuilles et s'évapore encore, etc.

On ne peut pas vivre (exister) sans eau, mais malheureusement, l'eau est mal distribuée: par exemple, en Afrique certaines régions n'ont pas assez d'eau[1],

mais en Inde, quand le Gange, le grand fleuve, déborde, il y a trop d'eau[2]. Aux États-Unis, nous avons quelquefois des périodes de sécheresse quand il n'y a pas de pluie ou, au contraire, des inondations, quand il y a trop de pluie. Mais en général, nous n'avons ni trop, ni trop peu[3] d'eau. Notre problème, c'est la pollution.

La pollution peut prendre plusieurs formes.

1. Les pluies acides

Quand les nuages passent au-dessus des zones industrielles, ils absorbent tous les gaz qui s'échappent (sortent) des cheminées et des voitures. Les nuages transportent ces gaz et les pluies qui tombent un peu plus loin sont des «pluies acides». Ces pluies acides causent la destruction des forêts et contaminent les lacs.

2. Les engrais[4]

Les agriculteurs utilisent beaucoup d'engrais, en général des phosphates, pour maintenir la fertilité du sol. Ces engrais chimiques sont entraînés[5] par les pluies jusque dans les lacs et les rivières. Ils polluent les rivières et les lacs parce qu'ils font pousser les plantes aquatiques[6]. Ces plantes prennent tout l'oxygène de l'eau. Sans oxygène, les poissons ne peuvent pas vivre et disparaissent. Les engrais polluent aussi les mers. Ils sont entraînés dans les mers par les rivières où ils nourrissent les algues. Ces algues se transforment en véritables «marées[7] rouges» et tuent[8] les poissons.

3. La marée noire

La marée noire est causée par le mazout[9] qui est jeté dans la mer par des pétroliers.

4. Les déchets[10] radioactifs

Il y a à notre époque plus de 100.000 tonnes de déchets radioactifs au fond de l'océan Atlantique et de l'océan Pacifique!

Il faut sauver l'eau. Il faut apprendre à conserver les réserves. Et surtout il faut apprendre à ne pas polluer, à ne pas verser les déchets toxiques dans l'eau. C'est le but[11] de beaucoup d'écologistes qui veulent protéger et sauver notre environnement.

Plusieurs formes de pollution

[1] assez d'eau *enough water*
[2] trop d'eau *too much water*
[3] nous n'avons ni trop, ni trop peu *we have neither too much nor too little*
[4] les engrais *fertilizers*
[5] entraînés *carried*
[6] ils font pousser les plantes aquatiques *they make aquatic vegetation grow*
[7] marées *tides*
[8] tuent *kill*
[9] le mazout *fuel oil*
[10] les déchets *waste*
[11] le but *the goal*

Après la lecture

A **La pollution.**   Vrai ou faux?

1. 65% de l'eau prend part au «cycle de l'eau».
2. On ne peut pas vivre sans eau.
3. Les marées rouges font disparaître les poissons.
4. La marée noire est causée par des algues.
5. Il y a des déchets radioactifs dans l'océan Pacifique.
6. Il faut apprendre à conserver les réserves d'eau.

B **Il faut sauver l'eau.**   Répondez.

1. Quels sont les risques de pollution de l'eau là où vous habitez?
2. Quelles sont les mesures adoptées par votre ville pour ne pas polluer l'eau ou pour la conserver? S'il n'y a pas de mesures adoptées, faites des recommandations.

LITTÉRATURE: APOLLINAIRE (1880-1918)

Guillaume Apollinaire a une vie très fantaisiste et mouvementée. Sa poésie reflète sa vie. Il voyage dans toute l'Europe—à Munich, Berlin, Prague, Vienne. Il s'intéresse à tous les mouvements intellectuels et artistiques de son époque. C'est la période avant la guerre de 1914, une période très riche en idées en tous genres. C'est le début du cubisme, par exemple. Les poètes et les artistes peintres (*painters*) discutent ensemble ces nouvelles idées. Apollinaire est l'ami des peintres Picasso, Vlaminck et Marie Laurencin. Apollinaire est un des premiers grands poètes français modernes. Il annonce les grands mouvements artistiques des années 20 (1920s).

Certains des poèmes d'Apollinaire sont des «calligrammes»: le poème est écrit en forme d'objet. *La cravate* est un exemple de ce genre de poème.

Avant la lecture

1. The poem is written in the shape of a tie. When do men or women wear ties? What impression does a tie convey?
2. What could a tie represent in terms of freedom and society?

Lecture

Après la lecture

A **Les vêtements.**   Répondez.

1. Qu'est-ce que vous mettez quand vous vous habillez «bien»?
2. Est-ce que vous jugez les gens d'après leurs vêtements?
3. D'après vous, est-ce qu'une école doit (*must*) imposer certaines normes vestimentaires?

B **Êtes-vous poète?**

Avec des amis «poètes», écrivez un calligramme.

En 1901-1902 Apollinaire est en Allemagne et rencontre une jeune Anglaise, Annie Playden. Mais Annie qui est mennonite émigre aux États-Unis.

Avant la lecture

1. Find out about the Mennonites.
2. In French, the word *bouton* means both button (for clothes) and bud (for flowers). In the last stanza of the poem, the poet makes a joke. See if you can explain what the joke is.

Lecture

ANNIE

Sur la côte du Texas
Entre Mobile et Galveston il y a
Un grand jardin tout plein de roses
Il contient aussi une villa
Qui est une grande rose

Une femme se promène souvent
Dans le jardin toute seule
Et quand je passe sur la route bordée
   de tilleuls°   *linden trees*
Nous nous regardons

Comme cette femme est mennonite
Ses rosiers et ses vêtements n'ont pas
   de boutons
Il en manque deux° à mon veston   *two are*
La dame et moi suivons le même rite   *missing*

«Apollinaire» par Picasso (Monument élevé à la mémoire du poète à Saint-Germain-des-Prés)

Après la lecture

■ **Discutons du poème.** Répondez.

1. The poet imagines his lost love in America. Find examples in the poem that show that this is just a fantasy.
2. In a typically French way, Apollinaire makes light of his emotion and sadness with a "joke." What is the only remaining link between the couple?

MÉTÉOROLOGIE: LA PRÉVISION DU TEMPS

Avant la lecture

1. Find a weather map in one of your newspapers.
2. Match the French and English terms for weather expressions by comparing the legend of your weather map with that of the French weather map below.

Lecture

Le matin, beaucoup de gens écoutent le bulletin météorologique à la radio ou le regardent à la télévision pour décider comment s'habiller.

La météo est la science qui étudie l'atmosphère: les vents, les pluies, les dépressions ou zones de basses pressions, et les anticyclones ou zones de hautes pressions. Pour prévoir le temps, les météorologistes doivent savoir[1] le temps qu'il fait sur tout le globe. Il y a trois centres météorologiques dans le monde qui rassemblent toutes les informations météorologiques; ils sont situés à Washington aux États-Unis, à Moscou en Russie et à Melbourne en Australie.

Le soleil chauffe la Terre[2]; la Terre à son tour chauffe l'air et forme l'atmosphère. Mais l'atmosphère n'est pas la même partout: il y a des masses d'air froid au-dessus des pôles, et des masses d'air chaud au-dessus de l'équateur. Quand les masses d'air passent au-dessus des mers ou des océans, elles absorbent de la vapeur d'eau. Il y a donc plusieurs catégories de masses d'air: froides et humides, froides et sèches, chaudes et humides, chaudes et sèches. Ces masses d'air pèsent de

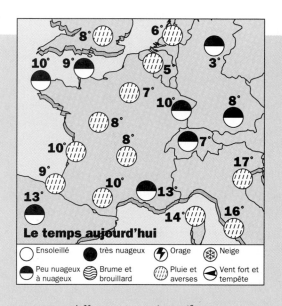

Le temps aujourd'hui

○ Ensoleillé	● très nuageux	Orage
Peu nuageux à nuageux	Brume et brouillard	Pluie et averses
		Neige
		Vent fort et tempête

manière différente sur le sol[3]. Dans un anticyclone, elles pèsent lourd[4]: c'est donc une zone de hautes pressions. Dans une dépression, elles ne pèsent pas lourd: c'est donc une zone de basses pressions. Dans un anticyclone, les masses d'air sont trop lourdes et ne peuvent s'affronter[5]. Le temps reste stable. Dans une dépression, les différentes masses d'air s'affrontent si elles sont différentes—une masse d'air froid va contre une masse d'air chaud, par exemple. Le front est la zone où les deux masses s'affrontent; il apporte de la pluie ou du vent.

Les vents sont des mouvements d'air entre les anticyclones (zones de hautes pressions) et les dépressions (zones de

Les cumulo-nimbus annoncent souvent un orage.

Les nimbo-stratus annoncent aussi le mauvais temps: pluie continue ou neige.

basses pressions). L'air est repoussé[6] par les anticyclones, mais il est aspiré[7] par les dépressions. Ce mouvement d'air est le vent.

Les nuages sont l'ensemble de particules d'eau très fines. Elles sont maintenues en suspension par les mouvements verticaux de l'air.

On peut souvent prévoir le temps d'après les nuages. La forme, la couleur et l'altitude donnent des renseignements relativement précis sur le temps.

[1] doivent savoir *must know*
[2] chauffe la Terre *heats the Earth*
[3] pèsent...sol *exert varying amounts of pressure on the surface of the Earth*
[4] lourd *heavily*
[5] s'affronter *collide*
[6] repoussé *pushed back*
[7] aspiré *pulled in*

Après la lecture

A **Le bulletin météorologique.** Donnez une définition en français pour les mots suivants.

1. la météorologie
2. les dépressions
3. les anticyclones
4. le front
5. le vent

B **La météorologie.** Répondez aux questions.

1. Qu'est-ce que la météorologie étudie?
2. Comment est-ce qu'on obtient les informations nécessaires?
3. Où sont les trois centres météorologiques?
4. Qu'est-ce qui arrive (*happens*) quand les masses d'air passent au-dessus des mers?
5. Quand est-ce que le temps reste stable? Quand est-ce qu'il pleut ou qu'il y a du vent?
6. De quelle autre manière est-ce qu'on peut prévoir le temps?

C **La carte du temps.** Faites la carte du temps pour les États-Unis pour la journée de demain (en français, bien sûr).

D **Savez-vous que...** Dans le système Celsius, 0° est la température où l'eau gèle, et 100° est la température où l'eau bout. Si vous voulez passer de degrés Celsius en degrés Farenheit ou vice versa, voici deux formules qui peuvent vous aider.

$9/5°C + 32 = °F$ Ex: $(9/5 \times 20°C) + 32 = 68°F$

$(°F-32) \times 5/9 = °C$ Ex: $(86°F - 32) \times 5/9 = 30°C$

Faites les calculs suivants.

1. 98.6° F= ___ ° C
2. 32° F= ___ ° C
3. 17° C = ___ ° F
4. 25° C = ___ ° F

CHAPITRE
13

LES SPORTS

OBJECTIFS

In this chapter you will learn to do the following:

1. talk about soccer and other sports
2. describe past actions
3. ask questions with "what"
4. express reactions
5. discuss some differences between sports in the U.S. and in France

MOTS 1

LE FOOT(BALL)

le but

un gardien de but

siffler

un arbitre

un terrain de foot(ball)

un ballon

des joueurs

un joueur

la tête

une équipe

le pied

les gradins

un stade

les deux camps

le camp adverse

un spectateur

Le stade est comble.
Il y a beaucoup de monde.
Les gradins sont pleins.

hier   aujourd'hui

Hier Nantes a joué contre Toulouse.
Le match a opposé Toulouse à Nantes.

Peyre a donné un coup de pied dans le ballon.

Roland a envoyé le ballon dans le but.
Il a marqué un but.

Exercices

A   Le stade est comble.   Répondez.

1. Il y a beaucoup de spectateurs dans le stade?
2. Les gradins sont pleins de spectateurs ou il y a beaucoup de places libres?
3. Le stade est comble?
4. Il y a beaucoup de monde dans le stade?
5. Le foot est un sport d'équipe. C'est un sport individuel ou collectif?

B   Un match de foot.   Répondez d'après les indications.

1. Dans un match de foot, il y a combien d'équipes? (deux)
2. Chaque équipe a combien de joueurs? (onze)
3. Il y a combien de joueurs sur le terrain? (vingt-deux)
4. Dans un match il y a combien de camps? (deux)
5. Le match est divisé en quoi? (mi-temps)
6. Il y a combien de mi-temps? (deux)
7. Chaque mi-temps dure combien de minutes? (quarante-cinq)
8. Qui garde le but? (le gardien de but)
9. Qu'est-ce que chaque équipe veut faire? (marquer un but)
10. Qui bloque ou arrête le ballon? (le gardien de but)

C   Toulouse contre Nantes.   Répondez par «oui».

1. Toulouse a joué contre Nantes?
2. Peyre a donné un coup de pied dans le ballon?
3. Peyre a passé le ballon à Roland?
4. Roland a envoyé le ballon dans le but?
5. Roland a marqué un but?
6. Le gardien n'a pas arrêté le ballon?
7. Roland a égalisé le score?
8. L'arbitre a sifflé?
9. Il a déclaré un penalty contre Toulouse?
10. Nantes a gagné le match?
11. Toulouse a perdu le match?

VOCABULAIRE

MOTS 2

D'AUTRES SPORTS

le panneau

le panier

lancer

le basket(-ball)

dribbler

le demi-cercle

Un joueur a dribblé le ballon.
Il a dribblé le ballon jusqu'au demi-cercle.

Un autre joueur a lancé le ballon dans le panier.

le volley(-ball)

par dessus le filet

le filet

le sol

Un joueur a servi.

Un autre joueur a renvoyé le ballon.

le cyclisme

des coureurs cyclistes

une course cycliste

un vélo

un coureur

un gagnant

une piste

une coupe

Leblanc (27) a gagné la course.
Boulet (28) a perdu la course.

Aux États-Unis le football américain est
un sport d'automne.

Le base-ball est un sport de printemps.

Exercices

A **Un match de basket.** Répondez.

1. On joue au basket-ball sur une piste ou sur un terrain?
2. Le basket-ball est un sport individuel ou un sport d'équipe?
3. Il y a cinq ou onze joueurs dans une équipe de basket-ball?
4. Pendant un match de basket les joueurs dribblent le ballon ou donnent un coup de pied dans le ballon?
5. Un joueur a dribblé le ballon jusqu'au panneau ou jusqu'au demi-cercle?
6. Un autre joueur a lancé le ballon dans le panier ou dans le but?

B **Le volley-ball.** Répondez par «oui» ou «non».

1. Une équipe de volley-ball a six joueurs?
2. Un joueur sert?
3. Un joueur du camp adverse renvoie le ballon?
4. Quand il renvoie le ballon, le ballon peut toucher le filet?
5. On renvoie le ballon par dessus le filet?
6. Le ballon peut toucher le sol?

C **C'est quel sport?** Identifiez.

> le base-ball
> le basket-ball
> le football
> le football américain
> le volley-ball

1. Aux États-Unis c'est un sport d'automne.
2. Aux États-Unis c'est un sport de printemps.
3. Le ballon ne peut pas toucher le sol.
4. Il y a cinq joueurs dans l'équipe.
5. Le joueur a donné un coup de pied dans le ballon.
6. Le joueur a renvoyé le ballon par dessus le filet.
7. Le gardien de but a bloqué le ballon.
8. Le joueur a servi.
9. Le joueur a lancé le ballon dans le panier.
10. Le joueur a marqué un but.

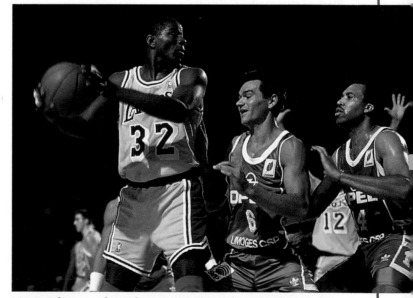

Magic Johnson et les Lakers jouent contre l'équipe de Limoges.

Greg Lemond, le premier Américain à gagner le Tour de France

D Une course cycliste. Choisissez.

1. Un vélo est ___.
   a. une bicyclette **b.** une voiture **c.** un stade

2. ___ roule à vélo.
   a. Une bicyclette **b.** Un coureur cycliste **c.** Un spectateur

3. Dans une course internationale, chaque équipe ___.
   a. gagne un trophée **b.** gagne la coupe **c.** représente son pays

4. Le gagnant de la course est ___.
   a. la coupe **b.** le champion **c.** le coureur

5. ___ gagnent de l'argent.
   a. Les professionnels **b.** Les amateurs **c.** Les spectateurs

6. ___ gagne.
   a. Le premier **b.** Le dernier
   c. Chaque équipe

7. On donne ___ au gagnant.
   a. la course **b.** la coupe
   c. la bicyclette

8. Dans une course cycliste les coureurs roulent sur ___.
   a. des gradins **b.** un terrain
   c. une piste

Activités de communication

Mots 1 et 2

A **C'est quel sport?** Give your partner several details about a sport without mentioning the name of the sport. Your partner will guess what sport you are describing. Then reverse roles.

> **Élève 1: Il y a cinq joueurs dans l'équipe. Les joueurs dribblent le ballon. Les meilleurs joueurs sont souvent très grands. Ils lancent le ballon dans le panier.**
> **Élève 2: C'est le basket-ball.**

B **Ton équipe favorite.** Ask your partner what his or her favorite team is and why. Reverse roles and report to the class.

> **Élève 1: Quelle est ton équipe favorite? Pourquoi?**
> **Élève 2: Mon équipe favorite de base-ball, c'est les Expos parce que je suis de Montréal. (Je n'ai pas d'équipe favorite de base-ball.)**

C **Un match de football.** Ask your partner several questions about the illustration using *qui, quel(le), est-ce que, combien,* and *où*. Then reverse roles.

Le passé composé des verbes réguliers

Describing Past Actions

1. You use the *passé composé* to express actions completed in the past. The *passé composé* is made up of the present tense of *avoir* and the past participle of the verb. Review the present tense of the verb *avoir.*

AVOIR	
j' ai	nous avons
tu as	vous avez
il/elle/on a	ils/elles ont

2. Study the following forms of the past participle of regular French verbs.

-er → -é		-ir → -i		-re → -u	
regarder	regardé	choisir	choisi	perdre	perdu
parler	parlé	réussir	réussi	vendre	vendu

Almost all past participles of French verbs end in the sound /é/, /i/, or /ü/.

PARLER	FINIR	PERDRE
j'ai parlé	j'ai fini	j'ai perdu
tu as parlé	tu as fini	tu as perdu
il/elle/on a parlé	il/elle/on a fini	il/elle/on a perdu
nous avons parlé	nous avons fini	nous avons perdu
vous avez parlé	vous avez fini	vous avez perdu
ils/elles ont parlé	ils/elles ont fini	ils/elles ont perdu

3. The *passé composé* is often used with time expressions such as:

> avant hier
> hier
> hier matin
> hier soir
> l'année dernière
> la semaine dernière

Study the following examples of the *passé composé*.

> **J'ai regardé le match à la télé hier soir.**
> **Nantes a joué contre Toulouse.**
> **L'année dernière Toulouse a gagné la coupe.**
> **Mais hier soir Toulouse a perdu le match.**
> **L'arbitre a puni Toulouse.**
> **Il a déclaré un penalty contre Toulouse.**
> **Les spectateurs ont applaudi.**

4. Note the placement of *ne... pas* in negative sentences with the *passé composé*. *Ne... pas* goes around the verb *avoir*.

> **Je *n*'ai *pas* parlé à Suzanne.**
> **Tu *n*'as *pas* regardé la télé?**
> **Il *n*'a *pas* entendu le téléphone.**

Exercices

A **Quel est le participe passé?** Donnez le participe passé.

1. habiter
2. quitter
3. parler
4. écouter
5. travailler
6. remplir
7. obéir
8. réussir
9. servir
10. dormir
11. perdre
12. vendre
13. attendre
14. répondre

B **Hier ou la semaine dernière.**
Donnez des réponses personnelles.

1. Hier matin tu as quitté la maison à quelle heure?
2. Avant les cours tu as rigolé avec tes copains?
3. Tu as parlé au prof de français?
4. La semaine dernière tu as passé un exâmen? Tu as réussi à l'examen?
5. Tu as répondu à toutes les questions?
6. Tu as quitté l'école à quelle heure hier?
7. Tu as attendu le bus devant l'école?

Le forcing

Encore une victoire pour l'équipe de Strasbourg. Les Niçois ont perdu leur troisième match.

STRASBOURG ET NICE 6–3

Après l'échec total de Lyon et le demi-échec face à Bourges, Nice a commis une troisième erreur en trois matchs. Les Strasbourgeois ont pratiqué un football collectif de qualité, se montrant patients et prudents pendant la première mi-temps. Le jeu niçois manquait de mouvement et de vitesse. Dortez se pose en rival sérieux de Peyre. Au début du match il a fait le forcing pour égaliser le score.

Ce n'est qu'après la mi-temps qu'il a marqué trois buts de suite. Et quels buts! On n'a jamais vu ça depuis le match légendaire qui Toulouse et Nantes

l'année dernière. Dortez avait mal à croire ce qu'il venait faire. Lors d'une interview apr le match il a dit: «Je dois être peu fou. C'est sûrement pour c que j'intéresse tout le monde lui est difficile de faire le hum quand son talent saute aux y Peyre, par contre, n'essaie m pas de cacher son ego. «Je plus fort que jamais,» a-t-il cisé l'autre jour. «Il est vra nous avons perdu trois m mais cela n'a pas d'import ou si peu. La semaine proc je vais pouvoir mont suis

C La fête d'Élisabeth. Complétez au passé composé.

1. Vendredi dernier Élisabeth ___ une fête. (donner)
2. Elle ___ à tous ses copains. (téléphoner)
3. Ses copains ___ au téléphone. (répondre)
4. Élisabeth ___ ses copains à la fête. (inviter)
5. Tous ses copains ___ son invitation. (accepter)
6. Yves et moi, nous ___ quelque chose à manger. (préparer)
7. Mais qui ___ les provisions? (acheter)
8. Tu ___ le menu? (choisir)
9. Non, Élisabeth ___ la fête et elle ___ le menu. (donner, choisir)
10. Tout le monde ___. (manger)
11. Vous ___ pendant la fête? (danser)
12. Oui, nous ___ et nous___. (danser, chanter)

D Un voyage en avion. On va imaginer que vous avez voyagé. Répondez.

1. Tu as voyagé l'année dernière?
2. Tu as voyagé avec Air France?
3. Tu as choisi classe économique ou première classe?
4. Tu as choisi une place côté couloir?
5. L'avion a décollé à l'heure?
6. Et il a atterri à l'heure?
7. Tu as voyagé avec un copain ou une copine?
8. Tu as attendu longtemps tes bagages?
9. La compagnie aérienne a perdu tes bagages?

E Un voyage en train. Mettez au passé composé.

1. J'attends le train.
2. Je voyage avec ma copine.
3. Nous attendons le train dans la salle d'attente de la gare.
4. J'achète un magazine au kiosque.
5. Je ne choisis pas de journal.
6. Ma copine achète un livre.
7. Nous entendons l'annonce du départ de notre train.
8. On annonce le départ au haut-parleur.
9. Le porteur descend nos bagages sur le quai.
10. Nous réussissons à trouver nos places dans la voiture onze.
11. Le contrôleur vérifie les billets.

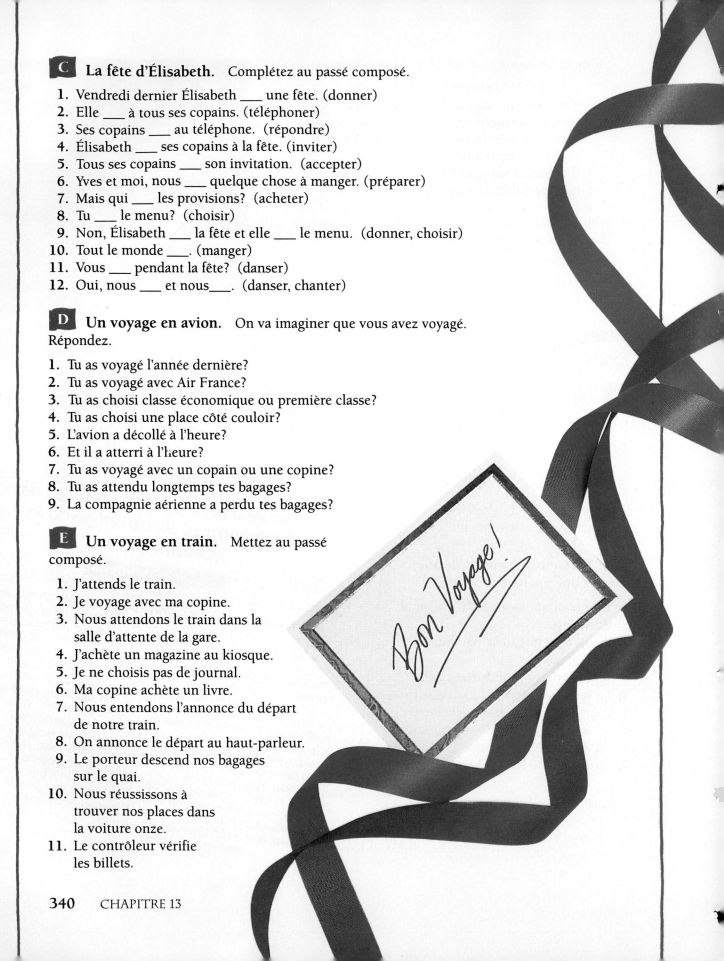

Bon Voyage!

1. *Qu'est-ce que* is another question or interrogative expression. It means "what" and refers to a thing.

> **Qu'est-ce que vous voyez?**
> **Qu'est-ce qu'il regarde?**
> **Qu'est-ce que vous avez?**

Note that *Qu'est-ce que vous avez?* also means "What's the matter?"

2. To ask "what?" in formal or written French you use *que* and invert the subject and verb.

> **Que voyez-vous?**
> **Que regarde-t-il?**
> **Qu'avez-vous?**

3. In informal French *qu'est-ce que* is used in exclamations.

> **Qu'est-ce qu'il est beau ce garçon!**   *How handsome that boy is!*
> **Qu'est-ce qu'elle est belle!**   *How beautiful she is!*
> **Qu'est-ce que je suis fatigué!**   *How tired I am!*

Exercices

A   **Comment? Qu'est-ce que tu fais?**   Posez des questions d'après le modèle.

> **J'écoute la radio.**
> *Comment? Qu'est-ce que tu écoutes?*

1. Je lis le journal.
2. Je regarde la télé.
3. Je fais des exercices.
4. Je fais les courses.
5. J'achète un cadeau.
6. Je lave la voiture.
7. Nous écrivons un poème.
8. Nous préparons le petit déjeuner.
9. Nous commandons une boisson.

B   **Des mini-conversations.**   Posez des questions et répondez d'après le modèle.

> **marquer/ un but**
>
> **Élève 1: Qu'est-ce que les joueurs ont marqué?**
> **Élève 2: Ils ont marqué un but.**

1. lancer / le ballon
2. dribbler / le ballon
3. envoyer / le ballon
4. perdre / le match
5. gagner / la coupe
6. égaliser / le score
7. gagner / de l'argent

CONVERSATION

Scènes de la vie   *Une retransmission sportive*

ROMAIN: Tu as regardé la télé hier soir?

CORINNE: Oui, j'ai regardé la retransmission du match France-Brésil.

ROMAIN: Tu parles de la victoire de la France sur le Brésil?

CORINNE: Voilà! La France a gagné un à zéro.

ROMAIN: Le Brésil a fait le forcing pour égaliser le score.

CORINNE: Oui, mais sans succès. À chaque fois Peyre a bloqué le ballon. Ce type est un gardien vachement fort.

ROMAIN: Qui a marqué le but pour la France? J'ai oublié.

CORINNE: Tu as oublié? Tu n'as pas de mémoire! Moi, je ne vais jamais oublier ça! Roland. C'est Roland qui a marqué le but.

Quel match alors!   Répondez d'après la conversation.

1. Qui a regardé la télé hier soir?
2. Qu'est-ce qu'elle a regardé à la télé?
3. Qui a joué contre la France?
4. Qui a gagné le match?
5. Quelle équipe a perdu le match?
6. Le Brésil a réussi à égaliser le score? Pourquoi pas?
7. Comment s'appelle le gardien de but français?
8. Qui a marqué le but pour la France?
9. Qui a oublié son nom?

20.30

20.25 TF1 22.35

Football

En direct de Rotterdam. Commentaires : Thierry Roland et Jean-Michel Larqué.

Feyenoord/AS Monaco

Demi-finale retour de la **Coupe d'Europe des vainqueurs de Coupes.** «Je crois sincèrement que l'on forme un groupe de joueurs très unis. Quand l'un est en difficulté, l'autre a la volonté de venir l'aider. C'est important comme état d'esprit, car cela veut dire qu'en Coupe d'Europe, où le mental compte énormément, on peut avoir confiance en la solidarité. Je pense qu'on a une équipe capable d'embêter beaucoup de monde.»
Rob Witschge, qui prononce ces paroles pleines de bon sens, sait de quoi il parle. Il connaît aussi bien le football néerlandais que le football français, pour avoir joué pendant deux ans à Saint-Etienne.

Désormais attaquant à Feyenoo l'ancien Stéphanois s'est parfai ment adapté au style défensif son équipe, qui ressemble én mément à celui de l'Ajax d'anta tous les défenseurs attaquent, to les attaquants défendent. Rés tat : les défenses adverses se tro vent confrontées à des vagues défe lantes bien difficiles à conteni Arsène Wenger, l'entraîneur de Monégasques, craint cette tactiqu du rouleau compresseur, il ne ! cache pas : «Feyenoord m'a fa forte impression. Cette formatio est très disciplinée. Et il éman d'elle une grande force physique.

B. H
En cas d'égalité à la fin du temps régle mentaire, il sera procédé aux prolonga tions et éventuellement aux tirs aux but.

20.30 C++ 21.00

Journal du cinéma

Présentation : Michel Denisot.

20.30 M6 20.40

Surprise-partie

Prononciation   *Liaison et Élision*

l'arbitre

1. You have already seen that in French certain words are pronounced differently depending on whether they are followed by a vowel or a consonant. There is either liaison or elision. Compare the following.

   les copains / les‿amis   je regarde / j'écoute

2. Liaison is the linking of a usually silent consonant to the following word when the word begins with a vowel or silent *h*. Liaison occurs with plural subject pronouns, plural articles, and plural possessive adjectives. Repeat the following.

   ils‿ont gagné   les‿équipes   des‿arbitres   mes‿amis

3. Elision is the linking of a consonant and a vowel sound. It is made by dropping the vowel at the end of a word before a vowel at the beginning of the next. Elision occurs with the articles *le* and *la*, with the pronoun *je*, and with the negative word *ne*. Repeat the following.

   l'arbitre   l'équipe   j'attends   j'ai gagné   Tu n'écoutes pas!

   les‿arbitres

   Now repeat and compare the following pairs of sentences.

   Vous‿avez perdu. / Vous n'avez pas perdu.
   J'ai fini. / Je n'ai pas fini.

Activités de communication

A   Le week-end dernier.   Tell your partner several things you did or didn't do last weekend, choosing from the verbs below. Then reverse roles.

acheter	dîner	jouer	regarder	téléphoner
attendre	dormir	manger	rigoler	travailler

B   Des exclamations!   Tell your partner the name of a well-known person, place, or thing. Your partner will give his or her opinion using *qu'est-ce que*. Then reverse roles. You may each take several turns.

   Élève 1: Michael Jordan.
   Élève 2: Qu'est-ce qu'il est grand!

C   Ton sport d'équipe favori.   Work with a partner. Take turns asking each other for the following information.

1. Quel est ton sport d'équipe favori?
2. Tu joues à ce sport ou tu préfères regarder les matchs à la télé?
3. Quelle est ton équipe favorite?
4. Ton équipe favorite a gagné beaucoup de matchs cette année?

LECTURE ET CULTURE

LES SPORTS EN FRANCE

Est-ce que les Français sont des sportifs sérieux? On peut dire que les sports collectifs intéressent les Français moins que les Américains ou les Russes, par exemple. Mais de nos jours, de plus en plus de Français pratiquent un sport. Le sport d'équipe le plus populaire en France, c'est le football ou, comme on dit souvent, le foot. Chaque grande ville a son équipe de foot. Des championnats nationaux et internationaux attirent[1] des fanas du monde entier. Mais le football en France, et en Europe en général, n'est pas le même que le football américain. D'abord le ballon est rond et les joueurs ne peuvent pas toucher le ballon avec les mains. Ils donnent un coup de tête ou un coup de pied dans le ballon pour envoyer le ballon dans le but de l'équipe adverse.

En France on pratique presque[2] tous les sports —le basket-ball, le volley-ball et le hand-ball. Mais il y a un sport qu'on ne pratique jamais: c'est le base-ball. Le base-ball n'est pas du tout populaire.

La France est le pays du cyclisme. Les courses dans les vélodromes attirent toujours beaucoup de monde. En juillet le célèbre Tour de France a lieu[3]. C'est une course internationale tout autour du[4] pays. Les coureurs cyclistes professionnels de tous les pays du monde participent au Tour de France. On donne au gagnant un trophée. On donne aussi une somme d'argent au nouveau héros international.

[1] attirent *attract*
[2] presque *almost*
[3] a lieu *takes place*
[4] tout autour du *all around*

79e Tour de France

Étude de mots

Quelle est la définition? Trouvez les mots qui correspondent.

1. un sport collectif
2. un sport individuel
3. le même
4. un joueur
5. le camp adverse
6. pratiquer un sport

a. le contraire de «différent»
b. faire du sport, jouer
c. l'opposition
d. un sport qu'on pratique seul
e. une personne qui pratique un sport
f. un sport d'équipe

Compréhension

A **Les sports.** Répondez par «oui» ou «non».

1. Les sports collectifs sont plus populaires en France qu'aux États-Unis.
2. Le sport d'équipe le plus populaire en France, c'est le football.
3. Le football est un sport collectif qu'on pratique en compétition.
4. Quand on joue au football américain on peut toucher le ballon avec les mains.
5. Le ballon de football en France est ovale.
6. Le base-ball est assez populaire en France.
7. Le cyclisme est plus populaire aux États-Unis qu'en France.
8. Le Tour de France a lieu au mois de septembre.

B **Les Français aiment les sports.** Répondez.

1. On pratique quels sports d'équipe en France?
2. Quel sport est-ce qu'on ne pratique jamais en France?
3. Quel sport est plus populaire en France qu'aux États-Unis?
4. Qu'est-ce que c'est, le Tour de France?
5. Qui participe au Tour de France?
6. Qu'est-ce qu'on donne au gagnant du Tour de France?

DÉCOUVERTE CULTURELLE

Il y a un sport qu'on pratique en France qui ressemble au football américain? Oui, mais ce n'est pas le foot. C'est le rugby. Le football américain ressemble au rugby.

Aux États-Unis toutes les écoles secondaires ont toujours des équipes de football américain et d'autres sports. En France, ce n'est pas le cas. Les sports ne sont pas très importants dans les lycées français. Il n'y a pas d'équipes organisées. Mais les élèves secondaires en France ont le mercredi après-midi libre et, grâce aux[1] associations sportives scolaires, ils peuvent profiter de leur temps libre pour faire du sport.

Les Françaises et les Français font de la gymnastique, du tennis et du jogging. Mais ce sont surtout les hommes qui jouent au foot.

[1] grâce aux *thanks to*

L'alpinisme est un sport très pratiqué en France **1**.

Voici des joueuses de volley-ball. Est-ce que l'arbitre regarde attentivement le match **2**?

En France aussi on aime faire du patin à roulettes sur les rampes **3**.

Le Tour de France commence et finit à Paris. Quel monument parisien célèbre est sur la photo **4**?

Voici un match de football à Bordeaux. C'est un match de nuit. Est-ce que les gradins sont pleins **5**?

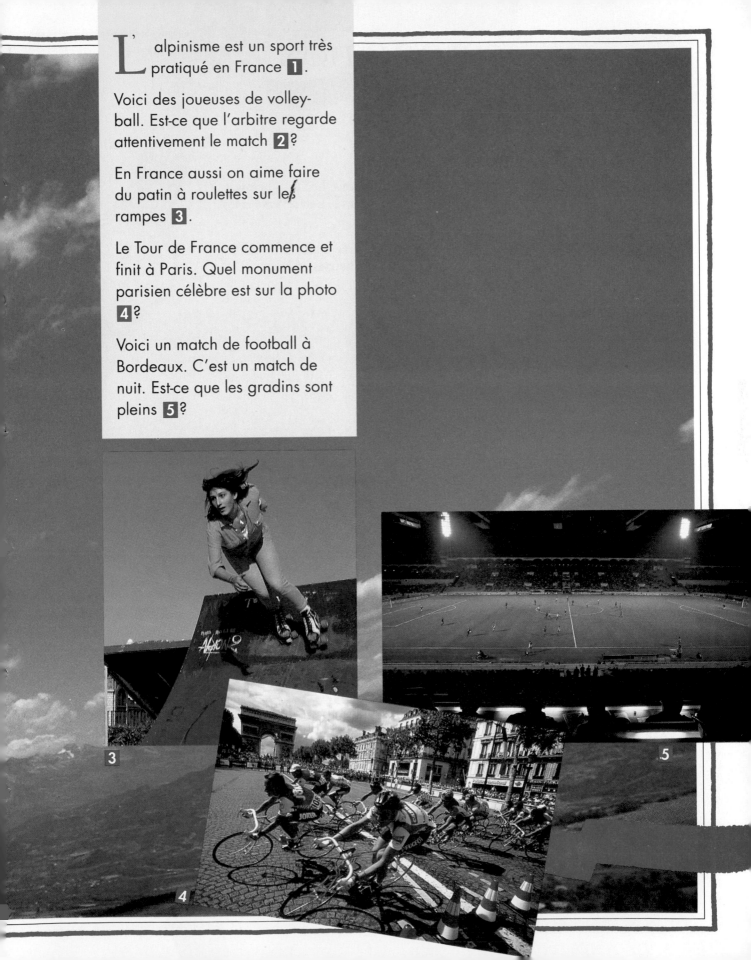

3

4

5

CULMINATION

Activités de communication orale

A **Le temps passé.** Using the time expressions and the verbs below, ask your partner several questions about his or her activities. Then reverse roles.

> quitter /ce matin
>
> Élève 1: Tu as quitté la maison à quelle heure ce matin?
> Élève 2: Ce matin j'ai quitté la maison à sept heures et quart.

VERBES	EXPRESSIONS DE TEMPS
étudier	ce matin
jouer	hier
perdre	hier soir
quitter	l'année dernière
regarder	la semaine dernière
téléphoner	pendant le week-end
travailler	
attendre	

B **Une enquête.** Divide into small groups and choose a leader. Using the list below, the leader will ask the others what they did last summer, take notes, and report to the class.

> Élève 1: Qui a voyagé en avion l'été dernier?
> Élève 2: Moi, j'ai voyagé en avion l'été dernier.

étudier le français	gagner beaucoup d'argent
jouer au tennis	voyager en avion / train / voiture
travailler	passer quelques semaines à la plage

Activité de communication écrite

Une invitation. Write a short note inviting a friend to go to a sports event with you. Be sure to include the following in your note.

1. Ask your friend if he or she would like to go to the sports event with you.
2. Tell your friend when and where the event is.
3. Say who is playing against whom.
4. Mention how you will get to the event.

Réintroduction et recombinaison

A **Mes vêtements.** Donnez des réponses personnelles.

1. Quelle est la couleur de ta chemise favorite ou de ton chemisier favori?
2. Quand tu achètes des chaussures, tu fais quelle pointure?
3. Tu achètes des vêtements prêt-à-porter ou sur mesure?
4. Si ton pantalon est trop large, tu as besoin de la taille au-dessus ou de la taille au-dessous?
5. Et s'il est trop serré, tu as besoin de quelle taille?

B **Raoul.** Répondez d'après le dessin.

1. Raoul est où?
2. Il parle à qui?
3. Que veut Raoul?
4. Qui met de l'essence dans le réservoir?
5. Qu'est-ce que la pompiste vérifie?

C **Serge roule en voiture.** Complétez.

1. Serge ___ bien. (conduire)
2. Il ___ le code de la route. (lire)
3. Il ___ que St.-Brieuc est assez loin d'ici. (dire)
4. Il ___ une carte postale de St.-Brieuc. (écrire)

D **Et vous aussi!** Récrivez les phrases de l'Exercice C en utilisant «vous».

Vocabulaire

NOMS
le foot(ball)
le terrain de football
l'équipe (f.)
le camp
le joueur
le gardien de but
le ballon
le but
l'arbitre (m.)
la tête
le pied

le basket(-ball)
le panier
le panneau
le demi-cercle

le base-ball
le volley-ball
le sol

le vélo
le cyclisme
le coureur cycliste
le coureur
la course
la piste
le stade
le gradin
le spectateur
le gagnant
la coupe

l'automne (m.)
le printemps

ADJECTIFS
adverse
comble
plein(e)

VERBES
dribbler
envoyer
lancer
opposer
siffler

AUTRES MOTS ET EXPRESSIONS
donner un coup de pied
marquer un but
contre
par dessus
jusqu'à
beaucoup de monde

hier
hier matin
hier soir
avant hier
l'année dernière

L'HIVER ET LES SPORTS D'HIVER

OBJECTIFS

In this chapter you will learn to do the following:

1. talk about skiing and ice skating
2. describe winter weather
3. describe past actions
4. ask "whom" or "what"
5. describe French and Canadian ski resorts

VOCABULAIRE

MOTS 1

UNE STATION DE SPORTS D'HIVER

un sommet

une montagne

une piste très raide

une vallée

des bosses (f.)

un télésiège

un chalet

une skieuse

des lunettes (f.)

un anorak

une écharpe

un bonnet

un skieur

un gant

un bâton

un ski

une chaussure
de ski

le ski de fond

le ski alpin

une piste de slalom

un moniteur   une monitrice

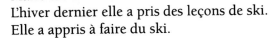

Marie est débutante.
L'hiver dernier elle a pris des leçons de ski.
Elle a appris à faire du ski.
Elle a eu un très bon moniteur.
Le moniteur a appris à faire du ski à Marie.
Elle a compris les instructions du moniteur.

Marie a mis son anorak.
Elle a mis ses gants, son écharpe
    et son bonnet.
Elle a mis ses skis.

Marie a descendu la piste.
Elle a descendu la piste verte.
La piste verte est pour les débutants.

Exercices

A **Marie a appris à faire du ski.** Répondez.

1. Marie a appris à faire du ski?
2. Qui a appris à Marie à faire du ski?
3. Elle a eu un très bon moniteur?
4. Elle a compris les instructions du moniteur?
5. Marie a mis son anorak?
6. Elle a mis ses gants, son écharpe et son bonnet?
7. Elle a mis ses chaussures de ski et ses skis?
8. Elle a descendu quelle piste?
9. La piste verte est pour les débutants?

B **Un sport fabuleux.** Répondez par «oui» ou «non».

1. Le ski est un sport d'été.
2. Les débutants ne font pas bien du ski.
3. Une piste très raide, c'est une piste avec des bosses.
4. Le moniteur ou la monitrice apprend à faire du ski aux débutants.
5. Les skieurs prennent le télésiège pour descendre la piste.
6. Les skieurs prennent le télésiège pour monter au sommet de la montagne.
7. On n'a pas vraiment besoin de pistes pour faire du ski de fond.
8. Les débutants descendent la piste de slalom.
9. Les skieurs et les skieuses portent souvent des lunettes.
10. Après le ski on va dans le chalet.

C **On fait du ski.** Répondez d'après les dessins.

1. C'est une station balnéaire ou une station de sports d'hiver?
2. C'est une plage ou une montagne?
3. C'est une piste ou une piscine?
4. C'est un skieur ou un nageur?
5. C'est un ski nautique ou un bâton?
6. C'est un maillot ou un anorak?
7. Elle fait du ski alpin ou du ski nautique?
8. Il fait du ski de fond ou du ski alpin?
9. C'est le sommet de la montagne ou la vallée?
10. C'est un gant ou une écharpe?

VOCABULAIRE

MOTS 2

EN HIVER

Il fait froid.
Le ciel est couvert.
Il neige.
Il gèle.
Le vent est très froid.

Quelle est la température
aujourd'hui?
Il fait deux (degrés
Celsius).

jouer dans la neige

lancer une
boule de neige

une patinoire

une patineuse

un patineur

le patinage

la glace

un patin à glace

Hier Robert a fait du patin.
Il a eu un petit accident.
Il a fait une chute.

Exercices

A Le petit accident de Robert. Répondez.

1. Robert a fait du patin ou du ski?
2. Il a mis ses patins ou ses skis?
3. Il a fait une chute sur la patinoire ou sur la piste de slalom?
4. Il a eu un petit accident ou un accident grave?

B Le temps en hiver. Répondez.

1. En hiver il fait froid ou il fait chaud?
2. Il neige en hiver ou en été?
3. Quand il neige, le ciel est couvert ou il fait du soleil?
4. Quand il neige, il fait chaud ou il fait froid?
5. Il gèle quelquefois en hiver?
6. Le vent est froid?
7. En général, quelle est la température dans ta ville en hiver?
8. Les températures en hiver sont basses ou élevées?

C Les sports d'hiver et d'été. Donnez des réponses personnelles.

1. Tu préfères l'été ou l'hiver?
2. Quelle est ta saison favorite?
3. Tu préfères les sports d'hiver ou les sports d'été?
4. Qu'est-ce que tu mets quand il fait très froid?
5. Tu as fait du ski? Où?
6. Tu aimes faire du ski?
7. Il y a une station de sports d'hiver près de chez toi?
8. Tu aimes jouer dans la neige?
9. Tu aimes lancer des boules de neige?
10. Tu aimes faire du patin?
11. Tu es bon patineur ou bonne patineuse?
12. Tu as des patins à glace?

D C'est le ski ou le patinage? Choisissez.

1. On pratique ce sport sur la glace.
2. On pratique ce sport sur la neige.
3. On descend une piste.
4. Les champions font du slalom.
5. On met des patins à glace.
6. On utilise des bâtons.
7. On pratique ce sport sur une patinoire.

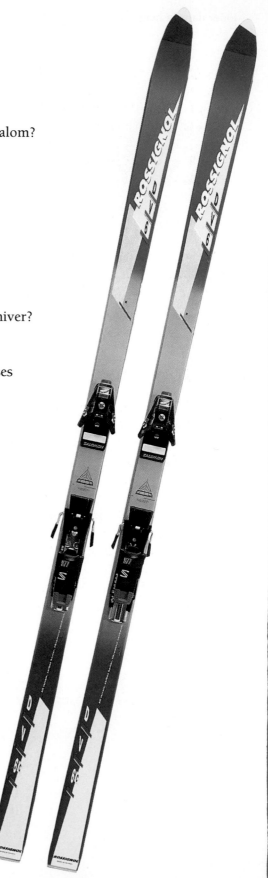

Activités de communication

A **À quels sports joue-t-on?** A French exchange student (your partner) has just arrived to spend a year at your school. He or she will ask you what the weather is like in your town in summer and winter and what activities people do during these seasons. Give him or her as much information as you can.

B **La météo: il va faire quel temps demain?** You would like to know what the weather is going to be like tomorrow. Find out the following from your partner:

1. if he or she heard or read the weather report (*la météo*) for tomorrow.
2. what the weather is going to be like. (If your partner hasn't heard or read the weather report, he or she should take a guess.)
3. what the temperature is going to be.
4. if your partner would like to do something with you, based on the weather report.

C **À la montagne.** Imagine that you and your partner are at a winter resort. Your partner will ask you what you did during the day. Using the list below, tell him or her several things you did, then reverse roles.

> Élève 1: Qu'est-ce que tu as fait aujourd'hui?
> Élève 2: D'abord j'ai pris des leçons de ski avec un moniteur.
>   Ensuite j'ai...

> descendre la piste
> faire du patin
> faire du ski
> jouer dans la neige
> lancer des boules de neige
> prendre le télésiège

D **Sur le télésiège.** On the chairlift you strike up a conversation with the person sitting next to you (your partner). Find out if he or she:

1. likes to ski and where.
2. skis often.
3. also likes cross-country skiing.
4. is a beginner or skis well.

STRUCTURE

Le passé composé des verbes irréguliers

Describing Past Actions

---

1. You have already learned the past participles of regular verbs in French which end with an /é/, /i/, or /ü/ sound. Note the past participles of the following irregular verbs which also end with an /i/ or /ü/ sound.

INFINITIF ➝	PARTICIPE PASSÉ
mettre	mis
permettre	permis
prendre	pris
comprendre	compris
apprendre	appris
dire	dit
écrire	écrit
conduire	conduit
avoir	eu
croire	cru
voir	vu
pouvoir	pu
vouloir	voulu
lire	lu

La ligne d'arrivée de la compétition de ski alpin à Val d'Isère

J'ai pris des leçons de ski.
J'ai appris à faire du ski.
J'ai compris toutes les instructions de la monitrice.
Elle a dit, «Bravo! Vous faites très bien du ski!»
J'ai eu de la chance. J'ai eu une très bonne monitrice.
Elle a écrit un livre sur le ski alpin. J'ai lu son livre.

2. The commonly used verbs *être* and *faire* also have irregular past participles.

être	été
faire	fait

J'ai fait un voyage à Megève l'année dernière.
J'ai été très content de pouvoir faire du ski.

3. Note the position of short adverbs such as *déjà*, *bien*, *trop*, and *vite* with the
   passé composé. They are placed between *avoir* and the past participle.

J'ai *déjà* mangé.	*I have already eaten.*
Il a *vite* fini son sandwich.	*He quickly finished his sandwich.*
Il a *bien* choisi son moniteur.	*He chose his instructor well.*

   Adverbs of time such as *hier* and *aujourd'hui* follow the past participle.

   Il a fait du ski *hier*.
   Mais il n'a pas fait de ski *aujourd'hui*.

Exercices

A **Gilles a fait du ski.** Répondez d'après les dessins.

Bonne chance!

1. Gilles a mis son anorak?
2. Il a dit «Bonne chance» à son ami?
3. Son ami a déjà fait du ski
   aujourd'hui?

4. Gilles a bien fait du ski?
5. Il a eu un accident?
6. Après l'accident Gilles a lu un livre pour les
   débutants?

B **Tu as dit quoi?** Complétez d'après le modèle avec «dire», «lire» ou «écrire».

> J'___ que j'___ ce que j'___.
> *J'ai dit que j'ai lu ce que j'ai écrit.*

1. Il ___ qu'il ___ ce qu'il ___.
2. Nous ___ que nous ___ ce que nous ___.
3. Tu ___ que tu ___ ce que tu ___.

4. Vous ___ que vous ___ ce que vous ___.
5. Elles ___ qu'elles ___ ce qu'elles ___.

C **Qu'est-ce qu'on a fait?** Répondez.

1. Est-ce que tu as lu le journal ce matin? Et tes parents?
2. Les élèves ont lu leur livre de francais avant l'examen?
3. Est-ce que tu as dit «Salut!» à tes copains ce matin?
4. Tes amis et toi avez dit «Au revoir!» à votre professeur de français hier?
5. La femme a dit «Zut!» quand elle a trouvé une contravention sur le parebrise de sa voiture?
6. Les élèves ont écrit des lettres à leurs grands-parents?
7. Ils ont écrit une composition au cours d'anglais?
8. Est-ce que tu as bien écrit cet exercice?

D **En route!** Complétez au passé composé.

Mon ami Laurent ___ (dire) que
_____1
Chamonix est une belle station de sports
d'hiver. Il ___ (lire) le Guide Michelin et
_____2
il ___ (voir) que Chamonix est loin de
__3
Paris. Mais il ___ (vouloir) y aller. Ses
____4
parents ___ (permettre) à Laurent
___5
de prendre leur voiture. Il ___ (prendre)
____6
leur voiture et il ___ (conduire) jusqu'à
___7
Chamonix. Il ___ (faire) le voyage avec
__8
son copain Alain qui ___ (être) très
___9
content de partir avec lui. Ils ___ (mettre)
____10
leurs skis sur la voiture. Ils ___ (prendre)
____11
l'autoroute. Ils n'___ pas ___ (avoir) de
___12
problème.

On va à la Mer de Glace près de Chamonix.

1. You use the pronouns *qui*, "whom," and *quoi*, "what," with prepositions such as *à*, *de*, *avec*, and *chez* to ask questions in French. *Qui* refers to a person and *quoi* refers to a thing. Study the following examples.

> **Tu parles à qui?**
> **Tu vas chez qui?**
> **Tu parles de quoi?**

2. Note the inversion in formal or written French.

INFORMAL	FORMAL
Vous parlez à qui?	**À qui parlez-vous?**
Vous allez chez qui?	**Chez qui allez-vous?**
Vous avez besoin de quoi?	**De quoi avez-vous besoin?**

Exercices

A **Comment? Je n'ai pas entendu.**   Répondez d'après le modèle.

> **Elle parle de sa sœur.**
> *Comment? Je n'ai pas entendu. Elle parle de qui?*

1. Elle parle de sa tante.
2. Elle parle de son prof.
3. Elle parle au moniteur.
4. Elle parle à son amie.
5. Elle est chez ses parents.
6. Elle va chez son copain.
7. Elle travaille avec sa cousine.
8. Elle parle de son travail.
9. Elle parle de ses vacances à la montagne.
10. Elle a besoin d'argent.
11. Elle a besoin de skis.

B **Au téléphone.**   Posez une question d'après le modèle.

> **Vous allez au cinéma avec votre amie.**
> *Avec qui allez-vous au cinéma?*

1. Vous téléphonez à votre amie.
2. Vous parlez à votre amie.
3. Vous parlez de choses sérieuses.
4. Vous laissez un message pour le frère de votre amie.

Un forfait-journée

CONVERSATION

Scènes de la vie *Tu as fait du ski?*

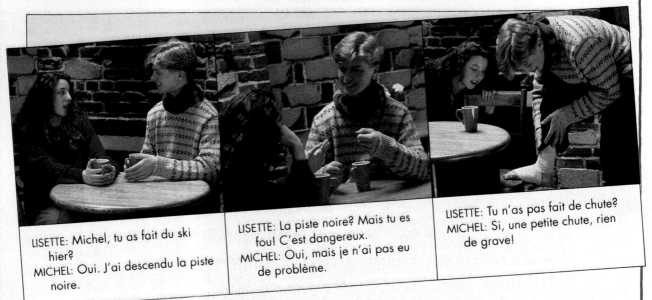

LISETTE: Michel, tu as fait du ski hier?
MICHEL: Oui. J'ai descendu la piste noire.

LISETTE: La piste noire? Mais tu es fou! C'est dangereux.
MICHEL: Oui, mais je n'ai pas eu de problème.

LISETTE: Tu n'as pas fait de chute?
MICHEL: Si, une petite chute, rien de grave!

 La piste noire. Répondez d'après la conversation.

1. Qui a fait du ski hier?
2. Il a descendu quelle piste?
3. La piste noire est facile ou difficile?
4. Les pistes noires sont des pistes très raides?
5. Michel a eu un problème?
6. Il a fait une chute?

Prononciation *Le son /r/ initial*

You have already practiced saying the /r/ sound in the middle or at the end of a word. You will now practice saying it at the beginning of a word. Repeat the following pairs of words.

> opéra / radio   mari / restaurant
> favori / rigoler   adoré / rez-de-chaussée

Now repeat the following sentences.

> C'est la radio qui réveille Richard.
> Pour rester en forme, Raoul ne regarde pas trop la télévison.
> Robert roule très vite dans sa Renault rouge.

une radio

Activités de communication

A **Au téléphone.** Ask your partner if he or she spoke on the telephone last night (or the night before). Ask whom your partner spoke to (*à qui*) and what they talked about (*de quoi*). Then reverse roles.

B **Le week-end dernier.** Choose three or four of the activities listed below and find out if your partner did any of them last weekend. If the answer is "yes," ask your partner some additional questions. Then reverse roles.

> Élève 1: Tu as vu un film le week-end dernier?
> Élève 2: Oui, j'ai vu un film.
> Élève 1: Tu as vu quel film?
> Élève 2: J'ai vu . . .

avoir un accident	inviter un copain ou une copine au cinéma
écrire une composition	jouer au football / base-ball / basket-ball, etc.
être à une fête	lire un journal / un magazine / un livre
étudier	parler au téléphone
faire tes devoirs	regarder un programme à la télé
faire un voyage	voir un film

C **J'ai appris à . . .** Tell your partner something you learned to do recently (last week, last summer, etc.). Your partner will ask you for the information below. Answer, then reverse roles.

1. when you learned to do the activity
2. where you learned
3. who taught you
4. if you took lessons
5. if you had a good instructor
6. if you understood the instructions

D **Au Canada.** Your Canadian pen pal has invited you to spend a week in Québec during the winter. Write back accepting or declining the invitation. Give several reasons why you can or cannot accept.

E **Mes vacances d'hiver.** Write a postcard to a friend telling about your mid-winter vacation. Include the following information.

1. where you are
2. who is with you
3. what the weather is like
4. what you have done
5. what you have liked and disliked
6. when you are going to return home

On fait beaucoup de ski au Canada.

LECTURE ET CULTURE

ON VA AUX SPORTS D'HIVER

En février dernier la classe de Madame Carrigan a fait un voyage au Canada. Les élèves ont eu une semaine de vacances. Ils ont pris le train de New York à Montréal. Ils ont passé trois jours à Montréal où ils ont parlé français. Montréal est la deuxième ville francophone[1] du monde, après Paris.

Après deux jours à Montréal ils ont pris le car[2] jusqu'au Parc du Mont-Sainte-Anne. Le Mont-Sainte-Anne est une station de sports d'hiver tout près de la jolie ville de Québec. Après leur arrivée à Sainte-Anne ils ont tous mis leur anorak et leurs chaussures de ski. Ils ont acheté leur ticket de télésiège. Ils ont pris le télésiège jusqu'au sommet de la montagne. Du sommet ils ont eu une vue splendide sur les montagnes et les vallées couvertes de neige. As-tu jamais[3] vu les montagnes couvertes de neige? C'est vraiment superbe!

Les bâtons à la main et les skis aux pieds, ils ont commencé à descendre une piste. Mais ils ont choisi la mauvaise[4] piste, une piste très raide, trop difficile pour des débutants. Qui a eu un accident? Le casse-cou[5] Michel? Mais oui, c'est lui! Il a fait une chute. Il a glissé jusqu'en bas[6] de la piste. Tous ses copains ont rigolé. Ils ont dit, «Michel, tu es une vraie boule de neige qui roule, roule, roule!»

[1] francophone   *French-speaking*
[2] le car   *the bus*
[3] jamais   *ever*
[4] mauvaise   *wrong*
[5] le casse-cou   *daredevil*
[6] a glissé jusqu'en bas   *slid to the bottom*

Le Mont-Sainte-Anne

Étude de mots

🚩 **Quel est le mot?** Choisissez.

1. Février est _____.
   a. un mois   b. une saison
2. Février est en ___.
   a. été   b. hiver
3. Montréal est une ville _____.
   a. francophone   b. française
4. Les chaussures de ski sont des _____.
   a. tennis   b. bottes
5. On met _____ quand il fait très froid.
   a. un maillot   b. un anorak

Compréhension

A **Une excursion.** Corrigez les phrases.

1. Les élèves de Madame Carrigan ont fait un voyage en France.
2. Ils ont pris l'avion.
3. Ils ont passé trois jours à Québec.
4. Québec est la deuxième ville francophone du monde.
5. Le Parc du Mont-Sainte-Anne est une station balnéaire.
6. Les élèves de Madame Carrigan font tous très bien du ski.

B **Un fait important.** Vous avez appris quelque chose d'important au sujet de Montréal. Qu'est-ce que c'est?

DÉCOUVERTE CULTURELLE

Quelques pays francophones ont des stations de sports d'hiver fabuleuses. En France, par exemple, il y a beaucoup de stations de sports d'hiver dans les Alpes et les Pyrénées. La Suisse est un pays célèbre pour le ski. Et n'oubliez pas que le français est une des langues officielles de la Suisse. En Suisse on parle français, allemand et italien. Et au Québec, la province francophone du Canada, il y a des stations de sports d'hiver superbes.

En France les écoles primaires ont des classes de neige. Les élèves vont dans une station de sports d'hiver. Le matin ils ont des cours. Ils étudient les maths, l'anglais, etc. L'après-midi, des moniteurs apprennent à faire du ski aux élèves. Il y a des classes de neige aux États-Unis? Vous croyez que c'est une bonne idée?

Dans les stations de sports d'hiver en France les pistes sont classées selon leur difficulté. Les couleurs indiquent le niveau, ou le degré, de difficulté.

PISTE	NIVEAU	TYPE DE SKIEURS
	facile	débutants
	moyen	bons skieurs
	difficile	très bons skieurs
	très difficile	très, très bons skieurs

Le hockey sur glace est un sport d'hiver très populaire, surtout au Canada. Et les joueurs canadiens sont parmi les meilleurs joueurs de hockey du monde **1**.

Courchevel est une grande station de sports d'hiver très célèbre dans les Alpes françaises. Tu veux faire du ski sur les pistes de Courchevel **2**?

Voici des gens dans une rue de Méribel pendant les Jeux Olympiques de 1992. Comme Courchevel, Méribel fait partie des Trois Vallées, une galaxie de stations de sports d'hiver dans les Alpes françaises **3**.

Voici le tricolore (le drapeau français) et le drapeau olympique. De quelles couleurs sont ces drapeaux **4**?

Voici des gens qui font du ski de fond dans la province d'Alberta au Canada **5**.

Ces deux couples prennent le télésiège jusqu'au sommet de la montagne **6**. Un des couples va faire du ski et l'autre couple va faire du surf des neiges. As-tu jamais fait du surf des neiges?

CULMINATION

Activités de communication orale

A **Sports d'hiver ou sports d'été?** Find out if your partner prefers winter or summer sports. Then ask which ones he or she likes and why. Reverse roles.

B **Sur la piste.** Imagine that you and your partner have just met on the ski slopes. Use the cues below to talk to each other.

1. Ask your partner to do something with you tomorrow. (Name the activity.)
2. Your partner wants to know where and at what time.
3. Your partner will either a) accept the invitation or b) decline, and suggest some other activity.

C **Miami et New York.** Imagine that you're from Miami and your partner is from New York. Contrast your two cities in winter. Talk about the weather, clothing, activities, and so on.

> Élève 1: À Miami il fait chaud en hiver.
> Élève 2: À New York il fait froid en hiver.

D **La location de skis.** You need to rent some ski equipment from the attendant (your partner) at a ski resort. Use the cues below to talk with your partner.

1. Greet each other.
2. Tell your partner what ski equipment you need and for how long.
3. He or she will ask your boot size.
4. Your partner will then ask what level skier you are.
5. Find out when you pay.

E **De quoi a-t-on besoin pour..?** Using the list below, ask your partner what one needs in order to do several of the following activities. Your partner will name as many things as possible. Then reverse roles.

Le Mont d'Arbois à Megève

> Élève 1: De quoi a-t-on besoin pour apprendre le français?
> Élève 2: On a besoin d'un bon professeur, d'un livre et de beaucoup de patience!

1. conduire une voiture
2. écrire une composition
3. faire du ski
4. faire un voyage
5. jouer au tennis
6. préparer un sandwich

Activité de communication écrite

■ **Une station de sports d'hiver idéale.** Write a paragraph describing an ideal winter resort (real or imaginary). Be sure to include the following information.

1. where it is located and how to get there
2. what the weather is generally like
3. what facilities there are (lifts, skating rinks, restaurants, etc.)
4. what else you can do there besides ski

Réintroduction et recombinaison

A **Un match de foot.** Mettez au passé composé.

1. Je joue au foot.
2. Je passe le ballon à Charles.
3. Il renvoie le ballon.
4. Le gardien bloque le ballon.
5. Nous ne marquons pas de but.
6. L'arbitre déclare un penalty.
7. L'équipe adverse marque un but.
8. Nous faisons le forcing pour égaliser le score.

B **La télé.** Complétez au passé composé.

1. Hier soir j'___ la télé. (regarder)
2. J'___ un film intéressant. (voir)
3. J' ___ la météo: demain, neige et froid, températures basses. (entendre)
4. À neuf heures mon copain Éric m' ___. (téléphoner)
5. Il n'___ pas ___ de bonnes nouvelles. (avoir)
6. Il ___ un examen et il n'___ pas ___ à l'examen. (passer, réussir)

Vocabulaire

NOMS

l'hiver (m.)
le vent
le ski (*skiing*)
le ski alpin
le ski de fond
le skieur
la skieuse
le (la) débutant(e)
le moniteur
la monitrice
la piste (raide)
la piste de slalom
la bosse

la station de sports d'hiver
le chalet
le télésiège
la montagne
le sommet
la vallée

le ski (*ski*)
le bâton
la chaussure de ski
l'anorak (m.)
le bonnet
l'écharpe (f.)
le gant

les lunettes (f.)

le patinage
le patin à glace
le patineur
la patineuse
la patinoire
la glace
l'accident (m.)
la chute

VERBES

apprendre à quelqu'un à faire quelque chose
descendre

AUTRES MOTS ET EXPRESSIONS

faire du ski
faire du patin
faire une chute
il fait __ degrés Celsius
il fait froid
il gèle
il neige

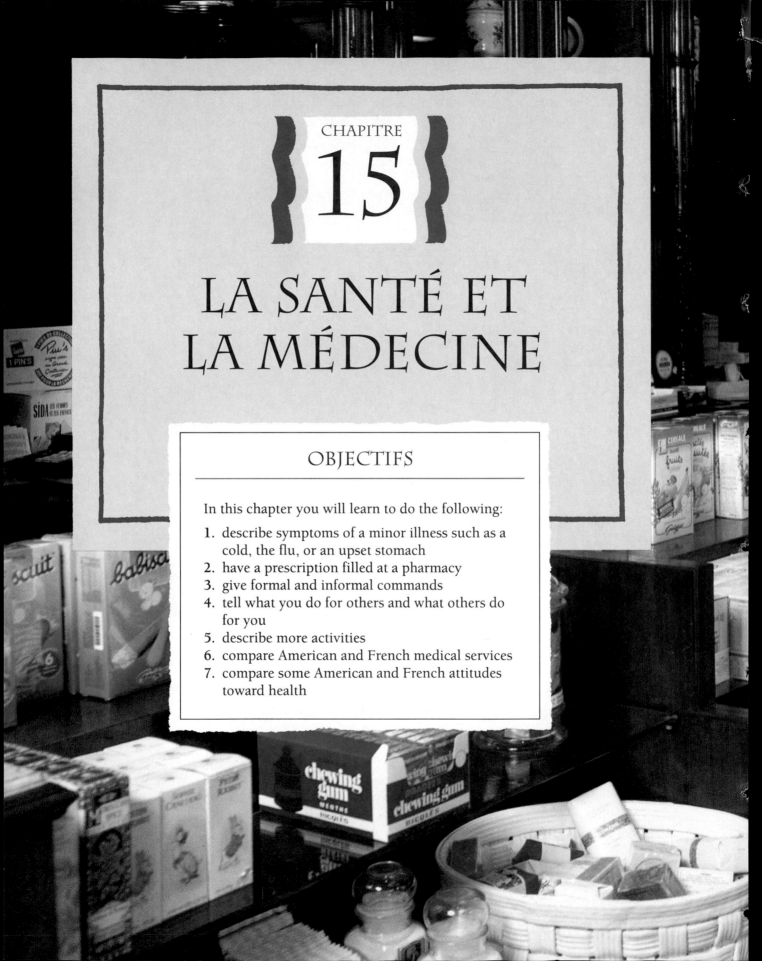

CHAPITRE

{ 15 }

LA SANTÉ ET
LA MÉDECINE

OBJECTIFS

In this chapter you will learn to do the following:

1. describe symptoms of a minor illness such as a cold, the flu, or an upset stomach
2. have a prescription filled at a pharmacy
3. give formal and informal commands
4. tell what you do for others and what others do for you
5. describe more activities
6. compare American and French medical services
7. compare some American and French attitudes toward health

VOCABULAIRE

MOTS 1

ON EST MALADE

les yeux (m.)

l'oreille (f.)

le nez

la bouche

la gorge

le ventre

avoir de la fièvre

Paul a un rhume.
Il est enrhumé.
Il éternue.

Atchoum!

un kleenex

Il tousse.

un mouchoir

Martin n'est pas en bonne santé.
Il est en mauvaise santé.
Il est très malade, le pauvre.
Il ne se sent pas bien.
Qu'est-ce qu'il a, le pauvre garçon?

Note: The expression *Qu'est-ce qu'il a?*
means "What's wrong with him?"

Miriam a la grippe.
Elle a de la fièvre.
Elle a des frissons.

Elle a mal à la tête.

Elle a mal au ventre.

Elle a mal aux oreilles.

Elle a le nez qui coule.

Elle a les yeux qui piquent.

Elle a la gorge qui gratte.

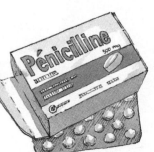

Christophe a très mal à la gorge. Il a une angine.

Note: Study the following cognates related to health and medicine.

allergique	de l'aspirine (f.)
bactérien(ne)	une infection
viral(e)	la pénicilline
une allergie	la température
un antibiotique	

Exercices

A **Qu'est-ce que c'est?** Identifiez.

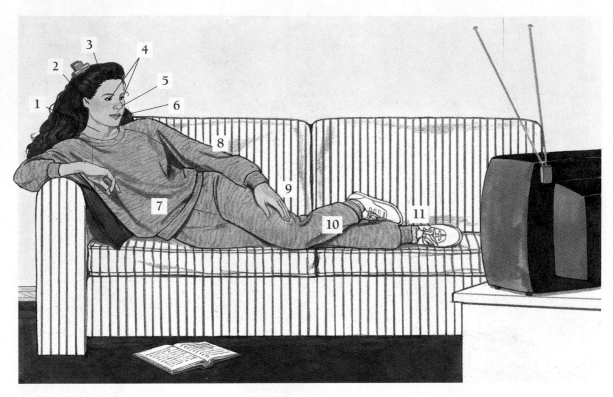

B **Qu'est-ce qu'elle a, la pauvre Miriam?** Répondez.

1. Miriam est très malade?
2. Elle ne se sent pas bien?
3. Qu'est-ce qu'elle a?
4. Elle a de la fièvre et des frissons?
5. Elle a la gorge qui gratte?
6. Elle a les yeux qui piquent et le nez qui coule?
7. Elle a mal à la tête?
8. Elle a mal au ventre?
9. Elle a mal aux oreilles?

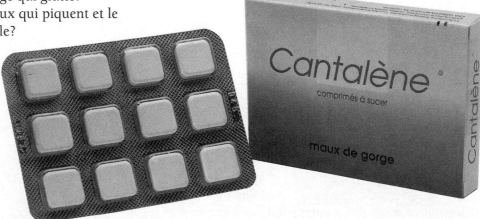

C   La santé.   Donnez des réponses personnelles.

1. Tu es en bonne santé ou en mauvaise santé?
2. Quand tu es enrhumé(e), tu as le nez qui coule?
3. Tu as les yeux qui piquent?
4. Tu as la gorge qui gratte?
5. Tu tousses?
6. Tu éternues?
7. Tu as mal à la tête?
8. Tu ne te sens pas bien?
9. Tu as de la fièvre quand tu as un rhume ou la grippe?
10. Quand tu as de la fièvre, tu as quelquefois des frissons?
11. Quand tu as mal à la tête, tu prends de l'aspirine?

D   On a mal.   Complétez.

1. On prend de l'aspirine. On a mal à la ___.
2. On a très mal à la gorge. On a une ___.
3. La ___ est un antibiotique.
4. On ne peut pas prendre de pénicilline quand on est ___ à la pénicilline.
5. On a une température de 40°C. On a de la ___.
6. Quand on est toujours malade, on est en ___.
7. Les ___ accompagnent souvent la fièvre.
8. On donne des antibiotiques comme la pénicilline pour combattre des infections bactériennes, pas ___.
9. Quand on a le nez qui coule, on a toujours besoin d'un ___ ou d'un ___.
10. Quand on a un rhume, on ___ et on ___.
11. Quand on a de la fièvre, on prend de l'___.
12. Quand on est enrhumé ou quand on écoute trop la musique, on a mal aux ___.

VOCABULAIRE

MOTS 2

CHEZ LE MÉDECIN

le médecin

un malade

une malade

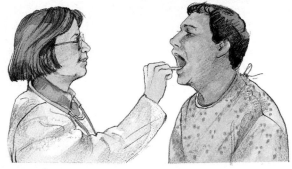

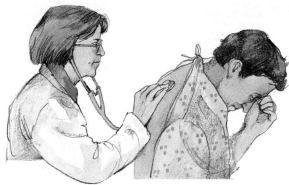

Le médecin examine le malade.
Le malade ouvre la bouche.
Le médecin examine la gorge du malade.

Elle ausculte le malade.
Il souffre, le pauvre.

Où avez-vous mal?

Ouvrez la bouche.

Toussez.

Respirez à fond.

Le médecin parle.

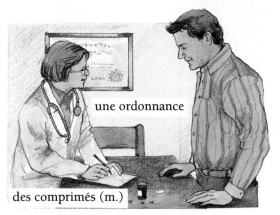

une ordonnance

des comprimés (m.)

le pharmacien
la pharmacienne

Le médecin me fait un diagnostic.
Elle me prescrit des antibiotiques.
Elle me fait une ordonnance.

Je suis à la pharmacie.
Qu'est-ce que la pharmacienne te donne?
Elle me donne des médicaments.

Note: You may use the following informal expressions to talk about health.

1. When you are not feeling well, you can say:

Je ne suis pas dans mon assiette aujourd'hui.

2. To tell someone he or she will soon be better, you can say:

Tu vas être vite sur pied.

3. When someone has a high fever, you can say:

Il a une fièvre de cheval.

4. To say "It hurts," you say:

Ça fait mal!

5. When you have a "frog in your throat," you can say:

J'ai un chat dans la gorge.

Exercices

A Chez le médecin. Choisissez.

1. Où est le malade?
   a. À l'hôpital.   b. Chez lui.   c. Chez le médecin.

2. Qui souffre?
   a. Le médecin.   b. Le malade.   c. Le pharmacien.

3. Qu'est-ce que le médecin examine?
   a. La bouche.   b. La gorge.   c. Le ventre.

4. Qu'est-ce que le malade ouvre?
   a. La bouche.   b. La gorge.   c. L'oreille.

5. Le médecin ausculte le malade. Comment respire-t-il?
   a. Il éternue.   b. À fond.   c. Bien.

6. Qui est-ce que le médecin ausculte?
   a. Le malade.   b. Le pharmacien.   c. La pharmacienne.

7. Que fait le médecin?
   a. Un diagnostic.   b. Des comprimés.   c. Des médicaments.

8. Qu'est-ce qu'il a, le pauvre malade?
   a. Une angine.   b. Mal au ventre.   c. Mal aux yeux.

9. Que fait le médecin?
   a. Un pharmacien.   b. Une ordonnance.   c. Un comprimé.

10. Qu'est-ce qu'elle prescrit?
    a. La pharmacie.   b. Des ordonnances.   c. Des antibiotiques.

11. Où va le malade pour acheter des médicaments?
    a. Chez le médecin.   b. À la pharmacie.   c. À l'ordinateur.

B Le médecin m'examine. Donnez des réponses personnelles.

1. Tu vas chez le médecin quand tu es très malade?
2. Le médecin te demande, «Où avez-vous mal»?
3. Quand tu as une angine, ça fait très mal?
4. Le médecin te dit, «Ouvrez la bouche»?
5. Il t'ausculte?
6. Il te dit, «Respirez à fond»?
7. Le médecin te fait un diagnostic?
8. Il te prescrit des comprimés?
9. Tu vas à la pharmacie pour acheter les médicaments?
10. Tu prends quelquefois des antibiotiques?

C Plus familier, s'il vous plaît. Dites d'une manière familière.

1. Je ne vais pas très bien aujourd'hui.   3. J'ai beaucoup de fièvre!
2. Tu vas bientôt te sentir mieux.   4. Je ne peux pas parler facilement.

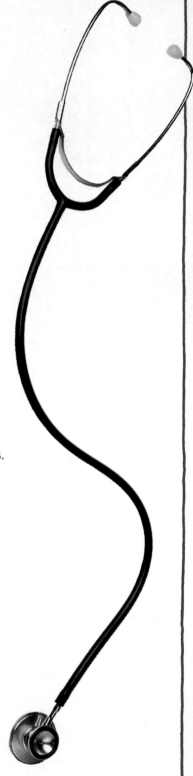

Activités de communication

Mots 1 et 2

A **Qu'est-ce que tu as?** Your partner was absent from school today due to illness. Call your partner to find out how he or she is feeling.

1. Ask what's wrong.
2. He or she will tell you a few symptoms.
3. Find out how your partner feels now.
4. Find out if he or she is going to school tomorrow.
5. Tell your partner something that happened at school today.
6. Your partner will ask you for the French homework.

B **Je ne suis pas dans mon assiette!** Yesterday you did something that made you feel ill today. Using List 1 below, tell your partner what you did. He or she will guess what's wrong with you, choosing from List 2.

1	2
lire pendant six heures	avoir le nez qui coule
manger trop de chocolat	avoir mal aux yeux
passer trop d'examens	avoir la gorge qui gratte
regarder trop la télé	avoir mal aux pieds
crier au match	être fatigué(e)
faire une longue promenade	avoir mal aux oreilles
étudier jusqu'à 3h du matin	avoir mal à la tête
écouter trop de musique	avoir mal au ventre
jouer dans la neige en tee-shirt	

Élève 1: Hier j'ai joué dans la neige.
Élève 2: Tu as le nez qui coule.

C **Quel médecin?** While on a trip to France, you get sick. Describe your symptoms. Your partner will look at the list of doctors at the *Hôpital Saint-Pierre* and tell you which one to call and what the phone number is.

Élève 1: J'ai mal au ventre.
Élève 2: Appelle le docteur Simonet au 43.89.39.25.

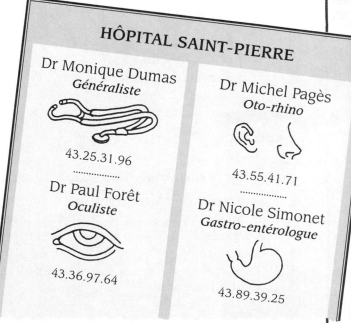

HÔPITAL SAINT-PIERRE

Dr Monique Dumas
Généraliste
43.25.31.96

Dr Paul Forêt
Oculiste
43.36.97.64

Dr Michel Pagès
Oto-rhino
43.55.41.71

Dr Nicole Simonet
Gastro-entérologue
43.89.39.25

STRUCTURE

Les pronoms *me, te, nous, vous*

Telling What You Do For Others and What Others Do For You

1. You have already seen the pronouns *me, te, nous,* and *vous* with reflexive verbs. These same pronouns function as objects of the verb.

Le médecin *te* voit?	Oui, il *me* voit.
Le médecin *t'*examine?	Oui, il *m'*examine.
Le médecin *vous* regarde?	Oui, il *me* regarde.
	Oui, il *nous* regarde.
Le médecin *te* fait une ordonnance?	Oui, il *me* fait une ordonnance.
Il *vous* parle?	Oui, il *me* parle.
	Oui, il *nous* parle.

2. Note that the object pronoun comes right before the verb of which it is the object. This is true even when there is a helping verb, such as *pouvoir, vouloir,* or *aller* in the sentence.

> Il *m'*examine.
> Il va *m'*examiner.
> Il peut *m'*examiner.

3. The object pronoun cannot be separated from the verb by a negative word.

> Il ne *vous fait* pas d'ordonnance.
> Il ne *nous examine* pas.
> Il ne *m'ausculte* jamais.

Exercices

A **Chez le médecin.** Donnez des réponses personnelles.

1. Quand tu vas chez le médecin, il te parle?
2. Il te regarde?
3. Il t'examine?
4. Il t'ausculte?
5. Il te fait un diagnostic?
6. Il te fait une ordonnance?
7. Il te prescrit des médicaments?
8. Il te prescrit des antibiotiques?
9. Le pharmacien te donne des médicaments?

B **Elle nous invite à la fête.** Répondez d'après le modèle.

Suzanne vous parle de sa fête?
Oui, elle nous parle de sa fête.

1. Elle vous téléphone?
2. Elle vous parle au téléphone?
3. Elle vous invite à la fête?
4. Elle vous dit l'heure de la fête?
5. Elle vous dit où elle habite?
6. Elle vous donne son adresse?

C **Elle ne nous invite pas à la fête.** Répondez par «non» aux questions de l'Exercice B.

D **Au rayon prêt-à-porter.** Complétez avec «vous» ou «me».

Je suis au rayon prêt-à-porter des Galeries Lafayette. La vendeuse ___ parle.
                                                                    1

Elle ___ demande:
        2

—Vous désirez?

—Je voudrais un chemisier, s'il ___ plaît. Je fais du 40.
                                  3

—D'accord. Je peux ___ proposer ces deux types de chemisiers.
                    4

—Ce chemisier bleu marine à manches longues ___ intéresse beaucoup.
                                             5

—Je ___ suggère la taille au-dessous alors. Ces chemisiers sont très grands.
     6

—D'accord. Je peux ___ payer avec une carte de crédit?
                    7

—Mais bien sûr!

E **Pourquoi ça?** Répondez d'après le modèle.

Élève 1: Il me regarde.
Élève 2: Il te regarde? Pourquoi?

1. Il me pose des questions.
2. Il me parle.
3. Il me téléphone.
4. Il me dit son numéro de téléphone.
5. Il me donne son adresse.

F **C'est ton anniversaire.** Donnez des réponses personnelles.

1. Tes copains vont te téléphoner le jour de ton anniversaire?
2. Ils vont te voir?
3. Ils vont t'inviter au cinéma ou au concert?
4. Ils vont te dire, «Bon anniversaire»?
5. Pour ton anniversaire, ils vont te faire un gâteau?

Les verbes comme *ouvrir* au présent et au passé composé

Describing More Activities

1. Although the verbs *ouvrir, souffrir, couvrir,* and *découvrir* have infinitives that end in *-ir,* they have the same endings as *-er* verbs in the present tense.

OUVRIR	SOUFFRIR
j' ouvre	je souffre
tu ouvres	tu souffres
il	il
elle } ouvre	elle } souffre
on	on
nous ouvrons	nous souffrons
vous ouvrez	vous souffrez
ils ouvrent	ils
elles ouvrent	elles } souffrent

2. The past participles of these verbs are irregular.

INFINITIF ⟶	PARTICIPE PASSÉ
ouvrir	ouvert
couvrir	couvert
découvrir	découvert
souffrir	souffert
offrir	offert

Pendant la nuit il a ouvert la fenêtre.
Hier le médecin a découvert la cause
de la maladie.

Guéris vite!

Exercices

A **Tu souffres?** Donnez des réponses personnelles.

1. Tu souffres quand tu es enrhumé(e)?
2. Tu souffres plus quand tu as un rhume ou quand tu as la grippe?
3. Tu prends de l'aspirine quand tu souffres d'une allergie?
4. Tu ouvres la bouche quand le médecin t'examine la gorge?
5. Tu ouvres les yeux quand le médecin t'examine les yeux?
6. Tu offres un bouquet de roses à ton amie malade?

B **Qu'est-ce qu'on fait?** Complétez avec «ouvrir» ou «offrir».

1. Nous ___ les yeux quand nous nous réveillons.
2. Elle ___ un livre à sa mère pour la Fête des Mères.
3. Vous ___ le magazine pour regarder les photos qui vous intéressent?
4. Vous ___ la bouche quand le médecin vous examine la gorge?
5. Ils ___ la bouche pour chanter.
6. J' ___ le livre et je commence à lire.
7. J'___ la fenêtre quand il fait chaud.
8. Tu ___ les cadeaux que tes amis t'___ pour ton anniversaire?

C **Il a été malade.** Répondez par «oui».

1. Charles a été malade?
2. Il a été à l'hôpital?
3. Le médecin a examiné Charles?
4. Charles a ouvert la bouche?
5. Le médecin a découvert la cause de sa maladie?
6. Il a couvert le pauvre Charles?
7. Le médecin a fait un diagnostic?
8. Charles a compris le diagnostic?
9. Le médecin a prescrit des médicaments?
10. Charles a pris les médicaments?
11. Il a pris trois comprimés par jour?
12. Il a beaucoup souffert?
13. Ses amis ont offert un petit cadeau à Charles?

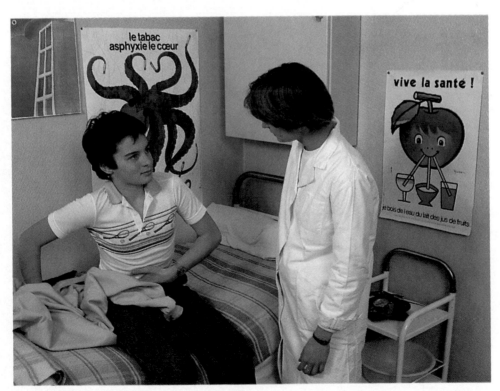

Une femme-médecin parle à son jeune patient.

L'impératif

Giving Formal and Informal Commands

1. You use the imperative to give commands and make suggestions. The forms are usually the same as the *tu, vous,* or *nous* form of the present tense. Note, however, that you drop the final *s* of the *tu* form of verbs ending in *-er,* including *aller.* The same is true for verbs like *ouvrir* and *souffrir,* which are conjugated like *-er* verbs. In commands the subject is omitted.

INFINITIF	TU	VOUS
regarder	regarde	regardez
aller	va	allez
ouvrir	ouvre	ouvrez
finir	finis	finissez
attendre	attends	attendez
prendre	prends	prenez
faire	fais	faites
dire	dis	dites

Marie, regarde le tableau! Va au tableau!
Madame, prenez des vitamines!
Roger et Vincent, faites attention!

2. To express "Let's . . .," you use the *nous* form of the verb without the subject.

   Dansons!
   Choisissons le menu touristique.

3. With commands, negative expressions go around the verb.

   Ne parle pas en classe.
   N'écoutez jamais ce disque.
   Ne disons rien.

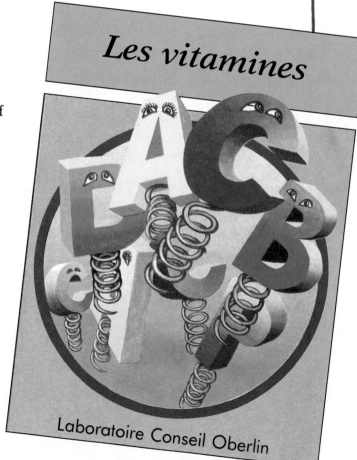

Les vitamines

Laboratoire Conseil Oberlin

Exercices

A **La loi, c'est moi!** Donnez un ordre à un copain ou à une copine d'après le modèle.

> **chanter**
> *Chante!*

1. danser
2. écouter la musique
3. parler français
4. travailler plus

5. préparer le dîner
6. commander un sandwich
7. ouvrir la porte

B **Et vous aussi!** Refaites l'Exercice A d'après le modèle.

> **chanter**
> *Chantez!*

C **Ne fais pas ça!** Donnez un ordre à un copain ou à une copine d'après le modèle.

> **regarder**
> *Ne regarde pas!*

1. lire le journal
2. écrire une lettre
3. prendre le métro
4. attendre dans la gare

5. descendre
6. aller vite
7. faire attention
8. entrer

D **Ne faites pas ça!** Refaites l'Exercice C d'après le modèle.

> **regarder**
> *Ne regardez pas!*

E **Allons-y!** Répondez d'après le modèle.

> **Vous voulez inviter Marie?**
> *Oui, invitons Marie!*

1. Vous voulez aller à la plage?
2. Vous voulez nager?
3. Vous voulez faire du ski nautique?
4. Vous voulez prendre le petit déjeuner?
5. Vous voulez aller au restaurant?
6. Vous voulez manger des fruits?

le stress

Laboratoire Conseil Oberlin

Stressé? N'oubliez pas de vous relaxer!

CONVERSATION

Scènes de la vie *Charlotte souffre*

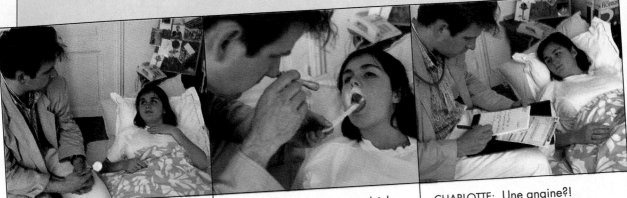

CHARLOTTE: Ah, docteur, qu'est-ce que je peux souffrir!
LE MÉDECIN: Où avez-vous mal? Quels sont vos symptômes?
CHARLOTTE: Qu'est-ce que je suis malade! J'ai les yeux qui piquent et la gorge qui gratte. Ça fait mal!

LE MÉDECIN: Vous avez mal à la tête?
CHARLOTTE: Ah, oui. J'ai mal partout. Et j'ai des frissons. J'ai froid.
LE MÉDECIN: Alors, vous avez de la fièvre. Je vais prendre votre température. Mais d'abord, je vais vous examiner. Ouvrez la bouche, s'il vous plaît. . . Oui, vous avez la gorge très rouge. Vous avez une angine.

CHARLOTTE: Une angine?!
LE MÉDECIN: Oui, ce n'est pas grave. Je vais vous faire une ordonnance. Je vous prescris des antibiotiques. Vous allez être vite sur pied.

Une angine. Répondez d'après la conversation.

1. Charlotte souffre beaucoup?
2. Elle a les yeux qui piquent?
3. Elle a la gorge qui gratte?
4. Elle a mal à la tête?
5. Où a-t-elle mal?
6. Elle a de la fièvre et des frissons?
7. Qu'est-ce que le médecin va prendre?
8. Qu'est-ce que Charlotte ouvre?
9. Elle a la gorge comment?
10. Qu'est-ce qu'elle a?
11. Qu'est-ce que le médecin prescrit?
12. Charlotte va être vite sur pied?

Docteur Henri ANSART

50, résidence du Bois du Four
78640 NEAUPHLE-LE-CHÂTEAU
(Yvelines)
Tél. 36.89.00.07   36.89.08.95

DUROSEL Charlotte

Hyconcil :

2 gélules matin et soir pendant 5 jours.

Locabiotal :

3 pulvérisations par jour.

Prononciation *Le son /ü/*

1. To say the sound /ü/, first say the sound /i/ but round your lips. Repeat the following words.

température	enrhumé	chaussure
voiture	descendu	

2. The sound /ü/ also occurs in combination with other vowels.

éternuer	lui	depuis
aujourd'hui	je suis	

Now repeat the following words and sentences.

> **Quelle est la température aujourd'hui?**
> **Luc conduit depuis huit ans.**
> **Il a mis ses chaussures dans la voiture.**

température

Activités de communication

A **Ah docteur, je suis très malade!**   Imagine you are sick with a cold, the flu, or a throat infection. When the doctor (your partner) asks you what's wrong, tell him or her several of your symptoms. Your partner will make a diagnosis and tell you what to do to get better.

> Élève 1: J'ai mal à la tête et j'éternue tout le temps.
> Élève 2: Vous avez un rhume. Prenez de l'aspirine et du bouillon
>   de poulet.

B **Je déteste ce cadeau!**   In your worst nightmare, what do the following people give you for your birthday? Your partner will ask you about each person. Answer, then reverse roles.

> Élève 1: Qu'est-ce que ta grand-mère t'offre pour ton
>   anniversaire?
> Élève 2: Elle m'offre des cassettes de Frank Sinatra.

tes parents	tes grands-parents
ton meilleur ami	ton frère
ta meilleure amie	ta sœur

C **Excusez-moi...**   You are supposed to take a French test today but you aren't feeling well. Write a note to your French teacher with the following information.

1. Say that you cannot take the test because you are ill.
2. Mention some symptoms you have.
3. Give the date and time you'd like to take the test.

UNE CONSULTATION OU UNE VISITE

Le pauvre Richard! Qu'est-ce qu'il est malade! Il tousse. Il éternue. Il a mal à la tête. Il a une fièvre de cheval. Il a des frissons. Il n'est pas du tout dans son assiette. Il n'est pas très courageux, notre Richard. Il veut prendre rendez-vous[1] chez le médecin, mais c'est le week-end. Son médecin ne donne pas de consultations.

Alors que faire? Pas de problème! Appelons S.O.S Médecins, un service qui envoie des médecins à domicile. Un médecin arrive chez Richard. Il examine Richard. Il ausculte le malade. Il prend sa température. Le médecin dit que Richard a la grippe. Mais ce n'est pas grave. Il va vite se sentir mieux. Le médecin fait une ordonnance à Richard. Il prescrit des antibiotiques: trois comprimés par jour, un à chaque repas[2].

Richard paie le médecin. Mais en France la Sécurité Sociale rembourse les honoraires des médecins, c'est-à-dire l'argent qu'on donne aux médecins. Les honoraires et tous les frais[3] médicaux sont remboursés de 80 à 100% (pour cent) par la Sécurité Sociale.

[1] prendre rendez-vous *make an appointment* [2] repas *meal* [3] les frais *expenses*

Étude de mots

Autrement dit. Dites d'une autre manière.

1. Richard a *beaucoup de fièvre.*
2. Il *ne se sent pas bien.*
3. Il veut *aller voir* le médecin.
4. Le médecin *ne voit pas de malades* pendant le week-end.
5. S.O.S Médecins envoie des médecins *chez les malades.*
6. Le médecin *écoute la respiration de* Richard.
7. La grippe n'est pas une maladie *sérieuse.*
8. Richard va vite *se sentir mieux.*

Compréhension

A **Vous avez compris?** Répondez par «oui» ou «non».

1. Richard est très courageux quand il est malade.
2. Il a beaucoup de fièvre.
3. Il a mal au ventre.
4. Richard veut aller chez le médecin.
5. Son médecin donne des consultations tous les jours.
6. Richard prend rendez-vous chez le médecin de S.O.S Médecins.
7. Le médecin prescrit des comprimés d'aspirine.
8. Les frais médicaux ne sont pas remboursés en France.

B **En France.** Qu'est-ce que vous avez appris sur les médecins et les services médicaux en France?

DÉCOUVERTE CULTURELLE

*L*a culture influence la médecine? Certainement. Par exemple, en France tout le monde parle de son foie[1]. Les Français disent souvent, «J'ai mal au foie». En Amérique on n'entend jamais «J'ai mal au foie». Pourquoi pas? Parce que, pour les Américains, une maladie du foie est quelque chose de grave. Mais quand un Français dit qu'il a mal au foie, il veut dire tout simplement qu'il a un trouble digestif. Ce n'est rien de grave. Il n'est peut-être pas dans son assiette aujourd'hui mais il va être vite sur pied.

Aux États-Unis on parle d'allergies. Beaucoup d'Américains souffrent d'une petite allergie. Les symptômes d'une allergie ressemblent aux symptômes d'un rhume. On éternue et on a souvent mal à la tête. Une allergie est désagréable, mais pas grave. En France, on parle moins souvent d'allergies. Vive la différence!

[1] le foie *the liver*

Les troubles digestifs

RÉALITÉS

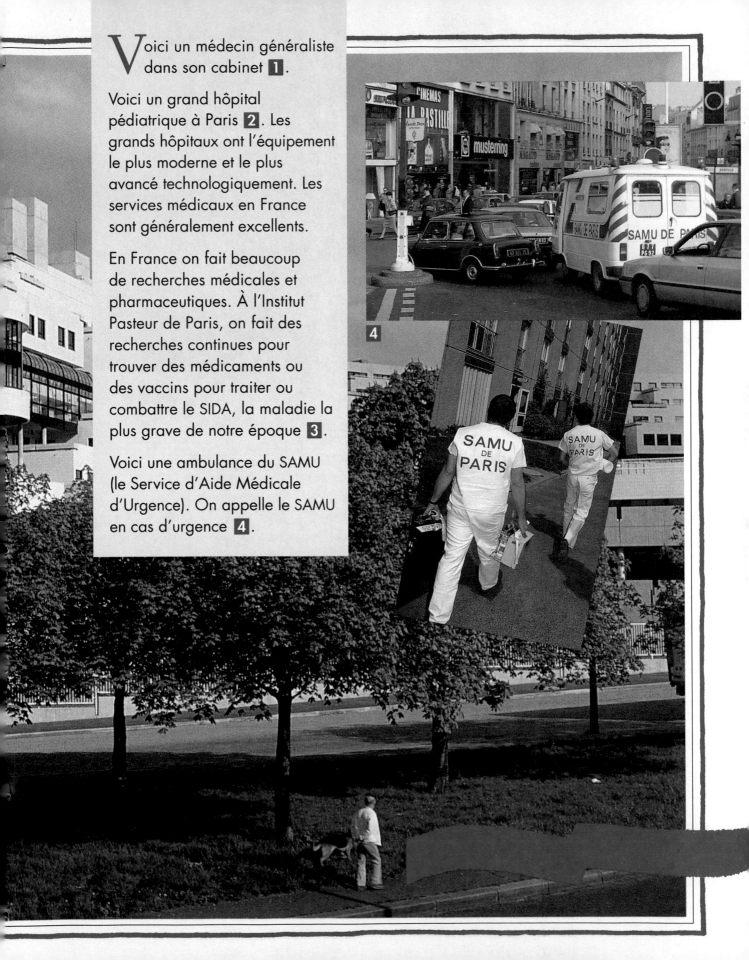

Voici un médecin généraliste dans son cabinet **1**.

Voici un grand hôpital pédiatrique à Paris **2**. Les grands hôpitaux ont l'équipement le plus moderne et le plus avancé technologiquement. Les services médicaux en France sont généralement excellents.

En France on fait beaucoup de recherches médicales et pharmaceutiques. À l'Institut Pasteur de Paris, on fait des recherches continues pour trouver des médicaments ou des vaccins pour traiter ou combattre le SIDA, la maladie la plus grave de notre époque **3**.

Voici une ambulance du SAMU (le Service d'Aide Médicale d'Urgence). On appelle le SAMU en cas d'urgence **4**.

CULMINATION

Activités de communication orale

A **Attention à la santé!** The health class is helping the teacher make up a quiz for the next class. Write down several health tips. When a student reads a tip aloud, another student must say whether it's a good or bad idea.

> Élève 1: Mange beaucoup de pâtisseries.
> Élève 2: C'est une mauvaise idée!

B **Qu'est-ce que tu me dis?** Suggest the following situations to your partner and ask what he or she would say in each case.

> t'offrir un bouquet de roses
>
> Élève 1: Je t'offre un bouquet de roses. Qu'est-ce que tu me dis?
> Élève 2: Je te dis, «Merci beaucoup, les roses sont magnifiques!»

1. te téléphoner à minuit
2. te proposer de sortir ensemble
3. te dire que j'ai besoin d'argent
4. te demander de faire mes devoirs pour moi
5. te donner un sandwich au pâté
6. te dire que je ne suis pas dans mon assiette

Activité de communication écrite

Tu es en bonne santé? Do you have good health habits? On a separate sheet of paper make a chart like the one below. For each statement, check the box that best describes you. Compare your results with those of a classmate.

Give yourself two points for each time you answered *souvent,* one point for each time you answered *de temps en temps,* and zero for each time you answered *jamais.* Scores: between 10 and 12, you take good care of yourself; between 4 and 6, you take fairly good care of yourself; below 4, you need to take better care of yourself.

	SOUVENT	DE TEMPS EN TEMPS	JAMAIS
1. Je mange des fruits et des légumes.			
2. Je prends des vitamines.			
3. Je pratique un sport.			
4. Je prends un bon petit déjeuner tous les jours.			
5. Je dors au moins huit heures par jour.			
6. Je porte des vêtements appropriés pour la saison.			

Réintroduction et recombinaison

A **Isabelle se sent très bien aujourd'hui!** Complétez au présent.

Qui ___ (dire) qu'Isabelle n' ___ (être) pas dans son assiette aujourd'hui? Ce
          1   2
n' ___ (être) pas du tout vrai. Elle ___ (aller) très bien. Elle ___ (se lever) de
     3   4   5
bonne heure, ___ (prendre) son petit déjeuner et ___ (quitter) la maison. Elle
               6   7
___ (vouloir) rester en forme. Elle ___ (aller) au gymnase où elle ___ (faire)
  8   9   10
de l'aérobic. Elle ___ (avoir) beaucoup de copains au gymnase. Ils ___ (mettre)
                    11   12
un survêtement et ils ___ (faire) de l'exercice ensemble.
                       13

B **Aux sports d'hiver.** Complétez au passé composé.

1. L'hiver dernier Sylvie et Maryse ___ (passer) une semaine à Val d'Isère dans
   les Alpes françaises.
2. Le premier jour elles ___ (mettre) leur anorak, leurs gants et leurs skis.
3. Elles ___ (prendre) le télésiège jusqu'au sommet de la montagne.
4. Malheureusement elles ___ (choisir) la mauvaise piste—une piste noire,
   très difficile.
5. Sylvie ___ (glisser) et ___ (faire) une chute.
6. Elle ___ (perdre) ses bâtons qui ___ (glisser) jusqu'en bas de la piste.
7. Deux garçons très sympa ___ (trouver) les bâtons et ils ___ (donner) les
   bâtons à Sylvie.
8. Les deux filles ___ (dire) «merci» aux garçons et ils ___ (faire) du ski
   ensemble toute la journée.

Vocabulaire

NOMS
la santé
la médecine
le médecin
le (la) malade
le (la) pauvre
l'allergie (f.)
l'angine (f.)
la température
la fièvre
les frissons (m.)
la grippe
le rhume
l'infection (f.)

le médicament
l'ordonnance (f.)

l'aspirine (f.)
l'antibiotique (m.)
la pénicilline
le comprimé
la pharmacie
le (la) pharmacien(ne)
le kleenex
le mouchoir

les yeux (m.pl.)
le nez
la bouche
l'oreille (f.)
la gorge
le ventre

ADJECTIFS
allergique

bactérien(ne)
enrhumé(e)
malade
viral(e)

VERBES
examiner
ausculter
respirer (à fond)
éternuer
tousser
couvrir
découvrir
offrir
ouvrir
souffrir

se sentir
prescrire

AUTRES MOTS ET EXPRESSIONS
avoir mal à
avoir un chat dans la gorge
avoir de la fièvre
avoir une fièvre de cheval
avoir les yeux qui piquent
avoir le nez qui coule
avoir la gorge qui gratte
être dans son assiette
être en bonne (mauvaise) santé
être vite sur pied
faire un diagnostic
faire une ordonnance
Ça fait mal.

16

LES LOISIRS CULTURELS

OBJECTIFS

In this chapter you will learn to do the following:

1. discuss movies, plays, and museums
2. indicate people, places, and things you know
3. tell what you know how to do
4. refer to people and things already mentioned
5. identify cities, countries, and continents
6. express "to come," "to come back," and "to become"
7. tell where people come from
8. contrast French and American cultural activities

VOCABULAIRE

MOTS 1

AU CINÉMA

un cinéma

14h 16h 18h

une séance

le guichet

l'écran

un dessin animé

une salle
de cinéma

Qui joue dans ce film?

les vedettes

un acteur

une actrice

un film étranger

On passe un film étranger à Paris.
On passe le film en V.O., c'est-à-dire
    en version originale.
On le voit en version originale avec
    des sous-titres français.

Le film est doublé.
La version originale est en anglais.
La version doublée est en français.

Qu'est-ce que tu vas faire?

les sous-titres (m.)

Tu préfères quels genres de films?

un documentaire   un film policier   un film d'horreur   un film de science-fiction

un film d'aventures   un film d'amour   une comédie   un drame

AU THÉÂTRE

une pièce de théâtre

le rideau

le décor

On monte une pièce.
C'est une comédie.

Comédie-Française

Molière
Le Tartuffe

Acte 1
  Scène 1
  Scène 2

Entracte
Acte 2
  Scène 1
  Scène 2

Acte 3
  Scène 1
  Scène 2

un costume

la scène

La pièce a trois actes.
Chaque acte a deux scènes.
Entre deux actes il y a un entracte.

Voici quelques genres de pièces:
    une tragédie
    un opéra
    une comédie musicale

l'entracte (m.)

Exercices

A **Fana de cinéma ou pas?** Donnez des réponses personnelles.

1. Tu es fana de cinéma? C'est-à-dire, tu aimes beaucoup voir des films?
2. Tu vas souvent au cinéma?
3. Il y a un cinéma près de chez toi?
4. La première séance est à quelle heure?
5. Il y a toujours un dessin animé avant le film?
6. Tu fais la queue devant le cinéma? Quels soirs spécialement?
7. Où est-ce que tu prends les billets?
8. Dans la salle de cinéma, tu préfères une place près de l'écran ou loin de l'écran?
9. Quel est ton acteur préféré ou ton actrice préférée?
10. Quelle est la vedette de ton film préféré?
11. Si tu vois un film étranger, tu préfères voir la version originale avec des sous-titres ou une version doublée?

B **Au cinéma.** Complétez.

1. Ce soir on ___ un très bon film au cinéma Rex.
2. C'est un film étranger. Il n'est pas doublé, il a des ___.
3. On ne passe pas le film en ___ originale.
4. La prochaine ___ commence à quelle heure?
5. Combien coûte le ___?

C **Tu aimes quels genres de films?** Donnez des réponses personnelles.

1. Tu préfères les documentaires ou les dessins animés?
2. Tu préfères les films policiers ou les films d'horreur?
3. Tu préfères les films d'aventures ou les films de science-fiction?
4. Tu préfères les comédies ou les drames?
5. Quand tu vas au magasin de vidéos, tu choisis généralement quel genre de films?

D **Des pièces et des films.** Complétez.

1. Au théâtre on ___ une pièce.
2. On voit un film au cinéma et on voit une pièce au ___.
3. Une pièce a des ___ et les ___ ont des ___.
4. Entre deux actes il y a un ___.
5. Un ___ joue le rôle de Roméo.
6. Une ___ joue le rôle de Juliette.
7. Le balcon de Juliette est le ___ d'une scène d'amour célèbre.
8. Les acteurs et les actrices portent des ___.
9. Le mot ___ en français signifie (veut dire) *scene* et *stage* en anglais.
10. Le ___ se lève à 20 heures.

E **Au théâtre.** Donnez des réponses personnelles.

1. Tu es fana de théâtre?
2. Tu vas souvent au théâtre?
3. Il y a un théâtre dans ta ville?
4. Ton école a un club d'art dramatique?
5. Tu es membre du club d'art dramatique?
6. Le club monte combien de pièces par an?
7. Cette année le club va monter quelle pièce?

F **Mes préférences.** Donnez des réponses personnelles.

1. Tu préfères les comédies ou les tragédies?
2. Tu aimes l'opéra?
3. Tu aimes les comédies musicales?
4. Tu as déjà joué dans une pièce?
5. Quel rôle as-tu joué?

Collections de la Comédie-Française

Comédie-Française

Molière
Le Malade imaginaire

VOCABULAIRE

MOTS 2

AU MUSÉE
une exposition d'art

la peinture

un tableau

une statue

la sculpture

une peintre

un peintre

des sculpteurs (m.)

une œuvre (f.)

Je sais le nom du peintre.
C'est Duval.
Je ne connais pas ce peintre
personnellement.
Je connais son œuvre, c'est-à-dire
ses tableaux.

Musée d'Art Moderne
Ouvert: du mardi au dimanche
de 9h à 18h
Fermé: le lundi

Moi, je connais bien le Musée d'Art
Moderne.
Je le visite souvent.
Je sais que le musée est fermé le lundi.
Il est ouvert tous les jours sauf le lundi.

Exercices

A Un peu de culture. Répondez d'après les dessins.

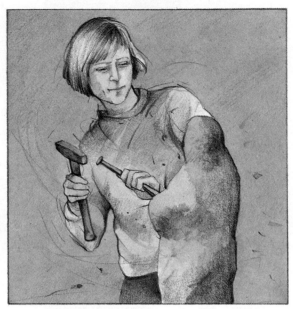

1. C'est un musée ou un théâtre?
2. Le musée est ouvert ou fermé?
3. C'est une exposition de peinture ou
   une exposition de sculpture?

4. Elle est peintre ou sculpteur?
5. C'est un tableau ou une statue?

B Qui le sait? Répondez.

1. Robert sait le nom du peintre?
2. Il connaît le peintre?
3. Il connaît l'œuvre du peintre?
4. Annick sait le nom du musée?
5. Elle connaît le musée?
6. Elle connaît le Musée d'Art Moderne?
7. Elle le visite souvent?
8. Elle sait que le musée est fermé le lundi?
9. Le Musée d'Art Moderne est ouvert tous
   les jours sauf le lundi?

Activités de communication

Mots 1 et 2

A Tu aimes le cinéma? You are talking to a French student (your
partner) in a café in Paris. He or she wants to know the following.

1. if you like movies
2. if you go to the movies often
3. if you have any favorite stars
4. what types of movies you like
5. how much it costs to go to the movies
   in the U.S.

B **Le théâtre.** A French exchange student at your school (your partner) is interested in theater. He or she wants to know the following.

1. if you like to go to the theater and what kinds of plays you like
2. if there are theaters in your town
3. if your school has a drama club
4. what play(s) the club is putting on or has put on this year

C **Les critiques.** Imagine that you are a movie critic for a French magazine. Write a short description of a few films of your choice. For each, indicate the type of film it is, who the actors are, and your opinion of the film. Your partner will guess what films you are reviewing.

> Élève 1: C'est un dessin animé. Les vedettes de ce film sont des animaux verts. C'est un film assez amusant.
> Élève 2: C'est les *Ninja Turtles*.

D **Mon film préféré.** Ask your partner what his or her favorite movies are and why. Then ask your partner the names of a few movies he or she hates and why. Reverse roles.

E **Au musée.** Read the descriptions of the five Paris museums listed below. Ask your partner which museum he or she might like to visit and why. (If your partner doesn't want to visit any of them, find out why.) Then reverse roles.

> Élève 1: Tu veux visiter quel musée?
> Élève 2: Je veux visiter le Centre Pompidou parce que j'aime l'art moderne.

F **Renseignements.** You are in Paris and would like to visit one of the museums listed in Activité E. Call the museum and ask the agent (your partner) for the following information. (He or she will answer using the information in Activité E.)

1. where the museum is
2. what time it opens and when it closes
3. what day it is closed
4. how much it costs to get in

LES MUSÉES

MUSÉE DE L'ARMÉE
Esplanade des Invalides. 45.55.37.70. Tous les jours de 10h à 18h. Entrée: 27F, Tarif réduit: 14F. (Musée accessible aux handicapés physiques).

CENTRE POMPIDOU (BEAUBOURG)
Rue Rambuteau. 42.77.12.33. Semaine de 12h à 22h. Samedi, dimanche et fêtes de 10h à 22h. Fermé le mardi. Tarif musée: 27F. Tarif réduit: 18F. *Le Musée National d'Art Moderne de l'après-impressionnisme à nos jours, plus des expositions temporaires, concerts, ballets, cinémathèque.*

MUSÉE DU LOUVRE
Rue de Rivoli. Ouvert tous les jours sauf le mardi de 9h à 18h. Entrée: 30F. Tarif réduit: 15F. *Six musées en un seul: antiquités gréco-romaines, égyptiennes, orientales, beaux-arts français, italiens et d'autres encore. En vedette, «la Vénus de Milo», et «la Joconde».*

MUSÉE DU SPORT
24, rue du Commandant Guilbaud. 40.45.99.12. Entrée: 20F. Tarif réduit: 10F. Ouvert tous les jours de 9h30 à 12h30 et de 14h à 17h. Fermé mercredi, samedi et fêtes. *Exposition permanente: Trésors et curiosités du sport.*

MUSÉE DU CINÉMA-HENRI LANGLOIS
Palais de Chaillot. 45.53.74.39. Tous les jours sauf mardi et fêtes. Visites guidées à 10h, 11h, 14h, 15h, et 16h. Entrée: 22F. Tarif réduit: 14F. *Documents sur le cinéma de 1895 à nos jours.*

STRUCTURE

| Les verbes *connaître* et *savoir* au présent | *Indicating People, Places, and Things You Know and What You Know How to Do* |

---

1. Study the following forms of the irregular verbs *connaître* and *savoir,* both of which mean "to know."

CONNAÎTRE	SAVOIR
je connais	je sais
tu connais	tu sais
il elle } connaît	il elle } sait
on	on
nous connaissons	nous savons
vous connaissez	vous savez
ils elles } connaissent	ils elles } savent

2. You use *savoir* to indicate that you know a fact.

> **Je sais le numéro de téléphone et l'adresse du cinéma.**
> **Je sais que le cinéma n'est pas loin d'ici.**
> **Il sait à quelle heure la séance commence.**

3. You use *savoir* + infinitive to indicate that you know how to do something.

> **Elle sait conduire.**
> **Tu sais danser?**

4. *Connaître* means "to know" in the sense of "to be acquainted with." You use it with people, places, and things. Compare the meanings of *savoir* and *connaître* in the sentences below.

> **Je sais son nom. C'est Nathalie. Je connais bien Nathalie.**
> **Je sais où elle habite. Elle habite à Grenoble. Je connais Grenoble.**
> **Je sais le nom de l'auteur. C'est Victor Hugo. Je connais son œuvre.**

Exercices

A **Qu'est-ce que tu sais?** Donnez des réponses personnelles.

1. Tu sais l'adresse de ton ami(e)? Il (Elle) habite quelle ville?
2. Tu connais la ville?
3. Tu sais le nom d'un bon restaurant? Quel est son nom?
4. Tu connais le restaurant?
5. Tu sais le nom de l'auteur de la tragédie de *Macbeth*? Quel est son nom?
6. Tu connais les pièces de Shakespeare?
7. Tu connais *Macbeth*?

B **On sait tout.** Complétez avec «savoir».

1. Moi, je ___ le nom du théâtre.
2. Et Paul ___ le numéro de téléphone du théâtre.
3. Paul et moi, nous ___ l'adresse du théâtre.
4. Mais nous ne ___ pas l'heure du lever de rideau.
5. Voilà Guy et Monique. Ils ___ à quelle heure la pièce commence.
6. Je ___ que le théâtre est fermé le dimanche.
7. Vous ___ quelle pièce on monte maintenant à la Comédie-Française?
8. Et toi, tu ___ qui joue le rôle principal dans cette pièce?

C **Qu'est-ce que tu sais faire?** Donnez des réponses personnelles.

1. Tu sais jouer au tennis?
2. Tu sais faire de l'aérobic?
3. Tu sais faire des costumes?
4. Tu sais organiser une très bonne fête?
5. Tu sais parler français?

D **Qui connaît quoi?** Complétez avec «connaître».

1. Je ___ bien la France.
2. Les élèves de Madame Benoît ___ la peinture française.
3. Mais ils ne ___ pas très bien la littérature française.
4. Tu ___ la culture française?
5. Et Paul, il ___ la culture française contemporaine?
6. Vous ___ l'art français?
7. Nous ___ les Impressionnistes comme Monet, Manet et Renoir.
8. Tu ___ l'œuvre du peintre Degas?
9. Ah, oui. Je ___ son œuvre. J'adore ses danseuses de ballet.

Auguste Rodin: «Les Bourgeois de Calais»

Les pronoms *le, la, les*

Referring to People and Things Already Mentioned

1. You have already learned to use *le, la, l',* and *les* as definite articles. These same words are also used as direct object pronouns. A direct object pronoun can replace either a person or a thing. Note that the direct object pronoun in French comes right before the verb.

Je sais le nom du film.	Je *le* sais.
Je vois le film.	Je *le* vois.
J'aime le film.	Je *l'*aime.
Je ne connais pas la vedette.	Je ne *la* connais pas.
Je lis les sous-titres.	Je *les* lis.
J'admire les costumes.	Je *les* admire.

2. Note the placement of the direct object pronoun in negative sentences. It cannot be separated from the verb by the negative word.

Tu connais l'auteur?	Non, je ne *le connais* pas.
Tu regardes la télé?	Je ne *la regarde* jamais.
Tu aimes les tragédies?	Je ne *les aime* pas du tout.

3. Remember that in sentences with a verb + infinitive, the pronoun comes right before the infinitive.

Nous pouvons lire les sous-titres.	Nous pouvons *les* lire.
Il ne peut pas comprendre le film.	Il ne peut pas *le* comprendre.

Exercices

A **Tu aimes les pâtisseries?** Donnez des réponses personnelles d'après le modèle.

> **les pâtisseries**
> *Les pâtisseries? Je les aime beaucoup.*
> *(Je ne les aime pas. Je les déteste!)*

1. les gâteaux
2. l'eau minérale
3. la viande
4. le bœuf
5. le poisson
6. la glace
7. les fruits
8. les crevettes
9. le poulet
10. les haricots verts

Paul Cézanne: «L'Assiette bleue-Abricots et Cerises»

B **On voit le film en version originale.** Complétez.

1. —On voit le film doublé ou en version originale?
   —On ___ voit en version originale.
2. —Tu sais le nom de la vedette?
   —Oui, je ___ sais.
3. —Tu connais la vedette?
   —Tu veux rigoler! Mais non, je ne ___ connais pas.
4. —Tu comprends le français?
   —Oui, je ___ comprends.
5. —Tu ___ comprends assez bien pour comprendre le film?
   —Non, mais il n'y a pas de problème. Il y a des sous-titres et je ___ lis
   quand je ne comprends pas le dialogue.

C **Qu'est-ce qu'il est beau!** Répondez d'après le modèle.

   Tu vois la statue?
   Oui, je la vois. Qu'est-ce qu'elle est belle!

1. Tu vois le théâtre?
2. Tu aimes la pièce?
3. Tu vois le tableau?
4. Tu entends le concert?
5. Tu vois le ballet?
6. Tu vois le film?
7. Tu lis le poème?
8. Tu vois le décor?
9. Tu regardes les costumes?
10. Tu vois la vedette?
11. Tu vois l'actrice?
12. Tu regardes les tableaux?

D **Qu'est-ce qu'on va faire?**
Répondez en utilisant «le», «la»
ou «les».

1. Après les cours tu vas prendre
   le bus?
2. Tu vas écouter la radio?
3. Tu vas faire les devoirs de
   français ce soir?
4. Tu vas regarder la télé?
5. Ton père ou ta mère va préparer
   le dîner?
6. Tes parents vont lire le journal?

Edgar Degas: «Deux Danseuses en Scène»

Les prépositions avec les noms géographiques

Identifying Cities, Countries, and Continents

You use the following prepositions to express "in" or "to" with geographical names.

1. *à* with the name of a city

> **Le Château de Versailles est bien sûr à Versailles.**
> **Le Musée du Louvre est à Paris.**
> **Je vais à New York pour aller au théâtre.**

2. *en* with the name of feminine countries and continents. Most countries and continents whose names end in silent *-e* are feminine. *Le Mexique* is one of the common exceptions.

> **Henri est en France.**
> **La France est en Europe.**
> **Carole va en Tunisie.**
> **La Tunisie est en Afrique.**
> **Shanghaï est en Chine.**
> **La Chine est en Asie.**

3. *au* with the name of masculine countries. Most countries whose names do not end in silent *-e* are masculine.

> **Il va faire du ski au Canada.**
> **Cancún est au Mexique.**
> **Tokyo est au Japon.**
> **Je passe mes vacances au Maroc.**
> **Lisbonne est au Portugal.**

4. *aux* with countries whose name is plural.

> **Marc fait un voyage aux États-Unis.**
> **Amsterdam est aux Pays-Bas.**

la France
la Tunisie
l'Espagne
la Chine
l'Italie
le Portugal
le Mexique
le Canada
le Japon
les États-Unis
le Maroc
les Pays-Bas

Exercices

A **Vous connaissez la géographie?**
Répondez en indiquant le pays.

1. Où est Paris?
2. Où est Rome?
3. Où est Madrid?
4. Où est Lyon?
5. Où est Tokyo?
6. Où est New York?
7. Où est Montréal?
8. Où est Lisbonne?

B Vous y allez quand? Posez une question d'après le modèle.

Nous allons à Antibes.
Ah oui? Vous allez en France quand?

1. Nous allons à Paris.
2. Nous allons à Cannes.
3. Nous allons à Amsterdam.
4. Nous allons à Barcelone.
5. Nous allons à Québec.
6. Nous allons à Shanghaï.
7. Nous allons à Miami.
8. Nous allons à Casablanca.

C C'est quel continent? Complétez.

1. Le Japon est ___ Asie et la Chine est ___ Asie aussi.
2. L'Italie et l'Espagne sont ___ Europe. Le Portugal est aussi ___ Europe.
3. Le Brésil, le Chili et l'Argentine sont ___ Amérique du Sud.
4. Les États-Unis et le Canada sont ___ Amérique du Nord.
5. Le Sénégal et la Côte d'Ivoire sont ___ Afrique.

D Les grands musées du monde. Complétez.

1. Le Musée du Prado est ___ Madrid ___ Espagne.
2. Le Musée du Louvre est ___ Paris ___ France.
3. Le Metropolitan Museum est ___ New York ___ États-Unis.
4. Le Musée Britannique est ___ Londres ___ Angleterre, c'est-a-dire ___ Grande-Bretagne.
5. Le Centre Pompidou est ___ Paris ___ France.
6. Le Rijksmuseum est ___ Amsterdam ___ Hollande, c'est-à-dire _ Pays-Bas.

La Fontaine Stravinski près du Centre Pompidou

Les verbes irréguliers *venir,* *revenir* et *devenir* au présent

Expressing "to come," "to come back," and "to become"

1. The verb *venir,* "to come," is irregular in the present tense. Study the following forms.

VENIR			
je	viens	nous	venons
tu	viens	vous	venez
il		ils	
elle	vient	elles	viennent
on			

Tu viens ce soir au théâtre?
Beaucoup de touristes viennent en France
en été pour visiter ses musées célèbres.
Venez avec nous!

2. Two other verbs conjugated like *venir* are *revenir,* "to come back," and *devenir,* "to become." *Devenir* is seldom used in the present.

Il revient à trois heures.

Exercices

A **Qui vient au cinéma?** Répondez par «oui».

1. Claude vient au cinéma avec nous?
2. Il vient avec Martine?
3. Liliane vient aussi?
4. Elle vient avec sa copine?
5. Elles viennent à vélomoteur?
6. Tu viens au cinéma aussi?
7. Tu viens avec un copain?
8. Ton copain et toi, vous venez à pied?

B **Ils reviennent cet après-midi.** Répondez d'après le modèle.

> Élève 1: Marie est là?
> Élève 2: Non, elle revient cet après-midi.

1. Mon père est là?
2. Mes copains sont là?
3. Sophie est là?
4. Le professeur est là?

La préposition *de* avec les noms géographiques

Telling Where People Come From

You use the following prepositions to express "from" with geographical names.

1. *de* with the name of a city, a feminine country, or a continent

> **Elle est de Bordeaux.**
> **Ses grands-parents viennent d'Italie.**
> **Mes grands-parents viennent d'Amérique du Sud.**

2. *du* with the name of a masculine country

> **Mon amie arrive du Japon ce soir.**
> **Son père revient du Maroc.**

3. *des* with a country whose name is plural

> **Ils arrivent des États-Unis.**

Exercices

A **D'où viennent tous ces touristes?** Répondez d'après le modèle.

> Italie
> *Ces touristes viennent d'Italie.*

1. Espagne
2. Rome
3. Nice
4. France
5. Tokyo
6. Japon
7. Maroc
8. Mexique
9. New York
10. États-Unis

B **D'où vient ta famille?** Donnez des réponses personnelles.

1. D'où viens-tu?
2. Ta famille et toi, d'où venez-vous?
3. D'où vient ton père?
4. D'où vient ta mère?
5. D'où viennent tes grands-parents?

La ville d'Oujda au Maroc

CONVERSATION

Scènes de la vie   *On va au cinéma*

DAVID: Carole, tu veux aller au cinéma?
CAROLE: Pourquoi pas? C'est une très bonne idée. On passe quel film?
DAVID: On a le choix. Il y a beaucoup de cinémas, tu sais! Tu préfères quels genres de films?

CAROLE: Moi, j'aime tous les films. Je suis fana de cinéma, une vraie cinéphile.
DAVID: Au Rex on passe un très bon film espagnol —en version originale avec des sous-titres, je crois.

CAROLE: Excellente idée! On peut travailler notre espagnol. La prochaine séance est à quelle heure?

 Des cinéphiles.   Répondez d'après la conversation.

1. Qui est fana de cinéma?
2. Elle aime quels genres de films?
3. On passe quel film au Rex?
4. Le film est doublé?
5. Qu'est-ce que les deux amis peuvent faire s'ils voient ce film?

Prononciation   *Les sons /ü/ et /u/*

It is important to make a clear distinction between /ü/ and /u/ since many words differ only in these two sounds. Repeat the following pairs of words.

> vous/vu   dessous/dessus   roue/rue   loue/lu   tout/tu

Now repeat the following sentences.

> **Vous avez vu ces statues?**
> **Tu vas souvent au musée?**
> **Cette comédie musicale est doublée.**

une roue

Activités de communication

A D'où viennent-ils? Working in groups, make a list of as many foreign celebrities as you can think of (world leaders, actors, athletes, etc.). Take turns asking students from another group where these people are from. Then reverse roles. The group with the most correct answers wins.

> **Élève 1: D'où viennent les Beatles?**
> **Élève 2: Ils viennent d'Angleterre. (Je ne sais pas. Je ne les connais pas.)**

B Où est...? Working in groups, make a list of as many famous foreign cities, museums, and geographical features as possible. Take turns asking students in another group to tell you where these things are. The group with the most correct answers wins.

> **Élève 1: Où est Montréal?**
> **Élève 2: Montréal est au Canada.**

C Je connais bien... Think of someone you know well in the class. Using the verbs *savoir* and *connaître*, tell your partner about this person without saying his or her name. Your partner will try to guess whom you are talking about. Include as much of the following information as you can.

1. son adresse et son numéro de téléphone
2. les cours qu'il ou elle a
3. les choses qu'il ou elle a dans sa chambre
4. les membres de sa famille
5. les activités qu'il ou elle aime faire

La Place Jacques Cartier à Montréal

> **Élève 1: Je sais qu'il aime le football américain et la musique rock. Je connais son frère Bob. Il habite dans la rue Kennedy...**
> **Élève 2: C'est Andy.**

D Moi, je sais chanter. Et toi? Think of several things that you know how to do well, then ask your partner if he or she knows how to do these things. If your partner doesn't know how, find out if he or she would like to learn.

> **Élève 1: Moi, je sais très bien chanter. Et toi?**
> **Élève 2: Je ne sais pas chanter.**
> **Élève 1: Tu veux apprendre à chanter?**

LECTURE ET CULTURE

LES LOISIRS CULTURELS EN FRANCE

*I*l est naturellement difficile de décrire[1] un adolescent américain typique. Et il est difficile aussi de décrire un adolescent français typique. Mais généralisons un peu! Disons que Chantal Brichant est une adolescente française typique. Que fait Chantal quand elle a du temps libre? Est-ce qu'elle lit? Oui, elle lit. Elle lit beaucoup? Pas vraiment. On peut dire que les jeunes Français lisent un peu plus que les jeunes Américains, mais ils ne lisent pas énormément. Quand Chantal lit, qu'est-ce qu'elle choisit? Elle choisit des romans[2] et des bandes dessinées[3].

Chantal va au théâtre? Oui, de temps en temps. Dans toutes les grandes villes de France, et surtout à Paris, il y a des théâtres. Chaque année un certain nombre de pièces sont bien accueillies[4] par le public. Mais Chantal, comme la plupart des adolescents «typiques», va plus souvent au cinéma. Les Français voient beaucoup de films français, bien sûr, mais ils voient aussi pas mal de[5] films étrangers. On passe les grands films étrangers en exclusivité[6] dans les grands cinémas. Ces films sont souvent doublés, mais on peut les voir aussi en version originale avec des sous-titres.

Mais quel est le loisir préféré de Chantal et des Français «typiques»? La télévision? Mais oui! La télévision est de loin[7] le loisir culturel préféré des Français. Et les jeunes gens aiment aussi sortir avec leurs copains. Est-ce qu'il y a beaucoup de différences entre les Américains et les Français? Qu'est-ce que tu en penses?

[1] décrire *to describe*
[2] des romans *novels*
[3] des bandes dessinées *comic strips*
[4] bien accueillies *well-received*
[5] pas mal de *quite a few*
[6] en exclusivité *first run*
[7] de loin *by far*

Étude de mots

Le français, c'est facile. Trouvez cinq mots apparentés dans la lecture.

Compréhension

A Vous avez compris? Répondez.

1. Chantal lit quand elle a du temps libre?
2. Elle lit énormément?
3. Quel est le genre littéraire préféré des Français?
4. Il y a des théâtres en France? Où?
5. Chaque année il y a des pièces que le public aime?
6. Où est-ce qu'on passe les films étrangers en exclusivité?
7. Quel est le loisir préféré des Français?

B Les adolescents. Il est extrêmement difficile de décrire un adolescent français ou américain typique. Pourquoi?

DÉCOUVERTE CULTURELLE

LES MUSÉES

Les musées en France sont très fréquentés par les Français et par les touristes qui viennent du monde entier—d'Europe, d'Asie, d'Australie, d'Amérique et d'Afrique. À Paris il y a beaucoup de musées. Le Musée d'Orsay est une ancienne gare qui est aujourd'hui un musée extraordinaire où il y a une exposition permanente des peintres impressionnistes. Le Centre Pompidou (ou Beaubourg) a toujours des expositions d'art moderne. Il y a un nouveau Musée Picasso. Et la perle des musées français, c'est le Louvre.

Le dimanche, l'entrée dans les musées nationaux est à demi-tarif. Le dimanche, les gens viennent en foule admirer les peintures et les sculptures des artistes de tous les siècles[1] et de tous les pays du monde.

LES BANDES DESSINÉES

La lecture préférée des jeunes de 8 à 18 ans est la bande dessinée. La «B.D.» vient en tête[2] des romans policiers, d'espionnage et de science-fiction. Mais les bandes dessinées ne sont pas seulement pour les enfants. Il est certain que la grande majorité des jeunes Français lisent «Tintin», «Astérix» et «Lucky Luke». Quand ils deviennent adultes, ils continuent d'avoir «leurs» bandes dessinées. Beaucoup de bandes dessinées, comme, par exemple, «Les Frustrés» de la dessinatrice humoristique Claire Brétécher, critiquent la vie moderne.

[1] les siècles *centuries*
[2] vient en tête *rates above*

© Hergé/Casterman

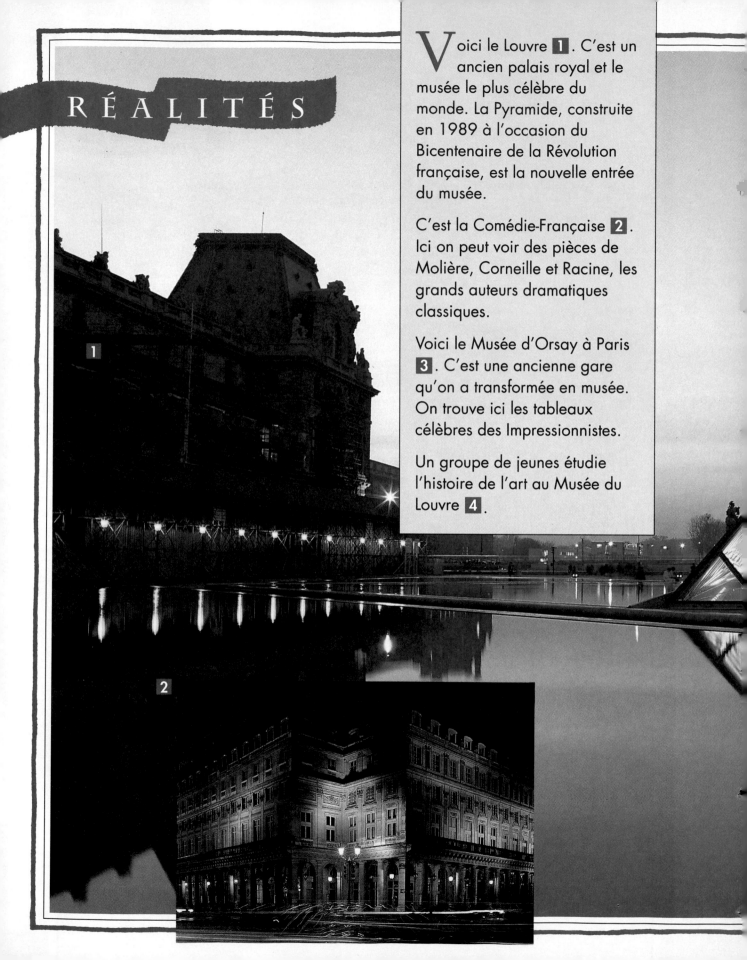

RÉALITÉS

Voici le Louvre **1**. C'est un ancien palais royal et le musée le plus célèbre du monde. La Pyramide, construite en 1989 à l'occasion du Bicentenaire de la Révolution française, est la nouvelle entrée du musée.

C'est la Comédie-Française **2**. Ici on peut voir des pièces de Molière, Corneille et Racine, les grands auteurs dramatiques classiques.

Voici le Musée d'Orsay à Paris **3**. C'est une ancienne gare qu'on a transformée en musée. On trouve ici les tableaux célèbres des Impressionnistes.

Un groupe de jeunes étudie l'histoire de l'art au Musée du Louvre **4**.

3

4

Activités de communication orale

A **Dans ta ville.** You have been asked to prepare a radio advertisement to attract French-speaking tourists to a cultural event (real or imaginary) that will take place in your town. Be sure to include the following information.

1. a brief description of the event
2. the date, time, and place
3. how and where to obtain tickets
4. price of the tickets
5. a statement encouraging people to attend

B **La télé.** Divide into small groups. The leader will interview the others to find out how much time they spend watching TV every day and what their favorite kinds of shows are. The leader will take notes and report to the class.

1. Tu regardes la télé combien d'heures par jour?
2. Quelles sortes de programmes est-ce que tu préfères regarder?

les sports	les clips (vidéos rock)
les comédies	les documentaires
les drames	les dessins animés
le journal télévisé	les séries
les films	

À la classe: Dans mon groupe, tout le monde regarde la télé deux ou trois heures par jour. On préfère les comédies...

C **Tu veux aller au cinéma avec moi?** Scan the following ads from a French movie guide. Select a movie you would like to see and invite your partner to go with you.

1. Ask your partner if he or she would like to see the movie you have selected.
2. Your partner wants to know where the movie is playing.
3. Tell him or her and give the time.
4. Your partner wants to know if the movie is dubbed or if it's in the original language with subtitles.
5. Tell your partner why you want to see this movie.
6. He or she will either accept your invitation or decline and suggest another film.

les salles

COMŒDIA
13, avenue Berthelot - Lyon 7ᵉ
Tél.:76.58.58.98

ROBIN DES BOIS
(Gran Ecran - Son Dolby Stéréo)
Tlj.: 13h50 - 16h30 - 19h15 - 22h

LA MANIERE FORTE (Son Dolby Stéréo)
Tlj.: 13h50 - 16h - 18h - 20h15 - 22h15

THELMA ET LOUISE
(Grand Ecran - Son Dolby Stéréo - V.O.)
Tlj.: 14h - 16h45 - 19h30 - 22h

SPARTACUS
(Grand Ecran -Son Dolby Stéréo - V.O.)
Tlj.: 14h30 - 20h15

LES TORTUES NINJA II
Tlj.: 14h - 16h - 18h - 20h - 21h45

UNE EPOQUE FORMIDABLE
+ Court métrage: "Le ridicule tue"
Tlj.: 14h - 16h - 18h - 20h - 22h

FOURMI LAFAYETTE
68, rue P. Corneille angle cours Lafayette - Tel. 78.60.84.

BRAZIL
Tlj. (sf. di.): 21h30 - di.: 19h4

SCENES DE MENAGE DAN UN CENTRE COMMERCIAL
Tlj.: 20h

TINTIN ET LE LAC AUX REQUINS
Me., sa., lu.:14h

ASTERIX ET LE COUP DU MENHIR
Me., sa., lu: 14h - di.: 15h 30

MAMAN, J'AI RATÉ L'AVION
Me., sa., di., lu.: 15h30

FANTASIA
Me., sa., di., lu.:15h30

ALICE
Sa.: 18h

JACQUOT DE NANTES
Me., sa., lu.: 15h30 - 21h30 - je., ve., ma.: 21h30 - di.: 17h45

Activité de communication écrite

Des renseignements, s'il vous plaît. You are going to spend a month in a French city of your choice. Write a letter to the tourist office (*le syndicat d'initiative*) to request information about cultural events during your stay. Be sure to include the following information.

1. your name and age
2. what cultural activities you like
3. when you will be in the city

Réintroduction et recombinaison

Je suis malade. Donnez des réponses personnelles.

1. Tu te sens bien aujourd'hui?
2. Quand tu es malade, tu te couches?
3. Aux États-Unis le médecin vient chez toi?
4. Le médecin te fait une ordonnance? Tu la donnes au pharmacien?
5. Quand le pharmacien te donne des comprimés, tu les prends avec un verre d'eau?
6. Quand tu es malade, tu ouvres un magazine et tu le lis?
7. Tu souffres beaucoup quand tu as la grippe?
8. Tu éternues et tu tousses quand tu es enrhumé(e)?

Vocabulaire

NOMS
le cinéma
le guichet
la séance
la salle de cinéma
l'écran (m.)
l'acteur (m.)
l'actrice (f.)
la vedette (m. et f.)
le film
le film policier
le film d'aventures
le film d'horreur
le film de science-fiction
le film d'amour
le film étranger
le dessin animé
le documentaire
le drame

le film en version originale (V.O.)
le film doublé
les sous-titres (m.)

le théâtre
la pièce
la scène (*stage*)
le rideau
le décor
le costume
l'acte (m.)
l'entracte (m.)
la scène (*scene*)
le genre
la comédie
la comédie musicale
la tragédie
l'opéra (m.)

le musée
l'exposition (f.)
la peinture
le (la) peintre
le tableau
la sculpture
le sculpteur
la statue
l'œuvre (f.)
le nom

ADJECTIFS
chaque
fermé(e)
ouvert(e)

VERBES
connaître
savoir

venir
revenir
devenir
visiter

AUTRES MOTS ET EXPRESSIONS
monter une pièce
passer un film
c'est-à-dire
entre
personnellement
sauf

RÉVISION

CHAPITRES 13-16

Conversation   *Le joueur de foot*

CHRISTINE: Tu connais le garçon là-bas?

SABINE: Je sais son nom—c'est Marc. Mais je ne le connais pas.

CHRISTINE: Je le vois tous les jours dans l'autobus.

SABINE: Et tu ne le connais pas!? Tu es trop timide! Je sais qu'il fait du foot tous les mercredis.

CHRISTINE: Comment tu sais ça?

SABINE: Il est dans l'équipe de mon frère. Il est gardien de but.

CHRISTINE: Il joue bien?

SABINE: Pas mal. Mais la semaine dernière, l'autre équipe a marqué trois buts et notre équipe a perdu zéro à trois!

Trois buts!   Répondez d'après la conversation.

1. Christine et Sabine connaissent le garçon?
2. Sabine sait son nom? Comment s'appelle-t-il?
3. Où est-ce que Christine le voit tous les jours?
4. Il joue à quoi?
5. Il est dans quelle équipe?
6. Il est gardien de but?
7. Est-ce que son équipe a gagné la semaine dernière? Pourquoi?

Structure

Les pronoms d'objet direct et indirect *me, te, nous* et *vous*

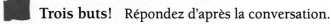

The pronouns *me, te, nous,* and *vous* function as both direct and indirect objects of the verb. Remember that *me* and *te* change to *m'* and *t'* before a vowel or silent *h*. Object pronouns always come right before the verb.

Le professeur *te* regarde?	Oui, il *me* regarde.
Le médecin *t'*examine?	Non, il ne *m'*examine pas.
Il va *vous* faire une ordonnance?	Oui, il va *nous* faire une ordonnance.

A   **Qu'est-ce qu'on fait?**   Répondez en utilisant «me» ou «nous».

1. Quand le médecin t'examine, il t'ausculte?
2. Quand tu as une angine, le médecin te prescrit des antibiotiques?
3. Tes copains te téléphonent quand tu es malade?
4. Tes professeurs vous admirent, toi et tes copains?
5. Ils vous donnent beaucoup de devoirs?
6. Ils vont vous voir l'année prochaine?

Les pronoms d'objet direct *le, la, les*

Review the following direct object pronouns *le, la, les*. Remember that *le* and *la* change to *l'* before a vowel or vowel sound. These pronouns can replace either people or things.

Je vois l'acteur.	**Je *le* vois.**
J'aime beaucoup cet acteur.	**Je l'aime beaucoup.**
Je vais regarder la télé.	**Je vais *la* regarder.**
Je n'aime pas les romans.	**Je ne *les* aime pas.**

B **Qu'est-ce qu'on fait?** Répondez en utilisant «le», «la», «l'» ou «les».

1. Vous connaissez les Impressionnistes?
2. Vous savez l'adresse du Musée d'Orsay?
3. Vous aimez les tableaux des Impressionnistes?
4. Qui aime la sculpture?
5. Tes copains et toi, vous aimez voir les films d'horreur?

C **Non.** Mettez à la forme négative d'après les indications.

1. Je les vois souvent. (ne... jamais)
2. Vous les aimez, ces gens? (ne... pas)
3. La télé, nous la regardons de temps en temps. (ne... jamais)
4. Le ballet? Nous voulons le voir. (ne... pas)

Les prépositions avec les noms géographiques

You use the following prepositions to express "in," "to," and "from" with geographical names.

1. *à* and *de* with cities

   Il habite à Paris. **Je viens de Rome.**

2. *en/au (aux)* and *de/du (des)* with countries, depending on whether the country is masculine or feminine, singular or plural.

	FÉMININ	MASCULIN
to	**Je vais en France.**	**Je vais au Brésil.** **Je vais aux États-Unis.**
from	**Je viens de France.**	**Je viens du Brésil.** **Je viens des États-Unis.**

Remember that, except for *le Mexique* and a few others, countries that end in a silent *e* are feminine.

D Quelle ville? Quel pays? Complétez.

1. Il est ___ Rome. Il habite ___ Italie.
2. Nous venons ___ Londres, mais nous n'habitons pas ___ Angleterre.
3. J'ai un appartement ___ Paris, mais je n'habite pas ___ France.
4. Ils vont tous les ans ___ Mexique.
5. L'Alhambra est ___ Grenade, ___ Espagne.
6. J'ai passé une semaine ___ Amsterdam ___ Pays-Bas.
7. Il vient ___ Maroc. Il est ___ Casablanca.
8. Tu viens ___ New York. Tu habites ___ États-Unis.

E Dans quel pays? Regardez la carte à la page 488. Choisissez une ville et répondez d'après le modèle.

> **Bruxelles**
>
> **Élève 1: Dans quel pays est Bruxelles?**
> **Élève 2: Bruxelles est en Belgique.**

Le passé composé des verbes réguliers et irréguliers

1. The *passé composé* is composed of two parts: the present tense of the verb *avoir* and the past participle of the verb. Review the forms of the *passé composé* of regular verbs.

PARLER	FINIR	VENDRE
j'ai parlé	j'ai fini	j'ai vendu
tu as parlé	tu as fini	tu as vendu
il / elle / on a parlé	il / elle / on a fini	il / elle / on a vendu
nous avons parlé	nous avons fini	nous avons vendu
vous avez parlé	vous avez fini	vous avez vendu
ils / elles ont parlé	ils / elles ont fini	ils / elles ont vendu

2. For the past participles of irregular verbs, see p. 360.

3. Remember that *ne... pas, ne... plus, ne... jamais* go around the verb *avoir.*

> **Tu n'as pas écouté le prof hier?**

F **Le match de foot.** Décrivez un match de foot imaginaire au *passé composé*. Utilisez les verbes et expressions suivants.

regarder	jouer	donner un coup de pied
marquer un but	passer le ballon	arrêter le ballon
égaliser le score	gagner	perdre

G **Les achats.** Vous avez acheté des vêtements. Décrivez ces vêtements à un copain ou une copine. Utilisez les verbes suivants.

acheter   coûter   prendre   trouver   aimer

L'impératif

Imperative forms are used to give commands or to make suggestions. They are the same as the *tu, nous,* and *vous* forms of the present tense. However, in the case of regular -*er* verbs and *aller,* you drop the final *s* of the *tu* form.

Travaille!	Attends un peu!	Fais ça!
Travaillons!	Attendons un peu!	Faisons ça!
Travaillez!	Attendez un peu!	Faites ça!

H **Le jeu de «Jacques a dit»** (*Simon says*). Vous donnez des ordres à vos camarades. Si vous dites d'abord «Jacques a dit», ils le font, mais si vous ne dites pas «Jacques a dit», ils ne le font pas.

(*Jacques a dit*): **Levez le bras droit! Fermez les yeux!** etc.

Activité de communication

Enquête sur les saisons. You want to know if your partner prefers summer or winter. On a separate sheet of paper, make a chart like the one below. Fill it out for both seasons. Compare your chart with your partner's and try to guess which season he or she prefers by asking questions about his or her choices.

Élève 1: Tu préfères le ski ou le ski nautique?
Élève 2: Je préfère le ski nautique.
Élève 1: Tu préfères l'été.

	L'HIVER	L'ÉTÉ
Vêtements		
Activités	le ski	le ski nautique
Équipement		
Nourriture		

MICROBIOLOGIE:
LOUIS PASTEUR ET L'INSTITUT PASTEUR

Avant la lecture

You have no doubt heard of pasteurized milk. The term comes from the name of the French chemist, Louis Pasteur, who invented the method of destroying harmful organisms without altering the milk. Find out how milk and other substances are pasteurized.

Lecture

«La vaccination de Joseph Meister»

Louis Pasteur (1822–1895)
Louis Pasteur est né en 1822 dans le Jura. Au collège, il n'est pas très bon élève. Il n'aime pas beaucoup ses cours, mais il aime le dessin. On l'appelle «l'artiste». Il veut devenir professeur et entre à l'École Normale, un institut qui forme les professeurs. Mais maintenant, il est passionné de sciences et passe son temps à faire de la recherche[1]. Il se spécialise en chimie.

En 1854, il commence à étudier ce que nous connaissons sous le nom de «microbes». Pasteur appelle ces microbes «germes» et il fonde une nouvelle science, la microbiologie. En 1873 Pasteur présente à l'Académie de Médecine un rapport qui révolutionne la médecine. Avant ce rapport de Pasteur, on croit que toutes les maladies terribles comme la typhoïde, le choléra et la fièvre jaune sont créées par le corps humain. C'est la théorie de la «génération spontanée». Mais Pasteur a fait des recherches sur les maladies du vin, de la bière et du ver à soie[2]. Il a compris que ces maladies n'arrivent pas toutes seules. Son idée, c'est que toutes les maladies sont causées par des micro-organismes. Ce sont des organismes très, très petits. On les baptise «microbes».

Pour Pasteur, les microbes sont partout. Il dit aux chirurgiens[3] de se laver les mains avant d'opérer, de bien laver aussi leurs instruments, c'est-à-dire de pratiquer l'asepsie. Malheureusement peu de[4] gens l'écoutent. Pourquoi? Parce qu'il n'est pas médecin. Il est chimiste et biologiste. Mais Pasteur ne s'arrête pas là. Il continue ses recherches. Il veut lutter[5] contre les microbes. Ses recherches sur les maladies infectieuses des animaux le conduisent à découvrir la vaccination. En 1885, il réalise le vaccin contre la rage[6]. On vaccine alors pour la première fois un être humain, un petit garçon de neuf ans—Joseph Meister—qui a été mordu[7] par un chien

enragé. C'est la victoire, après 40 ans de recherches.

[1] la recherche *research*
[2] du vin, de la bière et du ver à soie *wine, beer, and the silkworm*
[3] chirurgiens *surgeons*
[4] peu de *few*
[5] lutter *fight*
[6] la rage *rabies*
[7] mordu *bitten*

Laboratoire de culture cellulaire en masse dans des bioréacteurs à l'Institut Pasteur

L'Institut Pasteur (1888)

L'enthousiasme est grand, non seulement en France mais dans le monde entier.

L'Académie des Sciences reçoit[1] de l'argent de nombreux pays pour la construction d'un centre de recherches en microbiologie. L'Institut Pasteur est inauguré le 4 novembre 1888. Et qui est son concierge?[2] C'est… Joseph Meister. Les collaborateurs et élèves de Pasteur continuent son travail. En 1891 les docteurs Calmette et Guérin mettent au point[3] le BCG (Bacille de Calmette et Guérin), le vaccin contre la tuberculose. En 1894, le docteur Roux met au point un vaccin contre la diphtérie.

De nos jours, l'Institut Pasteur de Paris est célèbre dans le monde entier. En plus du centre de recherches, il a un hôpital pour les maladies infectieuses et un centre d'enseignement[4]. En 1983, c'est à l'Institut Pasteur que le docteur Montagnier a isolé le virus du SIDA (Syndrome Immuno-Déficitaire Acquis). Aujourd'hui à l'Institut, on continue à faire des recherches pour trouver une cure ou un vaccin contre cette terrible maladie.

[1] reçoit *receives*
[2] concierge *caretaker, concierge*
[3] mettent au point *come out with*
[4] enseignement *teaching*

Pasteur par Robert Thom

Après la lecture

A **Louis Pasteur.** Copiez ce formulaire (*data sheet*) sur Pasteur et remplissez-le.

NOM	
DATES	
ÉCOLE	
SPÉCIALISATION	
SUJET DU RAPPORT EN 1873	
DÉCOUVERTE EN 1885	

B **Enquête.** Que pensent vos camarades? Quelle est pour eux la plus grande découverte de Pasteur? Pourquoi?

C **Savez-vous que…** En France les enfants sont en général vaccinés contre les maladies suivantes: la diphtérie, le tétanos et la poliomyélite (un seul vaccin pour les trois); la tuberculose (le BCG); la coqueluche (*whooping cough*); la rougeole (*measles*); la rubéole (*German measles*) et les oreillons (*mumps*). Les deux premiers vaccins sont obligatoires et les autres sont recommandés. Et dans votre pays? Quels sont les vaccins recommandés?

ART: LES IMPRESSIONNISTES

Avant la lecture

1. What does the title of this text refer to?
2. Are any of these paintings familiar to you? Where did you see them?
3. How would describe them? Realistic? Dreamlike? Colorful?

Lecture

Entre 1870 et 1900, les arts, et en particulier la peinture, commencent à changer. Chaque année, le «Salon» est une grande exposition de peinture. Si les peintres veulent exposer leurs tableaux, ils leur faut être acceptés par un jury.

Nous sommes en 1873. Le jury vient de refuser[1] tout un groupe de jeunes peintres. Ils sont furieux et décident d'avoir leur propre exposition. Elle a lieu[2] en 1874. Le public est scandalisé et crie à la vulgarité: les couleurs sont trop vives, les paysages[3] sont trop «bizarres». Un des tableaux est intitulé «Impression: soleil levant[4]». De là le terme (péjoratif à l'origine) «les Impressionnistes». Qui sont ces jeunes peintres? En voici trois.

Claude Monet (1840–1926)
Lycéen au Havre, il aime faire les caricatures de ses professeurs sur ses cahiers. Le peintre Eugène Boudin les voit et encourage Monet à faire de la peinture. C'est une révélation pour lui. Il admire les jeux de la lumière[5] sur l'eau, sur tout le paysage. Pour mieux étudier les variations de la forme en fonction de la lumière, il peint le même sujet à différentes heures de la journée. La cathédrale de Rouen est une de ces séries.

Il passe la plus grande partie de sa vie dans sa maison de Giverny en Normandie où il reproduit dans son jardin les couleurs de ses tableaux.

Claude Monet: «La Cathédrale de Rouen, le Portail, Harmonie bleue»

Auguste Renoir: «Portrait de Margot»

Auguste Renoir
(1841–1919)

Il commence comme apprenti chez un décorateur de porcelaine à Paris. Il passe ses moments libres au musée du Louvre où il admire surtout les tableaux du peintre flamand Rubens. Renoir rencontre bientôt Claude Monet, qui l'encourage à peindre avec des couleurs moins sombres. Ils vont ensemble peindre à la campagne. Les Impressionnistes aiment peindre en plein air[6]. Comme tous les Impressionnistes, Renoir reçoit beaucoup de critiques. Il commence à douter, à se demander si les Impressionnistes ont raison[7]. Et pourtant Renoir est le premier Impressionniste reconnu par le public.

Edgar Degas (1834–1917)

Son père est un riche banquier qui est amateur d'art. Degas va régulièrement au Louvre où il copie les grands maîtres[8]. Degas aime le théâtre, l'opéra, la vie facile. Il devient ami avec les autres peintres impressionnistes, mais il n'a pas grand-chose en commun avec eux. Il n'aime pas peindre en plein air et il aime peindre des personnages et pas des paysages. On l'appelle souvent «le peintre des danseuses» parce qu'il a peint beaucoup de scènes où on voit des danseuses s'exercer avant le spectacle.

[1] vient de refuser *has just turned down*
[2] a lieu *takes place*
[3] les paysages *the landscapes*
[4] soleil levant *sunrise*
[5] les jeux de la lumière *the play of light*
[6] en plein air *outdoors*
[7] ont raison *are right*
[8] maîtres *masters*

Après la lecture

A **Les Impressionnistes.** Dites qui c'est: Monet, Renoir ou Degas?

1. Il aime beaucoup les tableaux de Rubens.
2. Il peint le même sujet à des heures différentes de la journée.
3. Son père est un riche amateur d'art.
4. Il n'aime pas peindre la nature.
5. Il commence par peindre sur de la porcelaine.
6. C'est un de ses tableaux qui leur donne leur nom.
7. Il peint souvent des danseuses.
8. Il aime beaucoup son jardin.

B **Une «Impressionniste» américaine.**
Faites un rapport sur la vie et l'œuvre de l'artiste peintre américaine Mary Cassatt (1845-1926).

Edgar Degas: «Dans les coulisses (Danseuses en bleu)»

HISTOIRE: TROIS EXPLORATEURS

Avant la lecture

La Nouvelle France included territories that covered most of the present-day United States. Although the French presence is not as prevalent as it used to be, it is still very much alive.

Lecture

Jacques Cartier

Robert Cavelier de la Salle

Jacques Cartier

Jacques Cartier est né à Saint-Malo en Bretagne en 1494. C'est une ville de marins[1] qui traversent souvent l'océan Atlantique pour aller pêcher[2]. Jacques Cartier est un marin audacieux, passionné des voyages: de Saint-Malo, il va au Portugal, au Brésil, à Terre-Neuve[3].

En 1534, le roi de France, François 1er, le charge d'une expédition pour découvrir des pays d'Orient où il y a de l'or et des pierres précieuses[4]. Jacques Cartier part avec deux bateaux et 61 marins. Vingt jours après, ils arrivent à Terre-Neuve. C'est un voyage très rapide pour l'époque[5]. Jacques Cartier revient au Canada encore deux fois. La troisième fois, en 1541, il construit un fort qui est devenu une grande ville: Québec.

Robert Cavelier de la Salle

Robert Cavelier de la Salle est le fils d'un riche marchand de Rouen, un grand port de Normandie. La Salle est passionné de l'Amérique et lit tous les rapports des explorateurs qu'il peut trouver. Il rêve[6] de descendre le Mississippi jusqu'au golfe de Mexique. En 1679, il réalise son rêve: il part de Fort Frontenac sur le Saint-Laurent avec six canots qui transportent 23 Français, 18 Indiens, 10 squaws et 3 enfants. Ils traversent les lacs Ontario, Érié, Huron et Michigan. Ils descendent l'Illinois et le Mississippi, et finalement ils arrivent dans le delta du Mississippi en 1682. La Salle prend possession de la région au nom du roi de France et appelle ces nouveaux territoires «La Louisiane» en l'honneur du roi Louis XIV.

John Charles Frémont

John Charles Frémont est né à Savannah en Géorgie en 1813. Son père est un aristocrate français qui est parti en Amérique pendant la Révolution de 1789 pour échapper à la guillotine. Le jeune Frémont est très intelligent. Il est surtout très bon en mathématiques, mais il aime aussi l'aventure et le danger. Il devient d'abord professeur de maths, mais sur un bateau de guerre[7]. Il devient ensuite l'assistant d'un mathématicien français, Nicolas Nicollet, qui fait le levé topographique[8] des territoires du Nord, entre le Mississippi et le Missouri. Mais à l'époque, c'est la conquête de l'Ouest qui passionne les esprits. Frémont est le candidat idéal pour cette longue route inconnue de plus de 3 500 kilomètres. Frémont rassemble alors à Saint-Louis une équipe de 19 «voyageurs» canadiens qui connaissent bien les fleuves et les forêts. Il est aussi accompagné par un topographe allemand, Preuss, et un guide, Kit Carson. Ils partent en juin 1842. Lorsqu'il revient dans l'Est, il rapporte beaucoup de notes. Sa femme Jessie écrit deux livres d'après ses notes. Les livres sont aussi illustrés de cartes des régions traversées. Ces deux livres font de Frémont et de son guide Kit Carson des héros nationaux et la conquête de l'Ouest est commencée.

[1] marins *sailors*
[2] aller pêcher *to go fishing*
[3] Terre-Neuve *Newfoundland*
[4] de l'or et des pierres précieuses *gold and precious stones*
[5] l'époque *the times, the age*
[6] rêve *dreams*
[7] guerre *war*
[8] fait le levé topographique *is surveying*

John Charles Frémont

Après la lecture

A **Trois explorateurs.** Vrai ou faux?

1. Jacques Cartier a descendu le Mississippi.
2. Il a fondé Québec.
3. Cavelier de la Salle est né en France.
4. Le nom «Louisiane» vient du nom du roi Louis XIV.
5. Le père de Frémont a été guillotiné.
6. Frémont a écrit deux livres.

B **Les voyages des explorateurs.** Regardez la carte et racontez les voyages des trois explorateurs.

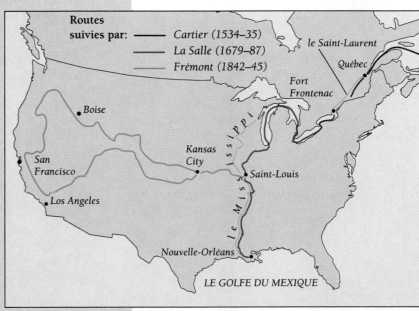

Routes suivies par:
— Cartier (1534–35)
— La Salle (1679–87)
— Frémont (1842–45)

le Saint-Laurent
Québec
Fort Frontenac
Boise
Kansas City
Saint-Louis
San Francisco
le Mississippi
Los Angeles
Nouvelle-Orléans
LE GOLFE DU MEXIQUE

OBJECTIFS

In this chapter you will learn to do the following:

1. check into and out of a hotel
2. describe past actions
3. tell what you do for another person or for other people
4. describe various kinds of hotels in France

VOCABULAIRE

MOTS 1

À L'HÔTEL

le hall

un escalier

la réception

la réceptionniste

une porte

le réceptionniste

une fiche d'enregistrement

une chambre avec salle de bains

une chambre à un lit

une chambre pour une personne

une chambre qui donne sur la cour

une chambre à deux lits

une chambre pour deux personnes

Lindsay est arrivée à l'hôtel.
Elle est entrée dans le hall.

Elle est allée à la réception.
Elle a montré son passeport à la réceptionniste.
Elle a rempli la fiche d'enregistrement.
La réceptionniste lui a donné la clé.

Elle a monté ses bagages.
Elle est montée au troisième étage.
Elle a pris l'ascenseur, pas l'escalier.

Elle a ouvert la porte de sa chambre avec la clé.

Elle est descendue une heure plus tard.

Elle est sortie.

Elle est rentrée à neuf heures du soir.

Exercices

A Qu'est-ce que c'est?
Répondez d'après les dessins.

1. C'est un hôtel ou une chambre?

2. C'est la réception ou la réceptionniste?

Fiche d'enregistrement

Nom:_____ Prénoms: _____

Né le: _____

Départment: _____

Profession: _____

Domicile habituel: _____

_____

Nationalité: _____

Signature: _____

3. C'est une clé ou une fiche d'enregistrement?

4. C'est un ascenseur ou un escalier?

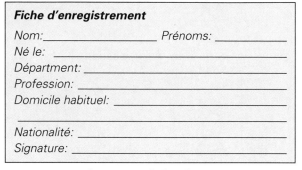

5. C'est une porte ou une chambre?

6. C'est une chambre à un lit ou à deux lits?

7. C'est une chambre qui donne sur la cour
ou sur la rue?

B À l'hôtel. Répondez.

1. Lindsay est arrivée à l'hôtel?
2. Elle est entrée dans le hall?
3. Elle a parlé à la réceptionniste?
4. Elle lui a montré son passeport?
5. Lindsay a rempli la fiche d'enregistrement?
6. La réceptionniste lui a donné la clé?
7. Lindsay a monté ses bagages?
8. Elle est montée par l'ascenseur?
9. La chambre est au troisième étage?
10. C'est une chambre avec salle de bains?
11. Lindsay est descendue une heure plus tard?
12. Elle est sortie?
13. Elle est rentrée à neuf heures du soir?

C Le touriste. Choisissez la bonne réponse.

1. À l'hôtel le touriste remplit ___.
   a. la fiche   b. la chambre   c. la clé
2. Pour monter dans sa chambre il prend ___.
   a. le lit   b. l'ascenseur   c. la porte
3. Il ouvre la porte de sa chambre avec ___.
   a. l'escalier   b. le lit   c. la clé
4. Il prend une douche dans ___.
   a. la salle de bains   b. le hall
   c. le petit déjeuner
5. Il dort dans ___.
   a. le lit   b. l'escalier
   c. la salle de bains
6. Le matin il se lève et prend ___.
   a. la fiche   b. le petit déjeuner
   c. la cour

ALTEA
— HÔTEL —

PETIT DÉJEUNER
Merci de passer votre commande ce soir.
Bonne nuit.

Le petit déjeuner est servi dans votre chambre de quart d'heure en quart d'heure de 7 heures à 11 heures.
Merci de faire votre choix et suspendre votre fiche à l'extérieur de votre porte.

Chambre N°____   Signature _____

PETIT DÉJEUNER COMPLET
Jus d'orange, croissant, petit pain, beurre, confiture ou miel, yaourt, fruit ou compote au choix.

❑ THÉ
❑ THÉ CITRON   ❑ DÉCAFÉINÉ
❑ THÉ AU LAIT   ❑ CAFÉ   ❑ CHOCOLAT
                  ❑ CAFÉ AU LAIT ❑ LAIT FROID
                                  ❑ LAIT CHAUD

...us vous suggérons notre petit déjeuner buffet qui vous sera servi au Coffee Shop dès 7 heures 30.

ALTEA
— HÔTEL —

Ne Pas
Déranger

MOTS 2

une facture

les frais (m.)

une carte de crédit

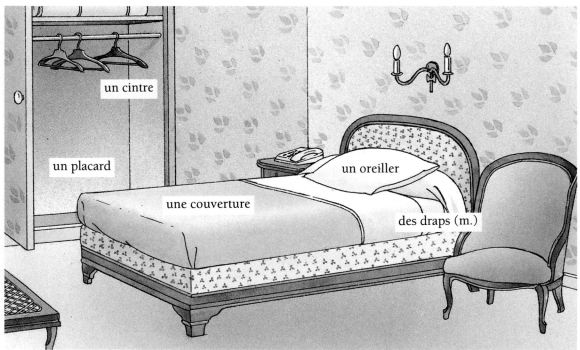

un cintre

un placard

une couverture

un oreiller

des draps (m.)

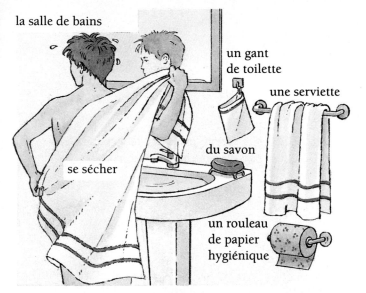

la salle de bains

un gant
de toilette

une serviette

du savon

se sécher

un rouleau
de papier
hygiénique

Lindsay est restée une semaine
    à l'hôtel.
Elle a libéré la chambre.

Elle est descendue à la réception.
Elle a demandé la facture.
Elle a vérifié les frais.

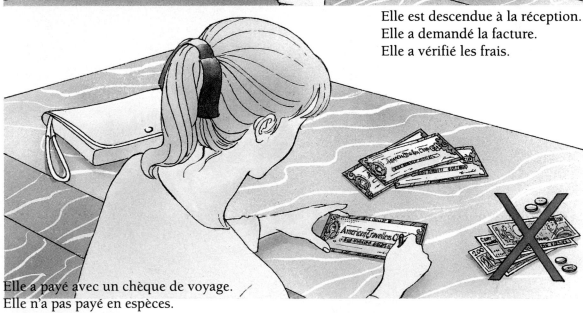

Elle a payé avec un chèque de voyage.
Elle n'a pas payé en espèces.

Exercices

A **Elle a libéré la chambre.** Répondez.

1. Lindsay a libéré la chambre?
2. Elle est descendue à la réception?
3. Elle a voulu payer?
4. Elle a demandé la facture?
5. Elle a parlé au caissier ou à la caissière?
6. Elle a vérifié les frais?
7. Elle a payé en espèces?
8. Elle a payé avec une carte de crédit?
9. Elle a payé la facture comment?

B **J'ai besoin de quoi?** Complétez.

1. Je vais me laver. J'ai besoin de ___ et d'un ___.
2. J'ai pris une douche. Maintenant je vais me sécher. J'ai besoin d'une ___.
3. Je vais mettre ma veste et mon pantalon dans le placard. J'ai besoin de ___.
4. Je vais me coucher mais il fait froid dans la chambre. J'ai besoin d'une autre ___.
5. Je préfère dormir avec deux ___. J'ai besoin d'un autre ___.
6. Ah, zut! J'ai besoin d'un rouleau de ___.
7. La chambre n'est pas prête (*ready*). Il n'y a pas de ___ sur le lit.

C **À l'hôtel?** Où sont les objets suivants—dans la chambre, dans la salle de bains, dans le placard ou à la caisse?

1. l'oreiller
2. le cintre
3. la facture
4. le papier hygiénique
5. la carte de crédit
6. le gant de toilette
7. les draps
8. la couverture
9. le savon
10. la serviette

Activités de communication
Mots 1 et 2

A **On prépare un voyage.** The French Club is planning a trip to Toulon in the South of France. Using each of the options below, find out what kind of hotel and room your partner would like and why. Then reverse roles. Report to the class about each other's preferences.

1. Un petit hôtel confortable ou un grand hôtel de luxe?
2. Un hôtel avec piscine ou court de tennis?
3. Un hôtel près ou loin de la mer?
4. Un hôtel avec discothèque?
5. Une chambre avec salle de bains?
6. Une chambre qui donne sur la cour ou sur la mer?
7. Une chambre pour deux, trois ou quatre personnes?

B **Comment réserver une chambre.** A family friend has asked you to phone a Montreal hotel to make reservations for her and her husband. Use the information on the right when you make the call. Your partner will play the role of the hotel employee.

Nom de l'hôtel: Hôtel St Laurent
Nom des clients: Joanne et Michael Burke
Type de chambre: à deux lits, avec salle de bains
Dates: du 15 au 22 mai
Prix de la chambre $ 85 canadiens
Carte de crédit: Visa 550-8165-98-3

C **Quelle catastrophe!** You have checked into a French hotel that is under new management. Several items are missing from the room. Call the desk clerk (your partner), give your name and room number, and tell what's missing. Say why you need the item immediately. He or she will try to resolve the problem. Then reverse roles.

> Élève 1: Bonjour, monsieur (madame). Je m'appelle M. Scott. Je suis dans la chambre 233. Il n'y a pas de draps sur mon lit. Je suis très fatigué et je veux dormir maintenant.
> Élève 2: Alors je vous donne des draps tout de suite.

STRUCTURE

Le passé composé avec *être*   *Describing Past Actions*

1. You have already learned that you form the *passé composé* of most verbs
   with the verb *avoir* and the past participle.

   > **Elle a parlé au caissier.**
   > **Elle a rempli la fiche.**
   > **Elle a demandé la facture.**
   > **Elle a vérifié les frais.**

2. With certain verbs, however, you use *être* as the helping verb rather than
   avoir. Many verbs that are conjugated with *être* express motion to or from a
   place.

arriver	Il est arrivé.	descendre	Il est descendu.
partir	Il est parti.	aller	Il est allé en ville.
entrer	Il est entré.	venir	Il est venu.
sortir	Il est sorti.	revenir	Il est revenu.
monter	Il est monté.	rentrer	Il est rentré.

3. Remember that with the *passé composé* the *ne...pas* goes around the verb
   être.

   > **Paul *n*'est *pas* arrivé à l'heure.**
   > **Je *ne* suis *pas* sorti.**

4. The past participle of verbs conjugated with *être* must agree with the subject
   in number (singular or plural) and gender (masculine or feminine). Study
   the following forms.

MASCULIN	FÉMININ
Je suis sorti.	Je suis sorti*e*.
Tu es sorti.	Tu es sorti*e*.
Il est sorti.	Elle est sorti*e*.
Nous sommes sortis.	Nous sommes sorti*es*.
Vous êtes sorti(*s*).	Vous êtes sorti*e*(*s*).
Ils sont sortis.	Elles sont sorti*es*.

Exercices

A Un voyage à Avignon.   Répondez par «oui».

1. Monique est allée à Avignon?
2. Elle est arrivée à la Gare de Lyon à 10h.
3. Elle est allée sur le quai?
4. Elle est montée en voiture?
5. Le train pour Avignon est parti à l'heure?
6. Le train est arrivé à Avignon à l'heure?
7. Monique est descendue du train à Avignon?
8. Elle est sortie de la gare?
9. Elle est allée à l'hôtel?
10. Elle est entrée dans le hall de l'hôtel?

B À l'école.   Donnez des réponses personnelles.

1. Tu es allé(e) à l'école ce matin?
2. Tu es arrivé(e) à l'école à quelle heure?
3. Tu es venu(e) à l'école comment?
4. Tu es entré(e) dans l'école?
5. Tu es allé(e) à ton premier cours?
6. Tu es sorti(e) de l'école à quelle heure hier?
7. Tu es allé(e) manger quelque chose avec tes copains après les cours?
8. Tu es rentré(e) à la maison tout de suite après?

C Au cinéma.   Mettez au passé composé.

1. Michel et sa sœur vont au cinéma.
2. Ils partent à l'heure.
3. Ils montent dans le bus.
4. Ils arrivent au cinéma.
5. Ils descendent du bus.
6. Ils vont au guichet.
7. Ils entrent dans le cinéma.
8. Ils sortent du cinéma après le film.
9. Ils vont au café.
10. Ils rentrent chez eux à minuit.

D Qui est sorti?   Donnez des réponses personnelles.

1. Le mois dernier, tes copains et toi, vous êtes allés au cinéma?
2. Vous y êtes allés comment? En voiture? En bus?
3. Vous êtes toujours partis à l'heure?
4. Vous êtes arrivés quelquefois en retard?
5. Après le film vous êtes allés manger quelque chose?
6. Vous êtes souvent rentrés chez vous assez tard?

E Un séjour.   Complétez au passé composé.

Ce matin Marc ___ (arriver) à Paris avec ses copains. Ils ___ (sortir) de la gare
                    1   2
et ___ (trouver) un taxi. Ils ___ (aller) à l'hôtel. Quand ils ___ (arriver) à
     3   4   5
l'hôtel, ils ___ (entrer) dans le hall. Ils ___ (aller) à la réception et tout le
             6   7
monde ___ (remplir) et ___ (signer) une fiche d'enregistrement. La
        8   9
réceptionniste ___ (donner) les clés à Marc. Marc et ses copains ___ (monter)
                10   11
au quatrième étage à pied. Ils ___ (prendre) l'escalier. Ils ___ (mettre) leurs
                                12   13
bagages dans leur chambre et ___ (sortir) tout de suite après.
                                14

F **Une excursion.** Mettez au passé composé.

MATHIEU: Tu ____ (aller) en Normandie avec Laure, n'est-ce pas?

THÉRÈSE: Oui, nous y ____ (aller).

MATHIEU: Comment avez-vous trouvé le Mont-Saint-Michel?

THÉRÈSE: C'est vraiment impressionnant. Nous ____ (sortir) de notre petit hôtel à huit heures du matin et nous ____ (arriver) au Mont vers 9h.

MATHIEU: Vous ____ (monter) à la basilique?

THÉRÈSE: Oui, et nous ____ (sortir) sur la terrasse. De là, la vue est superbe.

MATHIEU: Mon frère et moi ____ (aller) au Mont-Saint-Michel l'année dernière et je suis d'accord avec toi—c'est formidable!

Le Mont-Saint-Michel

D'autres verbes avec *être* au passé composé

Describing Past Actions

Although the following verbs do not express motion to or from a place, they are also conjugated with *être*.

rester	**Il est resté huit jours.**	*He stayed a week.*
tomber	**Il est tombé.**	*He fell.*
devenir	**Il est devenu malade.**	*He became sick.*
naître	**Elle est née en France.**	*She was born in France.*
mourir	**Elle est morte en 1991.**	*She died in 1991.*

Exercices

A **Être ou ne pas être.** Donnez des réponses personnelles.

1. Tu es né(e) quel jour?
2. Tu es né(e) à l'hôpital?
3. Tu es né(e) dans quel hôpital?
4. Ta mère est restée combien de jours à l'hôpital?
5. Où tes parents sont-ils nés?
6. Tu as des grands-parents? Où sont-ils nés?

B **Vous êtes maladroit!** Regardez les dessins et dites qui est tombé où.

l'enfant
L'enfant est tombé dans le jardin.

1. tu

2. Michel

3. tes copains

4. nous

5. vous

C **Aux Jeux Olympiques.** Complétez au passé composé.

1. Sophie ___ (aller) à Albertville en France pour participer aux Jeux Olympiques.
2. Elle ___ (rester) quinze jours dans les Alpes.
3. Elle est patineuse. Pendant la compétition elle n'___ pas ___ (tomber).
4. Mais toutes les autres patineuses ___ (tomber).
5. Alors Sophie ___ (gagner) la médaille d'or.
6. Elle ___ (devenir) championne olympique.
7. Après les Jeux elle ___ (rentrer) au Canada où elle ___(devenir) très célèbre.

Le passé composé: *être* ou *avoir*   *Describing Past Actions*

The verbs *descendre, monter, passer, rentrer,* and *sortir* are conjugated with *être* in the *passé composé* when they are not followed by an object. They are conjugated with *avoir,* however, when they are followed by a direct object. Study the following pairs of sentences. Note the differences in meaning.

WITHOUT OBJECT

Elle est descendue.

Nous sommes montés au deuxième étage.

Ils sont sortis hier soir.

WITH OBJECT

Elle a descendu *son sac à dos.*

Nous avons monté *nos bagages.*

Ils ont sorti *leur passeport.*

Exercices

A **Christine est arrivée.** Répondez par «oui».

1. Christine est arrivée à l'hôtel?
2. Elle est allée à la réception?
3. Elle a sorti son passeport et sa carte de crédit?
4. Elle est montée dans sa chambre?
5. Elle a pris l'escalier?
6. Elle a monté ses bagages?
7. Elle est descendue?
8. Elle est sortie?
9. Elle est allée au musée?
10. Elle est rentrée à l'hôtel à onze heures du soir?

B **En route!** Complétez au passé composé avec «avoir» ou «être».

1. Isabelle et Janine ___ (sortir) de la maison à neuf heures.
2. Elles ___ (sortir) tous leurs bagages sur le trottoir.
3. Elles ___ (attendre) le taxi.
4. Quand le taxi ___(venir), elles ___(mettre) leurs bagages dans le coffre.
5. Puis les deux filles ___(monter) dans le taxi.
6. À la gare elles ___ (descendre) du taxi et ___ (descendre) leurs bagages sur le quai.
7. Elles ___ (sortir) leurs billets et ___ (monter) dans le train.

Les pronoms *lui, leur*

Telling What You Do for Others

1. *Lui* and *leur* are indirect object pronouns. Observe the difference between a direct object and an indirect object in the following sentences.

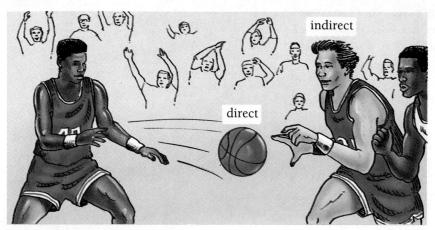

Pierre lance *le ballon à Gilles*.

Marie donne *l'argent à son copain*.

In the above sentences, *le ballon* and *l'argent* are direct objects. *Gilles* and *son copain* are indirect objects, introduced by *à*.

2. You use the pronoun *lui* to replace *à* + a person (singular).

Je parle *à Marie.*	**Je lui parle.**
Je parle *à Luc.*	**Je lui parle.**
Il lance le ballon *à l'autre joueur.*	**Il lui lance le ballon.**
Il ne renvoie pas le ballon *à la fille.*	**Il ne lui renvoie pas le ballon.**

3. You use the pronoun *leur* to replace *à* + more than one person.

Je téléphone *à Roger et à Olivier.*   **Je leur téléphone.**
Je téléphone *à Catherine et à Jeanne.*   **Je leur téléphone.**
L'arbitre parle *aux filles.*   **L'arbitre leur parle.**

4. As with other object pronouns, *lui* and *leur* cannot be separated from the verb by a negative word.

Je ne *lui parle* pas.
Il ne *leur téléphone* pas.

5. Remember that in sentences with a verb + infinitive, the pronoun comes right before the infinitive.

Je vais *lui* téléphoner.
Je ne veux pas *leur* offrir de cadeaux.

FRANCE TELECOM
600 AGENCES
PARTOUT
EN FRANCE
TELECARTE 50

Exercices

A   **Guy offre un cadeau.**   Refaites les phrases d'après le modèle.

> **Guy offre un cadeau** *à sa nouvelle amie française.*
> *Guy lui offre un cadeau.*

1. Guy offre un cadeau *à Danielle.*
2. Il donne le cadeau *à Danielle* au restaurant.
3. Elle est contente. Elle dit «merci» *à Guy.*
4. Elle téléphone *à sa copine Sandrine* pour décrire le cadeau.
5. Danielle dit *à sa copine,* «Guy est sympa, n'est-ce pas?»
6. Sandrine répond *à Danielle,* «Oh, oui, c'est un garçon vraiment chouette!»

B   **Un match de foot.**   Complétez avec «lui» ou «leur».

1. Il lance le ballon à Gilles?
   Oui, il ___ lance le ballon.
2. Les joueurs parlent à l'arbitre?
   Oui, ils ___ parlent.
3. Et l'arbitre parle aux joueurs?
   Oui, il ___ parle.
4. L'arbitre explique les règles aux joueurs?
   Oui, il ___ explique les règles.
5. L'employée au guichet parle à un spectateur?
   Oui, elle ___ parle.
6. Le spectateur pose une question à l'employée?
   Oui, il ___ pose une question.
7. L'employée vend des billets aux spectateurs?
   Oui, elle ___ vend des billets.

C   **Personnellement.**   Répondez en utilisant «lui» ou «leur».

1. Tu parles à tes professeurs?
2. Tu dis «bonjour» à ton professeur de français?
3. Tu vas téléphoner à tes copains ce week-end?
4. Tu aimes parler à tes copains au téléphone?
5. Tu parles souvent à tes copains?
6. Tu vas écrire à ta grand-mère?
7. Tu écris souvent à ta grand-mère?

CONVERSATION

Scènes de la vie *À la réception de l'hôtel*

LINDA: Bonjour, Madame. J'ai réservé une chambre pour deux personnes.
LA RÉCEPTIONNISTE: C'est à quel nom, s'il vous plaît?
LINDA: Au nom de Collins.

LA RÉCEPTIONNISTE: Vous avez votre confirmation?
LINDA: Oui, je l'ai. La voilà. *(Elle lui montre sa confirmation.)*
LA RÉCEPTIONNISTE: Merci. J'ai une très jolie chambre au troisième qui donne sur la cour.

LINDA: C'est une chambre à deux lits?
LA RÉCEPTIONNISTE: Oui, avec salle de bains.
LINDA: C'est combien, la chambre?
LA RÉCEPTIONNISTE: Trois cent cinquante francs. Et le petit déjeuner est compris. Voilà votre clé.

Une jolie chambre d'hôtel.   Répondez d'après la conversation.

1. Linda veut une chambre pour combien de personnes?
2. Elle parle à qui?
3. Elle a réservé une chambre?
4. Qu'est-ce qu'elle a montré à la réceptionniste?
5. La chambre est à quel étage?
6. Elle donne sur la rue?
7. C'est une chambre à combien de lits?
8. La chambre a une salle de bains privée?
9. C'est combien la chambre?
10. Le petit déjeuner est compris ou pas?

Prononciation   *Les sons /ó/ et /ò/*

It is important to make a clear distinction between the closed sound /ó/ as in «mot» and the open sound /ò/ as in «sort». Repeat the following pairs of words.

nos / note   mot / mort   dôme / dort   beau / bonne

Hôtel de Bordeaux

Now repeat the following sentences.

Claude ne dort pas beaucoup.
Paul sort beaucoup trop.
Il n'y a pas d'eau chaude dans la chambre 14.

Activités de communication

A   Au voleur!   Imagine that one of the rooms in your hotel in Paris was burglarized. The house detective (your partner) asks you and all the other guests what you did from the time you left your room this morning until the time you returned this afternoon. Give a full account of your activities.

Élève 1: À quelle heure est-ce que vous êtes sorti(e) de la chambre?
Élève 2: Je suis sorti(e) à dix heures et demie.
Élève 1: Où est-ce que vous êtes allé(e)?
Élève 2: Je suis allé(e) au troisième étage chercher mes copains.
Élève 1: Qu'est-ce que vous avez fait ensuite?

B   Qu'est-ce qu'on fait pour toi?   Think of a friend or family member you like very much. What does this person do for you? What do you do for him or her? Use the following verbs.

acheter	écrire	préparer
apprendre	faire	répondre
dire	parler	servir
donner	poser des questions	téléphoner

Mon amie Sylvie me donne de jolis cadeaux pour mon anniversaire. Elle me téléphone presque tous les soirs...Moi, je lui écris des lettres pendant les vacances.

C   Une enquête: Tu es né(e) quand?   Divide into groups. The leader will find out who is the oldest and the youngest in his or her group by asking the group members when they were born.

Élève 1: Judy, tu es née quand?
Élève 2: Je suis née le 17 août 1981...
Élève 1 (*à la classe*): Judy est née le 17 août 1981. Meredith est née le 30 janvier 1982. Judy est la plus âgée et Meredith est la plus jeune de notre groupe.

LECTURE ET CULTURE

L'HÔTEL DE LA GARE

Monique est arrivée avec quelques copines à Nice. Elles sont descendues du train et sont allées tout de suite au syndicat d'initiative. Le syndicat d'initiative est un bureau de tourisme qui se trouve souvent dans les gares ou près des gares. Les touristes vont au syndicat d'initiative pour trouver une chambre d'hôtel dans la ville où ils sont arrivés, s'ils n'ont pas réservé de chambre à l'avance.

Monique a expliqué à l'employée du syndicat d'initiative que ses copines et elle sont étudiantes. Elles ne veulent pas aller dans un hôtel de grand luxe qui coûte très cher. Pas de problème: l'employée a téléphoné à l'Hôtel de la Gare où elle a réservé une chambre pour les filles. L'Hôtel de la Gare est un hôtel confortable mais pas trop cher. Et il est où, l'Hôtel de la Gare? En face de[1] la gare, bien sûr! Il y a un Hôtel de la Gare dans beaucoup de villes en France.

Monique et ses copines sont sorties de la gare, elles ont traversé la rue et sont arrivées à l'hôtel en deux minutes. Elles ont rempli les fiches d'enregistrement et ont monté leurs bagages à la chambre. Elles sont redescendues tout de suite après et sont allées visiter la ville de Nice.

[1]en face de *across from*

Étude de mots

A **Le français, c'est facile.** Trouvez cinq mots apparentés dans la lecture.

B **C'est-à-dire...** Trouvez les mots ou expressions qui correspondent.

1. le syndicat d'initiative
2. réserver
3. expliquer
4. les bagages
5. cher

a. qui coûte beaucoup
b. les sacs à dos, les valises
c. un bureau de tourisme
d. dire
e. louer à l'avance

GRAND HOTEL DE LA GARE ★NN

BAR — RESTAURANT
33230 SAINT - MÉDARD - DE - GUIZIÈRES
57.69.60.14

Christian BIRON
PROPRIÉTAIRE
CHEF DE CUISINE

ÉTAPE V. R. P.
SÉMINAIRES - NOCES
BANQUETS DIVERS
SALLE de 25 à 200 Couverts
-15 CHAMBRES-

R. C. S. A 341530111   IMP. BOAT

Compréhension

 Un séjour à Nice. Répondez.

1. Monique et ses copines sont arrivées où?
2. Elles sont allées à Nice comment?
3. Quand elles sont arrivées à la gare, où sont-elles allées?
4. Pourquoi sont-elles allées au syndicat d'initiative?
5. L'employée du syndicat d'initiative a téléphoné à quel hôtel?
6. Où est l'hôtel?
7. Les filles sont allées à l'hôtel?
8. Elles sont allées à l'hôtel à pied, en autobus ou en taxi?
9. Qu'est-ce qu'elles ont fait quand elles sont arrivées à l'hôtel?
10. Qu'est-ce que le syndicat d'initiative?
11. Qu'est-ce que vous avez appris au sujet des hôtels de la Gare?

DÉCOUVERTE CULTURELLE

En France les hôtels sont classés par le ministère du Tourisme selon leur confort et leur luxe.

★★★★L	HÔTEL DE GRAND LUXE
★★★★	HÔTEL DE PREMIÈRE CLASSE, TOUT CONFORT
★★★	HÔTEL TRÈS CONFORTABLE
★★	HÔTEL CONFORTABLE
★	HÔTEL AU CONFORT MOYEN, SIMPLE MAIS CONVENABLE[1]

LIGUE FRANÇAISE POUR LES
AUBERGES DE LA JEUNESSE
38, Bd RASPAIL 75007 PARIS
TÉL. (1) 45 48 69 84
FAX   45 44 57 47

Quelle catégorie d'hôtel est la plus chère? Et la moins chère?

En France, il y a beaucoup de pensions qui sont souvent très agréables. Une pension est un hôtel simple à caractère familial.

Les jeunes qui voyagent en France aiment aller dans des auberges de jeunesse[2]. Les auberges de jeunesse ont des dortoirs[3] et ne coûtent pas très cher. Beaucoup de randonneurs[4] et cyclistes louent une chambre (ou un lit) dans une de ces auberges, qui se trouvent souvent près des villes. Les jeunes voyageurs les aiment beaucoup parce que dans les auberges de jeunesse ils peuvent faire la connaissance de[5] jeunes gens qui viennent de beaucoup de pays différents.

[1] moyen...convenable *moderately priced, no-frills hotel*
[2] des auberges de jeunesse *youth hostels*
[3] des dortoirs *dormitories*
[4] randonneurs *hikers*
[5] faire la connaissance de *meet*

RÉALITÉS

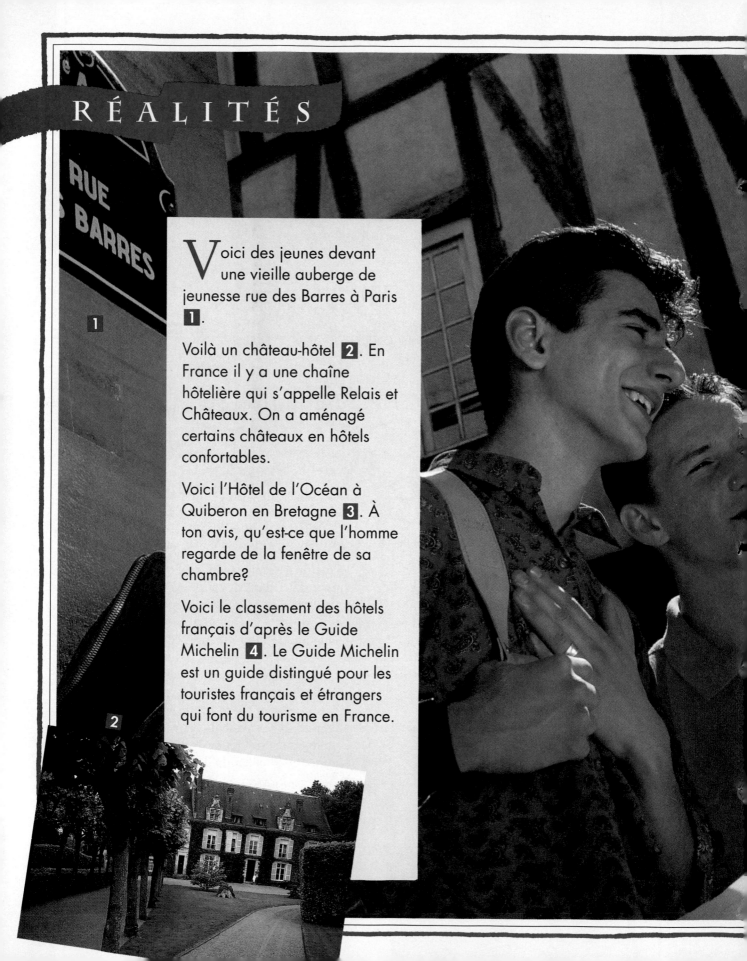

Voici des jeunes devant une vieille auberge de jeunesse rue des Barres à Paris **1**.

Voilà un château-hôtel **2**. En France il y a une chaîne hôtelière qui s'appelle Relais et Châteaux. On a aménagé certains châteaux en hôtels confortables.

Voici l'Hôtel de l'Océan à Quiberon en Bretagne **3**. À ton avis, qu'est-ce que l'homme regarde de la fenêtre de sa chambre?

Voici le classement des hôtels français d'après le Guide Michelin **4**. Le Guide Michelin est un guide distingué pour les touristes français et étrangers qui font du tourisme en France.

HOTEL DE L'OCÉAN

3

4

MICHELIN

🏛️	Grand luxe	🍴🍴🍴🍴🍴
🏛️	Grand confort	🍴🍴🍴🍴
🏛️	Très confortable	🍴🍴🍴
🏠	De bon confort	🍴🍴
🏠	Assez confortable	🍴
🏡	Simple mais convenable	

❀❀❀	La table vaut le voyage
❀❀	La table mérite un détour
❀	Une très bonnne table
Repas	Repas soigné à prix modérés 100/130
☕	Petit déjeuner
enf. 55	Menu enfant

🏠 🍴	Menu à moins de 75 F

CULMINATION

Activités de communication orale

A **Des vacances formidables.** Using the following question words and phrases, ask your partner about a great vacation he or she once had. Then reverse roles.

1. où 3. avec qui
2. quand 4. quelles activités

B **Allons en France.** Your partner is planning a trip to France and is going to stay in one of the hotels pictured below. Ask your partner which of the hotels he or she prefers and why. Then reverse roles.

Auberge de Combreux

Combreux
Val de Loire

21 chambres de 210 à 350 F
Petit déjeuner   30F
Demi-pension   280F

Auberge pleine de charme en forêt, près des châteaux de la Loire. À l'hôtel vélo, tennis, piscine, practice de golf.

Hôtel Idéal Mont Blanc

Combloux
Haute-Savoie

Ouvert: été et hiver
26 chambres de 310 à 365F
Petit déjeuner   37F
Demi-pension   277F
Pension complète 322 F

Chalet grand confort dans les Alpes. Séjour idéal pour les sports d'été ou d'hiver.

Hôtel de Paris

34, boulevard d'Alsace
Cannes, Côte d'Azur

45 chambres de 250 à 580F
Petit déjeuner 35F en salle,
50F en chambre par personne
Hôtel de grand confort en ville. Près de la mer. Chambres avec télé couleurs, radio, salles de bains. Jardin avec piscine.

Hostellerie du Châteaux d'Agneaux

Avenue Sainte-Marie
Agneaux, Normandie

12 chambres de 300 à 600F
Petit déjeuner   37F
Demi-pension   450F
Pension   550F

Trente km. de la plage. Sur la route du Mont-St.-Michel. Confort, calme avec tennis et sauna.

Activités de communication écrite

A **Une publicité.** Write an ad for a hotel (real or imaginary) using the ads above as a guide.

B **Mon journal intime.** Write a diary entry describing your activities last weekend.

C **Une vie antérieure.** Imagine you lived in another century. Write a short paragraph telling where and when you were born and died.

Réintroduction et recombinaison

Les loisirs culturels. Donnez des réponses personnelles.

1. Tu es sorti(e) le week-end dernier ou tu es resté(e) à la maison?
2. Si tu es sorti(e), avec qui es-tu sorti(e)?
3. Tu es allé(e) au cinéma le mois dernier?
4. Tu as vu quel film? Avec quels acteurs?
5. Tes copains et toi, avez-vous déjà visité un musée? Quel musée?
6. Vous avez admiré quels peintres ou quels sculpteurs?
7. Tu connais la Statue de la Liberté? Tu sais dans quelle ville des États-Unis elle est?
8. Si tu vas en France, qu'est-ce que tu veux visiter?
9. Tu veux voir une pièce à la Comédie-Française? Quel genre de pièce, une comédie ou une tragédie?
10. Si tu vas voir un film étranger, tu préfères le voir doublé ou en version originale avec des sous-titres?

Vocabulaire

NOMS
l'hôtel (m.)
le hall
l'escalier (m.)
la réception
le (la) réceptionniste
la personne
la fiche d'enregistrement
la facture
les frais (m.)
la carte de crédit
le chèque de voyage

la chambre
   à un lit
   à deux lits
la porte
le placard
le cintre
les draps (m.)

la couverture
l'oreiller (m.)
la salle de bains
le savon
le gant de toilette
la serviette
le rouleau de papier hygiénique

VERBES
monter
montrer
réserver
tomber
se sécher
mourir
naître

AUTRES MOTS ET EXPRESSIONS
donner sur
libérer la chambre
payer en espèces

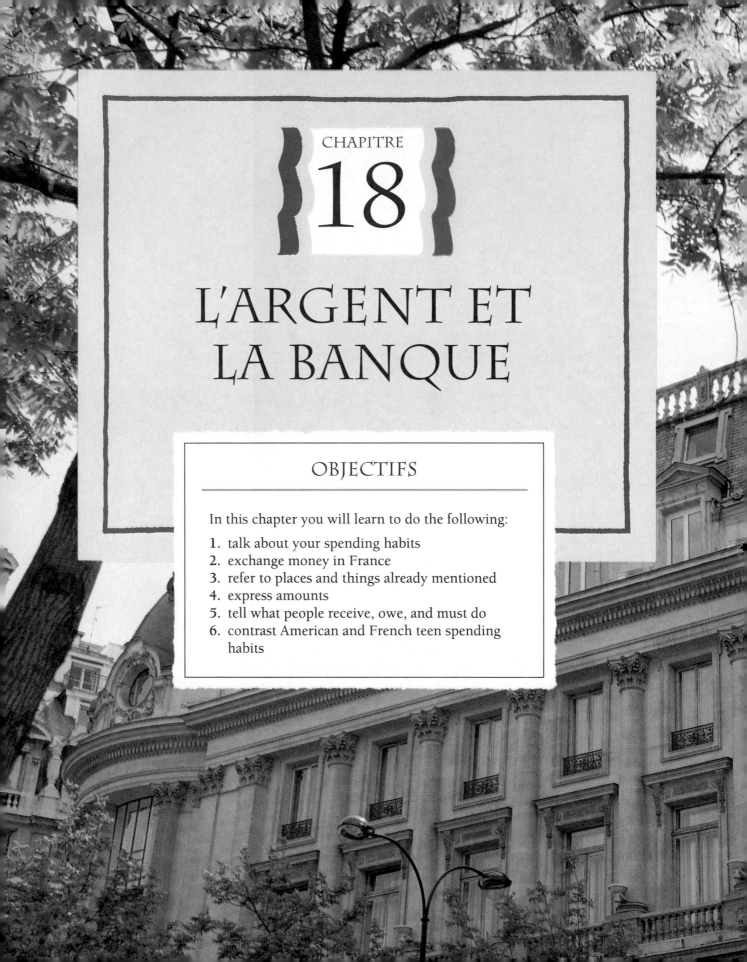

CHAPITRE

{18}

L'ARGENT ET LA BANQUE

OBJECTIFS

In this chapter you will learn to do the following:

1. talk about your spending habits
2. exchange money in France
3. refer to places and things already mentioned
4. express amounts
5. tell what people receive, owe, and must do
6. contrast American and French teen spending habits

VOCABULAIRE

MOTS 1

de l'argent liquide

un billet

une pièce

de la monnaie

un sac

un portefeuille

un porte-monnaie

Tu as de la monnaie?

Tu peux me faire de la monnaie?

Oui, j'en ai.

Oui, je peux.

une poche

À LA BANQUE

un chèque (bancaire)

signer un chèque

toucher
un chèque

SOCIÉTÉ NATIONALE

RELEVÉ DE COMPTE
1134580PT03941

3180

--- 39418 ---

code banque
30003
code guichet
03182
numéro de compte
0048039532

SYLVIE VIDAL
75 BOULEVARD DU TEMPLE
75010 PARIS

		DÉBIT	CRÉDIT	VALEUR
DATE	NATURE DE L'OPÉRATION			
2802	VIREMENT ÉPARGNE DECLIC 2802		608,00	010392

* CE RELEVÉ CONCERNE VOTRE *
CODEVI
* * * * * * * * * * * * * * * * * *

2.618.12

NOUVEAU SOLDE

un relevé de compte
d'épargne

Sylvie est allée à la banque.
Elle a ouvert un compte d'épargne.
Elle a versé de l'argent sur son compte.

AU BUREAU DE CHANGE

le cours du change

ETATS UNIS \5,00 F
ITALIE
ALLEMAGNE
JAPON

Steve est allé au bureau de change.
Il y est allé pour changer de l'argent.
Il a changé de l'argent?
Oui, il en a changé.
Il a donné des dollars.
Et il a reçu des francs français.

la monnaie française

Exercices

A **Qu'est-ce que c'est?** Identifiez.

2. C'est de l'argent liquide ou un chèque de voyage?

1. C'est un chèque bancaire ou une carte de crédit?

4. C'est un sac ou une poche?

5. C'est un portefeuille ou un porte-monnaie?

3. C'est un billet ou une pièce?

7. Elle signe le chèque ou elle touche le chèque?

6. C'est une banque ou un bureau de change?

8. Il fait de la monnaie ou il change de l'argent?

B Au bureau de change. Répondez.

1. Où est-ce que Steve est allé?
2. Il a de la monnaie américaine ou de la monnaie française?
3. Il a changé de l'argent?
4. Il a changé combien de dollars?
5. Quel est le cours du change?
6. Steve a reçu combien de francs pour ses dollars?

C Mon argent. Donnez des réponses personnelles.

1. Tu as de l'argent sur toi?
2. Tu as combien d'argent sur toi?
3. Tu mets ton argent dans ton portefeuille?
4. Tu mets des pièces ou des billets dans ton portefeuille?
5. Tu mets les pièces dans un portefeuille, dans un porte-monnaie ou dans ta poche?
6. Ton portefeuille est dans ta poche ou dans ton sac?
7. En général, tu paies en espèces, par chèque ou avec une carte de crédit?
8. Tu as un compte d'épargne?
9. Tu regardes ton relevé de compte chaque mois?
10. Tu verses de l'argent sur ton compte?

ODYSSEE
LE COMPTE DES 13-18 ANS

LA POSTE
BOUGEZ AVEC LA POSTE

VOTRE BANQUE CONFORTABLEMENT CHEZ VOUS

BNP

Tous vos comptes en direct sur Minitel

TELESERVICE BNP

VOCABULAIRE

MOTS 2

Voici Lise.
Elle aime mettre de l'argent de côté.
Elle ne dépense pas tout son argent.
Elle fait des économies.

Et voilà Denis.
Denis n'a pas d'argent.
Il est fauché.
Il veut emprunter de
    l'argent à Lise.

Tu peux me prêter
de l'argent?

Oui, je peux
te prêter de
l'argent.
Tu en veux
combien?

Denis rembourse Lise.
Il lui rend son argent.

Note: Here are some informal words referring to money.

le fric	l'argent
50 balles	50 francs
Il est fauché.	Il n'a pas d'argent.
Il a plein de fric.	Il a beaucoup d'argent.

Exercices

A **C'est qui?** Décidez si c'est Lise ou Denis.

1. Il / Elle dépense tout son argent.
2. Il / Elle met de l'argent de côté.
3. Il / Elle fait des économies.
4. Il / Elle a un compte d'épargne.
5. Il / Elle est toujours fauché(e).
6. Il / Elle emprunte de l'argent à un(e) ami(e).
7. Il / Elle prête de l'argent.
8. Il / Elle rembourse l'argent qu'il/elle emprunte.

B **L'argent et toi!** Donnez des réponses personnelles.

1. Tu travailles?
2. Tu gagnes de l'argent? Tu as de l'argent de poche?
3. Qu'est-ce que tu fais pour gagner de l'argent? Tu travailles dans le jardin des voisins? Tu laves des voitures? Tu gardes des enfants? Tu aides ton père ou ta mère?
4. Tu dépenses tout ton argent de poche ou tu en mets de côté?
5. Tu as un compte d'épargne? Dans quelle banque?
6. De temps en temps, tu empruntes de l'argent à tes parents?
7. Quand tu dois de l'argent à tes parents, tu les rembourses toujours?
8. Tu leur rends vite l'argent?

C **Un peu d'argot.** Dites la même chose d'une autre manière.

DAVID: Tu as *du fric?*
MARIE: Tu me demandes si j'ai *du fric*. Tu sais bien que *je suis toujours fauchée*.
DAVID: Et tu me dois cinquante *balles*.
MARIE: Oui, je sais. Mais tu n'en as pas besoin. Tu as *plein de fric*.
DAVID: C'est pas la question.
MARIE: D'accord. Je te rends les cinquante *balles* demain.

D **Quel est le nom?** Choisissez le mot qui correspond.

1. épargner   a. le versement
2. économiser   b. le remboursement
3. verser   c. le prêt
4. changer   d. l'épargne
5. dépenser   e. l'emprunt
6. emprunter   f. des économies
7. prêter   g. la dépense
8. rembourser   h. le change

Activités de communication

Mots 1 et 2

A Ton argent et toi. A French exchange student at your school (your partner) wants to know about American teens and money. Answer his or her questions, then reverse roles.

1. Tu gagnes de l'argent? Comment?
2. Tes parents te donnent de l'argent de poche?
3. Pour quoi est-ce que tu dépenses ton argent?
4. Tu mets de l'argent de côté?

B Au bureau de change. You are at a foreign exchange office in France and want to change 50 dollars into francs. The exchange rate is five francs to the dollar. Act out the following scene with the teller (your partner).

1. Greet the teller and say what you want.
2. Ask what the exchange rate is today.
3. The teller asks if you have traveler's checks or cash. (If you have traveler's checks, the teller asks you to sign them.)
4. The teller asks you for your passport.

C Quel cours du change! You and your partner are French tourists visiting the U.S. Fortunately for you, the current exchange rate is five francs to the dollar. Make a list of several gifts you'd like to buy for your friends and family in France. Tell your partner how much each of your gifts costs in dollars. He or she will tell you the price in francs. Then reverse roles.

> Élève 1: Je voudrais acheter une cassette pour ma sœur. Ça coûte 9 dollars. Ça fait combien en francs?
> Élève 2: Ça fait 45 francs.

D Un petit problème. You'd like to buy or do something but you can't afford it at the moment. Your friend (your partner) might be able to help you out.

1. Tell your partner you'd like to borrow money.
2. Your partner wants to know how much and why.
3. Your partner asks when you can pay him or her back.
4. Say when you can pay the money back and how you'll get it.

STRUCTURE

Le pronom *y*
Referring to Places Already Mentioned

1. You have already used the pronoun *y* with the verb *aller* to refer to a place just mentioned. *Aller* cannot stand alone.

> **Tu vas au restaurant?**
> **Oui, j'y vais.**
> **On y va ensemble?**

2. You also use the pronoun *y* to replace any location introduced by *à* or another preposition.

> **Tu vas *à Paris?***   **Oui, j'y vais.**
> **Henri monte *sur la tour Eiffel?***   **Oui, il y monte.**
> **Il est *à l'Hôtel Racine?***   **Oui, il y est.**
> **Il veut entrer *dans l'hôtel?***   **Oui, il veut y entrer.**
> **Tu veux aller *en France?***   **Oui, je veux y aller.**
> **Ils peuvent dîner *chez leurs amis?***   **Oui, ils peuvent y dîner.**

3. With the *passé composé*, *y* comes before the helping verb.

> **Ils sont entrés *dans le musée?***   **Oui, ils y sont entrés.**
> **Elle est montée *au troisième étage?***   **Oui, elle y est montée.**
> **Elle a vu de beaux tableaux *au musée?***   **Oui, elle y a vu de beaux tableaux.**

4. Note the placement of *y* in negative sentences.

PRÉSENT	**Je *n'y vais pas.***
VERBE + INFINITIF	**Je ne vais pas *y aller.***
PASSÉ COMPOSÉ	**Je n'y *suis* pas allé(e).**

Exercices

A **Au gymnase.** Répétez la petite conversation.

BÉATRICE: Tu vas au gymnase?
HÉLÈNE: Oui, j'y vais tous les samedis.
BÉATRICE: Ton copain y va aussi?
HÉLÈNE: Oui, il y va aussi. Il y va souvent.

B **On y va?** Répondez d'après les dessins en utilisant «y».

1. David est allé au bureau de change?
2. Il est allé au bureau de change le matin?
3. Il est allé au bureau de change pour changer de l'argent?
4. Il est arrivé au bureau de change avant l'ouverture?
5. Il a attendu devant le bureau?
6. Il a attendu cinq minutes devant le bureau?
7. Quand le bureau a ouvert, David est entré dans le bureau?
8. Il a fait la queue devant la caisse?

C **À l'école.** Donnez des réponses personnelles en utilisant «y».

1. Tu vas à l'école tous les jours?
2. Tu prépares tes leçons à la maison?
3. Tu parles français au cours de français?
4. Tu parles français au cours d'anglais?
5. Tu attends tes amis dans la cour?
6. Tu mets tes livres dans ton sac à dos?
7. Tu vas à l'école à pied?
8. Tu aimes aller chez tes copains après les cours?
9. Tu veux aller chez eux aujourd'hui?

Y, *lui* ou *leur*

Referring to People and Things Already Mentioned

1. You also use the pronoun *y* to replace *à* + a thing.

Georges répond *à la lettre?*	Oui, il y répond.
Anne a répondu *au téléphone?*	Non, elle n'y a pas répondu.

2. If the preposition *à* is followed by a person, you use *lui* or *leur*, not *y*.

Georges répond *à Marie.*	Il *lui* répond.
Anne a répondu *à ses amis.*	Elle *leur* a répondu.

Exercices

A **Il a téléphoné.** Répondez en utilisant «y».

1. Paul a téléphoné à l'hôtel?
2. Paul a répondu à la question?
3. Il a obéi à la règle?
4. Paul a réussi à l'examen?
5. Paul a participé au match?

B **Y, *lui* ou *leur*?** Complétez.

1. Tu as répondu à la lettre?
   Oui, j'___ ai répondu.
2. Tu as répondu à vos cousins?
   Oui, je ___ ai répondu.
3. Sa sœur a répondu à une petite
   annonce? Oui, elle ___ a répondu.
4. Elle a répondu à sa mère?
   Oui, elle ___ a répondu.
5. Elle a téléphoné à ses copains?
   Oui, elle ___ a téléphoné.
6. Tes copains et toi, vous avez obéi
   au professeur? Oui, nous ___ avons obéi.
7. Vous avez obéi aussi aux règles
   de l'école? Oui, nous ___ avons obéi.

Le pronom *en*

Referring to Things Already Mentioned

1. You use the pronoun *en* to replace a noun that is introduced by *de* or any form of it: *du, de l', de la, des.*

Vous avez *de la monnaie?*	Oui, j'en ai.
	Non, je n'en ai pas.
Richard veut *de l'argent?*	Oui, il en veut.
	Non, il n'en veut pas.
Il va changer *des francs?*	Oui, il va en changer.
	Non, il ne va pas en changer.
Il a besoin *d'argent?*	Oui, il en a besoin.
	Non, il n'en a pas besoin.
Il a parlé *de ses finances?*	Oui, il en a parlé.
	Non, il n'en a pas parlé.
Il est venu *de la banque?*	Oui, il en est venu.
	Non, il n'en est pas venu.
Il y a *des* bureaux de change en ville?	Oui, il y en a.
	Non, il n'y en a pas.

Exercices

La fête de Laurence. Répondez d'après le dessin.

Laurence sert du coca?
Oui, elle en sert.

1. Elle sert de l'eau minérale?
2. Elle sert des sandwichs?
3. Elle sert de la pizza?
4. Elle sert de la salade?
5. Elle sert du fromage?
6. Elle sert des chocolats?
7. Elle sert de la glace?
8. Elle sert de la mousse au chocolat?

Oui, j'en ai. Donnez des réponses personnelles en utilisant «en».

1. Tu as de l'argent dans ton portefeuille?
2. Tu as de la monnaie dans ta poche?
3. Tu reviens de la banque?
4. Tu as des billets?
5. Tu as des pièces?
6. Tu as besoin d'argent?
7. Tu veux gagner de l'argent?
8. Tu parles de l'argent?
9. Tu as emprunté de l'argent à tes parents?
10. Tu as prêté de l'argent à tes amis?

C **Dans le réfrigérateur.** Répondez d'après le modèle.

> **du coca**
>
> Élève 1: Il y a du coca dans ton réfrigérateur?
> Élève 2: Oui, il y en a dans mon réfrigérateur. (Non, il n'y en a pas.)

1. de l'eau minérale
2. de la glace
3. des légumes surgelés
4. du jambon
5. des tartes
6. de la viande

D'autres emplois du pronom *en*

Expressing Amounts

1. Note that you also use the pronoun *en* with numbers and expressions of quantity. They cannot stand alone in French. They must be accompanied by *en*.

   Tu as combien de magazines?   J'*en* ai *deux.*
   Et tu as beaucoup de livres?   Oui, j'*en* ai *beaucoup.*

2. Here are some other expressions of quantity. Note the use of *en* with them.

   J'*en* ai *une paire.*
   J'*en* ai *une douzaine.*

   J'*en* ai *très peu.*   *very few, very little*
   J'*en* ai *assez.*   *enough*
   J'*en* ai *quelques-uns (-unes).*   *a few*
   J'*en* ai *plusieurs.*   *several*
   J'*en* ai *trop.*   *too much, too many*

Exercice

 J'en ai assez. Donnez des réponses personnelles en utilisant «en».

1. Tu as combien de paires de chaussures?
2. Tu en as assez?
3. Tu as combien de billets d'un dollar? Tu en as quelques-uns?
4. Tu en as assez pour acheter un coca?
5. Tu as beaucoup d'argent ou peu d'argent dans ton portefeuille?
6. Tu as plusieurs cours aujourd'hui?
7. Tu as trop de devoirs tous les soirs?
8. Tu as beaucoup de cassettes de ton groupe de rock préféré ou tu en as seulement quelques-unes?

Les verbes *recevoir* et *devoir*

Saying What People Receive, Owe, and Must Do

1. Study the following forms of the present tense of the irregular verbs *recevoir*, "to receive," and *devoir*, "to owe."

RECEVOIR	DEVOIR
je reçois	je dois
tu reçois	tu dois
il elle on } reçoit	il elle on } doit
nous recevons	nous devons
vous recevez	vous devez
ils elles } reçoivent	ils elles } doivent

> Je reçois beaucoup de cadeaux pour mon anniversaire.
> Elle reçoit beaucoup de lettres.

> Nous devons de l'argent à la banque.
> Mon ami me doit de l'argent.

2. When followed by an infinitive, the verb *devoir* also means "must" or "to have to."

> Il m'a prêté de l'argent. Je dois lui rendre son argent.
> Elle a un examen difficile demain. Elle doit étudier ce soir.

3. Note the past participles of these verbs.

> J'ai *reçu* cent dollars.
> J'ai *dû* étudier pour réussir à l'examen.

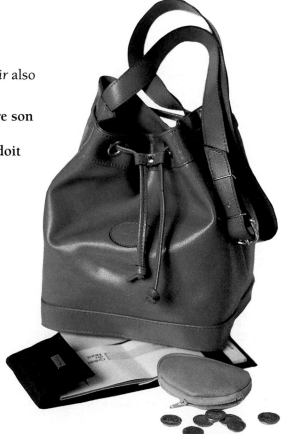

Exercices

A Je sais que je lui dois de l'argent. Mettez au pluriel d'après le modèle.

Je lui dois vingt francs.
Nous lui devons vingt francs.

1. Je lui dois de l'argent.
2. Je lui dois cent dollars.
3. Si je reçois mon chèque aujourd'hui, je vais le rembourser.
4. Je sais que je dois lui rendre l'argent que je lui dois.

Un distributeur automatique de billets.

B Je dois aller au bureau de change. Répondez.

1. Si tu as besoin de francs, tu dois aller au bureau de change?
2. Si j'ai besoin de francs, je dois y aller aussi?
3. On doit y aller ensemble?
4. Le dollar est à cinq francs. Si je change vingt dollars, je reçois combien de francs?
5. Si un Français change cent francs, il reçoit combien de dollars?
6. Les Français reçoivent leur salaire en dollars ou en francs?
7. Les Américains reçoivent leur salaire en dollars ou en francs?
8. Tu as déjà reçu un salaire?
9. Tu as reçu combien?

C On doit faire beaucoup de choses. Complétez au présent avec «devoir» ou «recevoir».

Dans la vie, on ____ faire beaucoup de choses et ce n'est pas toujours agréable!
                    1
Moi, tous les matins je ____ me lever à six heures et demie. Je ____ préparer le
                          2   3
petit déjeuner. Ma sœur, Aurélie ____ donner à manger au chien. Nous ____
                                  4   5
quitter la maison à huit heures pour aller à l'école. Le soir nous ____ aider
                                                                    6
notre mère à préparer le dîner. Après le dîner nous ____ faire nos devoirs.
                                                      7
Nous ____ beaucoup travailler tous les jours! Mais chaque semaine nous ____
     8   9
de l'argent de poche de nos parents. Tes copains et toi, vous ____ de l'argent de
                                                              10
poche de vos parents? Qu'est-ce que vous ____ faire tous les jours pour en
                                          11
avoir? Vous travaillez? Une question de plus! Qu'est-ce que vous faites de
l'argent que vous ____? Vous le dépensez ou vous mettez quelques dollars de
                   12
côté? Vos parents vous disent que vous ____ faire des économies?
                                        13

CONVERSATION

Scènes de la vie *Au bureau de change*

ROBERT: Je voudrais changer vingt dollars en francs français, s'il vous plaît.

LE CAISSIER: Vous avez des chèques de voyage ou de l'argent liquide?
ROBERT: Des chèques de voyage. Le dollar est à combien aujourd'hui?
LE CAISSIER: À cinq francs quatre-vingts.

ROBERT: Très bien.
LE CAISSIER: Votre passeport, s'il vous plaît. Et signez votre chèque. Votre adresse à Paris?
ROBERT: Hôtel Molière, rue Molière dans le 1er arrondissement.

A **Des francs, s'il vous plaît.** Répondez d'après la conversation.

1. Où est-ce que Robert est allé?
2. Il veut changer combien de dollars?
3. Il va changer des chèques de voyage ou de l'argent liquide?
4. Il veut changer des dollars en quelle monnaie?
5. Quel est le cours du change?
6. Le caissier veut voir son passeport?
7. Robert est à quel hôtel à Paris?

B **Qu'est-ce qu'il a fait?** Corrigez les phrases.

1. Robert est allé à la banque.
2. Il a changé de l'argent liquide.
3. Il a changé cinquante francs.
4. Il a reçu des dollars.
5. Le caissier a voulu voir sa carte de crédit.

6523

LA POSTE
DCV-01

ACHAT ☐ **VENTE** ☐ **DE BILLETS ETRANGERS**

à M _Laporte, Robert_
(nom, prénom) _Hôtel Molière_
(adresse) _Rue Molière_
Paris   75001

DEVISE	CODE	MONTANT		COURS	CONTRE-VALEUR
				5,3500	1,0,7,0,0,
USD	03190	2000		COMMISSION	,1,2,8,
A _Paris_ , LE _26/06_				NET	1,0,5,7,2

SIGNATURE DU CLIENT,

Robert Laporte

Prononciation *Les sons /p/, /t/, /k/*

1. Repeat the following words with the initial French sounds /p/, /t/, and /k/.

   payer   pour   temps   taxi   quand   calme

2. Repeat the following words with the final French /p/, /t/, and /k/.

   nappe   soupe   carte   contente   banque   fric

3. Now repeat the following sentences.

   Philippe a plein de fric à la banque.
   Tes parents vont payer avec une carte de crédit?

payer avec une
carte de crédit

Activités de communication

A Malheureusement. Work with a partner. Take turns telling each other several things you would like to do but can't because there's something else you must do first. Reverse roles.

> Élève 1: Je voudrais aller au match de tennis mais je ne peux pas parce que je dois faire mes devoirs de maths.
> Élève 2: Et moi, je voudrais regarder la télé mais je ne peux pas parce que je dois aider ma mère.

B Faisons les valises. Write down at least five items of clothing you would pack for a one-week stay in France next summer. Compare your list with your partner's and see if you've packed the same items.

> Élève 1: Moi, j'ai trois paires de jeans. Et toi, tu en as combien?
> Élève 2: J'en ai deux. Et j'ai six tee-shirts. Toi, tu en as combien?

C Où suis-je? Think of a place. Your partner will try to guess which place you're thinking of by asking questions with *y*. Then reverse roles.

D Il y en a combien? Your partner wants to know if there are a lot of the following at your school. Answer with *beaucoup, assez, quelques-un(e)s, très peu,* or *trop.* Then reverse roles.

   bons professeurs
   élèves sportifs ou sportives
   élèves brillant(e)s
   clubs intéressants
   cours intéressants
   examens difficiles

> Élève 1: À ton avis il y a beaucoup d'élèves amusants à l'école?
> Élève 2: À mon avis il y en a quelques-uns.

LECTURE ET CULTURE

LA SEMAINE DES JEUNES FRANÇAIS

Qu'est-ce qu'une semaine? Une période de sept jours? Oui, mais une «semaine» peut être aussi quelque chose d'autre. La semaine peut être de l'argent. La semaine est la somme d'argent qu'un jeune Français ou une jeune Française reçoit de ses parents. C'est de l'argent de poche. Les jeunes Français reçoivent combien d'argent pour leur semaine? On ne peut pas répondre d'une façon générale[1] à cette question. Ça dépend d'abord de la générosité des parents et ensuite de la situation économique de la famille. Nathalie Cassis, par exemple, reçoit 50 francs par semaine de ses parents. Qu'est-ce qu'elle fait avec les 50 francs qu'elle reçoit? Nathalie achète de temps en temps un tee-shirt ou une cassette. Elle achète pas mal de[2] cassettes parce qu'elle aime beaucoup la musique. Elle achète aussi des billets pour les concerts de ses chanteurs favoris. De temps en temps elle va au café prendre un pot[3] avec des copains et bien sûr il faut payer.

Ses parents ont ouvert un compte d'épargne pour Nathalie. Elle aime faire des économies et mettre de l'argent de côté. Quand fait-elle des versements sur son compte? Si elle reçoit de l'argent pour son anniversaire, elle en dépense une partie, pas tout, et met le reste de côté. Quand elle reçoit une très bonne note, ses parents lui donnent aussi un peu d'argent. Souvent elle le dépense mais quelquefois elle le verse sur son compte d'épargne. Tu as une semaine? Tu reçois combien d'argent? Qu'est-ce que tu fais avec ta semaine? Tu fais les mêmes choses que Nathalie?

[1] d'une façon générale   *in a general way*
[2] pas mal de   *a lot of*
[3] prendre un pot   *to have a drink (soda, tea, etc.)*

Étude de mots

Des définitions. Trouvez le mot dans la lecture.

1. une période de sept jours
2. pas vieux
3. le père et la mère
4. une manière
5. beaucoup
6. une personne qui chante
7. ne pas dépenser trop d'argent

Compréhension

A **Vrai ou faux?** Répondez par «oui» ou «non».

1. Tous les jeunes Français reçoivent de l'argent de leurs parents.
2. Tous les jeunes Français reçoivent la même somme d'argent.
3. Tous les jeunes Français ont un compte d'épargne.
4. Nathalie Cassis a un compte d'épargne.
5. Elle dépense tout son argent.

B **Vous avez compris?** Répondez d'après la lecture.

1. Combien d'argent de poche est-ce que les jeunes Français reçoivent de leurs parents? Ça dépend de quoi?
2. Qu'est-ce que Nathalie achète avec l'argent qu'elle reçoit?
3. Pourquoi achète-t-elle des cassettes?
4. Avec qui va-t-elle au café?
5. Qu'est-ce qu'elle y prend?
6. Qu'est-ce que les parents de Nathalie ont ouvert pour elle?
7. Quand Nathalie fait-elle des versements sur son compte?
8. Quelles sont les deux définitions du mot «semaine»?

DÉCOUVERTE CULTURELLE

La monnaie change d'un pays à l'autre. C'est le dollar aux États-Unis, mais pas en France. Chaque pays a sa monnaie nationale. Les monnaies étrangères s'appellent des «devises». La monnaie française est le franc français. À propos des francs, il y en a plusieurs: le franc belge, le franc suisse, le franc C.F.A. en Afrique et le franc antillais à la Martinique et à la Guadeloupe. Les devises n'ont pas toujours la même valeur. Il y a des fluctuations. Quelquefois le dollar est à dix francs français et quelquefois il tombe à cinq francs. Quand le dollar est à cinq francs,

tout est très cher pour les Américains en France. Et si le dollar est à dix francs, tout est bon marché pour eux. Pour toi, il vaut mieux aller en France quand le dollar est haut ou quand le dollar est bas? Quand est-ce que tu reçois le plus pour le dollar?

Des francs tahitiens

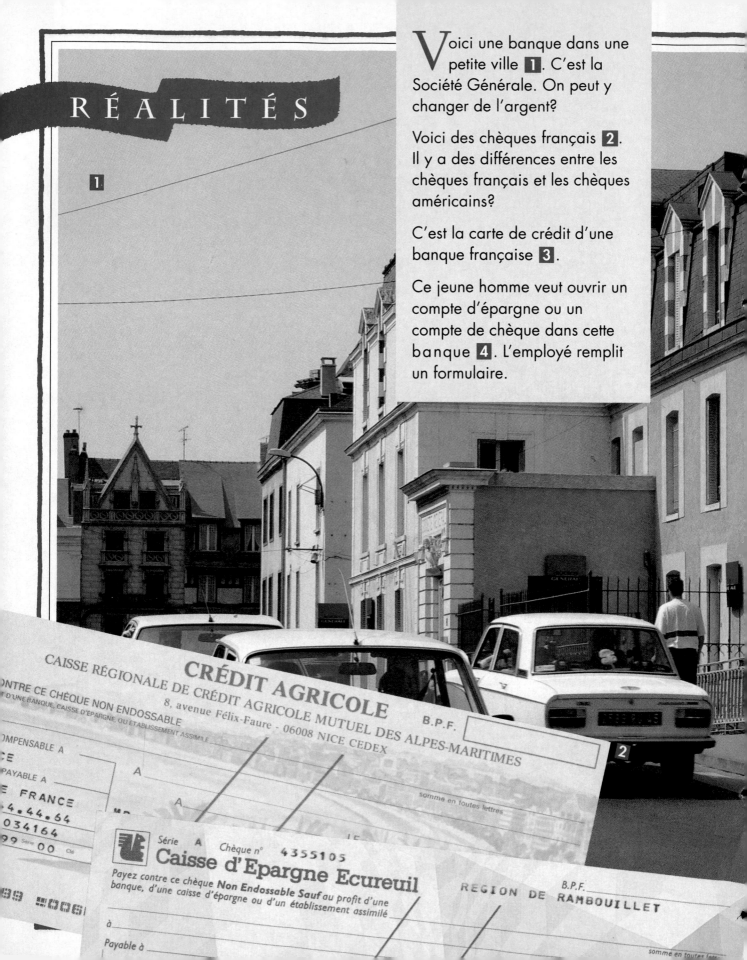

RÉALITÉS

1

Voici une banque dans une petite ville **1**. C'est la Société Générale. On peut y changer de l'argent?

Voici des chèques français **2**. Il y a des différences entre les chèques français et les chèques américains?

C'est la carte de crédit d'une banque française **3**.

Ce jeune homme veut ouvrir un compte d'épargne ou un compte de chèque dans cette banque **4**. L'employé remplit un formulaire.

2

CAISSE RÉGIONALE DE CRÉDIT AGRICOLE MUTUEL DES ALPES-MARITIMES

CRÉDIT AGRICOLE

CONTRE CE CHÈQUE NON ENDOSSABLE
SAUF D'UNE BANQUE, CAISSE D'ÉPARGNE, OU ÉTABLISSEMENT ASSIMILÉ

8, avenue Félix-Faure - 06008 NICE CEDEX

B.P.F.

OMPENSABLE A _____

PAYABLE A _____

A _____

E FRANCE
4.44.64
034164
99 Série 00 Cle

somme en toutes lettres

Série A   Chèque n° 4355105

Caisse d'Epargne Ecureuil

Payez contre ce chèque **Non Endossable Sauf** au profit d'une banque, d'une caisse d'épargne ou d'un établissement assimilé _____

REGION DE RAMBOUILLET

B.P.F. _____

à _____

Payable à

somme en toutes let

CULMINATION

Activités de communication orale

A **Qu'est-ce que tu as reçu?** Imagine you have received one of the items listed below. Help your partner guess which one you received by giving him or her a clue. Reverse roles.

un bulletin de notes   une facture
une carte d'anniversaire   une lettre d'amour
une carte postale

Élève 1: J'ai eu un «A» en français et un «B» en maths.
Élève 2: Tu as reçu ton bulletin de notes.

B **Rêves de voyage, voyages de rêve.** Work in small groups. Each person will write down several places he or she would like to visit, then exchange papers with the others. Tell whether you have already visited the places mentioned on the paper you've received. If you have not visited the places, tell whether or not you would like to, and why.

Montréal

Élève 1: Ah oui, je voudrais y aller. Je voudrais y aller en hiver parce que j'aime faire du ski. (J'y suis allé l'année dernière avec mes grands-parents.)

Activités de communication écrite

A **Es-tu comme la cigale ou la fourmi?** Are you careless with your money like the grasshopper or careful with it like the ant? Take the test and see what it reveals about you.

B **Mon budget idéal.** List all your purchases for a month. In what areas, if any, do you feel you don't have enough money to spend? Tell how much more you need and why.

Je n'ai pas assez d'argent parce que les vêtements chic coûtent cher. Moi, j'ai besoin d'au moins $100 par mois pour acheter de jolis vêtements!

TEST

1. **Pour avoir de l'argent de poche...**
   a. je ne fais rien. Mes parents me donnent de l'argent.
   b. je travaille dans un magasin, dans un restaurant, etc.
2. **Quand je vois quelque chose que j'aime beaucoup...**
   a. je l'achète impulsivement.
   b. je réfléchis avant de l'acheter.
3. **Quand je reçois de l'argent comme cadeau...**
   a. je le dépense tout de suite.
   b. j'en mets de côté.
4. **Quand je veux faire ou acheter quelque chose de spécial...**
   a. j'emprunte de l'argent à mes amis ou à mes parents.
   b. je mets de l'argent de côté à l'avance.
5. **Quand j'emprunte de l'argent à mes copains...**
   a. j'oublie souvent de les rembourser.
   b. je les rembourse tout de suite.
6. **Quand un ami a besoin d'argent...**
   a. je ne peux pas l'aider parce que j'ai déjà dépensé tout mon argent.
   b. je peux lui prêter de l'argent parce que j'en ai mis de côté.

SCORE:

Une majorité de *a*: Tu es une vraie cigale! Tu aimes beaucoup t'amuser dans la vie. Tu dois peut-être essayer de penser un peu plus au futur.

Une majorité de *b*: Tu es une petite fourmi, responsable et toujours bien organisé(e). Tu es sûr(e) de t'amuser assez dans la vie?

Réintroduction et recombinaison

A **À l'hôtel.** Répondez d'après les indications.

1. Où est-ce que Gilbert est allé? (à l'hôtel)
2. À qui a-t-il parlé? (au réceptionniste)
3. Il a demandé quel type de chambre? (pour une personne)
4. Qu'est-ce qu'il a rempli? (une fiche d'enregistrement) ·
5. À quel étage est la chambre? (au premier)
6. La chambre donne sur la rue ou sur la cour? (sur la cour)
7. Comment Gilbert est-il monté? (par l'escalier)
8. Qu'est-ce qu'il a monté? (ses bagages)

B **Le séjour de Robert.** Complétez avec «y» ou «en».

1. Robert est allé à l'hôtel?
   Oui, il ___ est allé.
2. Il est entré dans le hall?
   Oui, il ___ est entré.
3. Il est dans le hall maintenant?
   Oui, il ___ est.
4. Il va à la réception?
   Oui, il ___ va.
5. Il a des bagages?
   Oui, il ___ a.
6. Il a combien de valises?
   Il ___ a deux.
7. Robert monte dans sa chambre?
   Oui, il ___ monte.
8. Il reste une semaine à l'hôtel?
   Oui, il ___ reste une semaine.

L'Hôtel Carlton à Cannes

Vocabulaire

NOMS
l'argent de poche (m.)
l'argent liquide (m.)
le billet
la pièce
la monnaie
le chèque (bancaire)
le franc
la balle
le dollar
la banque
le compte d'épargne

le relevé de compte
  (d'épargne)
le bureau de change
le cours du change

la poche
le sac
le portefeuille
le porte-monnaie

VERBES
changer
emprunter
prêter
rembourser
signer
toucher
verser
devoir
recevoir
rendre

AUTRES MOTS ET EXPRESSIONS
avoir plein de fric
être fauché(e)
faire des économies
faire de la monnaie
mettre de l'argent de côté

assez
peu
plusieurs
quelques-un(e)s
trop

RÉVISION

CHAPITRES 17-18

Conversation *L'arrivée à l'hôtel*

M. BOUDREAU: Bonjour, Monsieur. Je m'appelle Michel Boudreau. J'ai réservé une chambre pour ce soir et demain.

L'EMPLOYÉ: Oui, Monsieur. Voilà. Une chambre avec salle de bains pour une personne. Vous êtes de quelle nationalité?

M. BOUDREAU: Je suis français.

L'EMPLOYÉ: Alors, si vous voulez bien remplir cette fiche, s'il vous plaît. *(Il lui donne la fiche.)* C'est votre premier voyage à Montréal?

M. BOUDREAU: Oh non. Je suis déjà venu plusieurs fois.

L'EMPLOYÉ: Si vous voulez changer de l'argent, il y a un bureau de change juste à côté.

M. BOUDREAU: Je sais. J'y suis allé avant de venir ici. Par contre, si vous avez la monnaie de 50 dollars canadiens... Je dois prendre un taxi...

L'EMPLOYÉ: Mais bien sûr, Monsieur.

 À l'hôtel. Répondez d'après la conversation.

1. Comment s'appelle le client?
2. Il est de quelle nationalité?
3. Qu'est-ce qu'il doit remplir?
4. M. Boudreau est déjà venu à Montréal?
5. Il est allé où avant d'arriver à l'hôtel? Qu'est-ce qu'il y a fait?
6. De quoi est-ce qu'il a besoin?
7. Pour quoi faire?
8. D'après vous, M. Boudreau habite au Canada?

Structure

Le passé composé avec *être*

1. Review the verbs that use *être* as a helping verb in the *passé composé*. Remember that they are mostly verbs of motion.

arriver	sortir	aller	devenir	tomber
partir	monter	venir	rentrer	naître
entrer	descendre	revenir	rester	mourir

2. Remember that the past participle of verbs conjugated with *être* agrees in gender (masculine or feminine) and in number (singular or plural) with the subject of the verb.

Elle est arrivée. **Nous sommes venus.**

A **Un groupe de jeunes en visite à Paris.**
Répondez d'après le modèle.

> **Alain (aller au Louvre)**
> *Alain est allé au Louvre.*

1. Caroline et Stéphanie (aller au Musée d'Orsay)
2. Olivier (monter sur la Grande Arche)
3. Bernadette (aller à Versailles)
4. Christian et Marc (descendre à pied du haut de la tour Eiffel)
5. Alain (rester tout l'après-midi au Louvre)

Le passé composé avec *être* ou *avoir*

Le Château de Versailles

In the *passé composé*, the verbs *monter, descendre, sortir,* and *rentrer* take either *être* or *avoir.* They take *avoir* when they have a direct object. Otherwise they take *être.*

> Il a monté ses bagages dans
> sa chambre.
>
> Il est monté dans sa chambre.

B **Le client et l'employée.** M. Delcour est un client de l'hôtel. Mlle Dubois travaille à l'hôtel. Dites qui a fait quoi. (Utilisez le passé composé.)

> monter dans sa chambre descendre pour changer de l'argent
> descendre les bagages sortir en ville
> monter le petit déjeuner sortir sa carte de crédit

Les pronoms d'objet indirect *lui* et *leur*

You use the indirect object pronoun *lui* to replace *à* + a person and the indirect object pronoun *leur* to replace *à* + more than one person. Remember that in negative constructions, the pronoun cannot be separated from the verb by a negative word.

> Je parle *à mon père.* Je *lui* parle.
> J'écris *à mes parents.* Je *leur* écris.
> Tu parles souvent *à Marie?* Je ne *lui parle* jamais!
> Elle va téléphoner *à ses amis?* Non, elle ne va pas *leur téléphoner.*

C **Personnellement.** Répondez en utilisant «lui» ou «leur».

1. Tu téléphones souvent à tes copains?
2. Tu vas téléphoner à un(e) ami(e) ce soir?
3. Tu aimes parler à tes amis?
4. Tes copains obéissent à leurs parents? Et toi?
5. Tu réponds à ton professeur quand il te pose une question?

Le pronom *y*

1. The pronoun *y* replaces any expression of location introduced by *à* or another preposition (*sur, en, dans, chez, en haut de, en bas de,* etc.).

<blockquote>

Tu vas *à Versailles?*   **Oui, j'y vais.**

Tu es allé *en haut de la*   **Oui, j'y suis allé.**
     tour Eiffel?

</blockquote>

2. Remember that *y* can also replace *à* + a thing, not referring to a place.

<blockquote>

Je vais répondre *à sa lettre.*   **Je vais y répondre.**

Elle ne fait pas attention   **Elle n'y fait pas attention.**
     aux autres voitures.

</blockquote>

3. In the *passé composé, y* comes before the helping verb.

<blockquote>

Il est entré dans l'hôtel?   **Oui, il y est entré.**

Elle a vu son nom sur la liste?   **Non, elle n'y a pas vu son nom.**

</blockquote>

D   **La visite de Paris continue.**   Répondez en utilisant «y».

1. Vous êtes allés à Paris?
2. Vous allez souvent en Europe?
3. Vous êtes montés en haut de la tour Eiffel?
4. Vous êtes entrés dans Notre-Dame?
5. Vous êtes descendus dans les Catacombes?
6. Vous rentrez bientôt aux États-Unis?

E   **Y, *lui* ou *leur*?**   Remplacez les mots en italique par «y», «lui», ou «leur».

1. Ils n'écrivent jamais *à leurs cousins.*
2. Marie-France répond *au téléphone.*
3. Le professeur pose des questions *aux élèves.*
4. Les élèves vont répondre *aux questions du professeur.*
5. Vous n'obéissez pas toujours *à votre mère.*
6. Gilles et Lisa disent «Joyeux anniversaire» *à Olivier.*
7. Michel a offert un cadeau *à Laurence.*
8. Tu n'as pas réussi *à l'examen.*
9. Carole et Luc n'ont pas changé 500 francs *au bureau de change.*
10. Nous sommes souvent tombés *sur la piste noire.*

Le pronom *en*

Review the object pronoun *en*. It replaces *de* (*du, de l', de la, des*) + a thing.

<blockquote>

Tu as *de l'argent?*   **Oui, j'en ai.**

Ils ont offert *des boissons?*   **Non, ils n'en ont pas offert.**

</blockquote>

F On fait un pique-nique. Répondez d'après le modèle.

Je voudrais du pain. (apporter)
Qui en apporte?

1. Je voudrais du coca. (acheter)
2. Je voudrais des sandwiches. (préparer)
3. Je voudrais de la citronnade. (faire)
4. Je voudrais des chips. (apporter)
5. Je voudrais de la limonade. (acheter)
6. Je voudrais de l'orangeade. (faire)

Les verbes *devoir* et *recevoir*

1. Review the forms of these two irregular verbs.

	DEVOIR	RECEVOIR
PRÉSENT	je dois tu dois il / elle / on doit nous devons vous devez ils / elles doivent	je reçois tu reçois il / elle / on reçoit nous recevons vous recevez ils / elles reçoivent
PARTICIPE PASSÉ	dû	reçu

2. Remember that *devoir* means "must" or "ought to" as well as "to owe."

G Questions d'argent. Complétez.

1. Si tu ___ (recevoir) un chèque demain, n'oublie pas de lui rendre l'argent que tu lui ___. (devoir)
2. Vous me ___ (devoir) encore 100 francs.
3. Nous ne voulons pas lui demander de l'argent; nous lui ___ (devoir) déjà 1.000 francs.
4. Vous ___ (recevoir) mon chèque la semaine dernière?
5. Ils ___ (recevoir) de l'argent de leurs parents toutes les semaines.
6. Je ___ (ne... jamais recevoir) votre chèque!

Activité de communication

■ Au syndicat d'initiative. Working with a partner, prepare a conversation between a student looking for an inexpensive hotel in Paris and an agent in the *syndicat d'initiative*.

LA FRANCE

La Mer d'Irlande

L'ANGLETERRE

La Mer du Nord

L'ALLEMAGNE

Amsterdam ✪

LES PAYS-BAS

la Tamise

Londres ✪

La Manche

Bruxelles ✪

Calais

Lille

LA BELGIQUE

Bonn ✪

le Rhin

Amiens

LE LUXEMBOURG

Luxembourg ✪

le Rhin

le Main

Les Îles Anglo-Normandes

Cherbourg

Le Havre

Rouen

la Seine

Reims

la Marne

Metz

la Meuse

Strasbourg

LES VOSGES

le Rhin

Caen

Paris ✪

la Seine

Troyes

Nancy

la Moselle

Brest

Rennes

Le Mans

Orléans

Chaumont

Ballon de Guebwiller 1424 m ▲

Mulhouse

la Loire

Dijon

la Saône

Besançon

LE JURA

L'AUTRIC

Angers

Tours

la

Nantes

L'Océan Atlantique

Poitiers

LA FRANCE

la Loire

Crêt de la Neige 1723 m ▲

le Lac Léman

Berne ✪

LA SUISSE

Vichy

le Rhône

Genève

La Rochelle

Limoges

Clermont-Ferrand

Lyon

Chamonix

Mont Blanc 4807 m

L'ITALIE

le Pô

la Dordogne

Le puy de Sancy 1886 m ▲

St-Étienne

LES

Grenoble

Bordeaux

la

LE MASSIF CENTRAL

Rodez

le Rhône

la Garonne

Bayonne

Toulouse

Montpellier

Nîmes

Avignon

Aix-en-Provence

Marseille

Nice

Cannes

MONACO

LES PYRÉNÉES

Vignemale 3298 m

L'ANDORRE

Perpignan

Toulon

L'Ebro

La Mer Méditerranée

La C

Ajaccio

L'ESPAGNE

488

Madrid ✪

N
O — E
S

0   100   200

Kilomètres

La Sardaig

LE MONDE FRANCOPHONE

L'Océan Pacifique

L'ASIE

LE LAOS
LE VIÊT-NAM
LE CAMBODGE

LE VANUATU
la Nouvelle-
Calédonie (Fr)

L'AUSTRALIE

L'EUROPE

LA BELGIQUE
LE LUXEMBOURG
LA SUISSE
MONACO
la Corse
(Fr)
L'ANDORRE
LA FRANCE
Paris

LE LIBAN

LA
TUNISIE

L'ALGÉRIE

LE MAROC

LA MAURITANIE
LE SÉNÉGAL
LA GUINÉE
LE
MALI
LE
NIGER
LE
TCHAD

BURKINA
FASO
LE BÉNIN
LE TOGO
LA CÔTE-
D'IVOIRE
LE CAMEROUN
LE GABON

L'AFRIQUE

LA RÉPUBLIQUE
CENTRAFRICAINE

DJIBOUTI

LE
CONGO
LE
RWANDA
LE
BURUNDI
LE ZAÏRE

LES
COMORES

LES
SEYCHELLES

L'Océan Indien

L'ÎLE MAURICE
la Réunion
(Fr)

Mayotte
(Fr)
MADAGASCAR

l'Île Amsterdam
(Fr)

l'Île St Paul
(Fr)

les Îles
Crozet
(Fr)

L'Océan
Atlantique

L'AMÉRIQUE
DU NORD

St-Pierre-
et-Miquelon
(Fr)

le Québec
(le Canada)

la Guadeloupe (Fr)
la Martinique (Fr)

HAÏTI

la Guyane
française (Fr)

L'AMÉRIQUE
DU SUD

la Louisiane
(les États-Unis)

L'Océan
Pacifique

la Polynésie
française (Fr)

Tahiti

L'ANTARCTIQUE

490

PRONONCIATION ET ORTHOGRAPHE

I. La transcription phonétique

The following are phonetic symbols used in this book.

[a]	la, là, avec	[ã]	dans, encore, temps
[é]	télé, chez, dîner, les	[õ]	non, regardons
[è]	elle, êtes, frère	[ẽ]	fin, demain
[i]	qui, il, lycée, dîne	[œ̃]	un
[ü]	tu, une		
[u]	vous, où, bonjour	[y]	fille, travailler
[ó]	au, beaucoup, allô		
[ò]	homme, alors	[sh]	chez, Michel
[œ́]	deux, veut	[zh]	je, âge
[œ̀]	heure, sœur	[g]	garder, goûter, Guy

II. L'alphabet français

a b c d e f g h i j k l m n o p q r s t u v w x y z
Voyelles: a e i(y) o u
Consonnes: b c d f g h j k l m p q r s t v w x z

III. Les accents

There are five written accent marks on French letters. These accents are part of the spelling of the word and cannot be omitted.

1. *L'accent aigu* (´) occurs over the letter *e*.

  le téléphone   élémentaire

2. *L'accent grave* (`) occurs over the letters *a, e,* and *u*.

  voilà   le frère   où

3. *L'accent circonflexe* (^) occurs over all vowels.

  le château   la fenêtre   le dîner   l'hôtel   août

4. *La cédille* (ç) appears only under the letter *c*. When the letter *c* is followed by an *a, o* or *u* it has a hard /k/ sound as in *ca*ve, *co*ca, *cu*lmination. The cedilla changes the hard /k/ sound to a soft /s/ sound.

  ça   garçon   commençons   reçu

5. *Le tréma* (¨) indicates that two vowels next to each other are pronounced separately.

  Noël   égoïste

VERBES

A. Verbes réguliers

INFINITIF	**parler** *to speak*	**finir** *to finish*	**répondre** *to answer*
PRÉSENT	je parle tu parles il parle nous parlons vous parlez ils parlent	je finis tu finis il finit nous finissons vous finissez ils finissent	je réponds tu réponds il répond nous répondons vous répondez ils répondent
IMPÉRATIF	parle parlons parlez	finis finissons finissez	réponds répondons répondez
PASSÉ COMPOSÉ	j'ai parlé tu as parlé il a parlé nous avons parlé vous avez parlé ils ont parlé	j'ai fini tu as fini il a fini nous avons fini vous avez fini ils ont fini	j'ai répondu tu as répondu il a répondu nous avons répondu vous avez répondu ils ont répondu

B. Verbes avec changements d'orthographe
(Verbs with spelling changes)

INFINITIF	**acheter**[1] *to buy*	**appeler** *to call*	**commencer** *to begin*
PRÉSENT	j'achète tu achètes il achète nous achetons vous achetez ils achètent	j'appelle tu appelles il appelle nous appelons vous appelez ils appellent	je commence tu commences il commence nous commençons vous commencez ils commencent
INFINITIF	**manger**[2] *to eat*	**payer**[3] *to pay*	**préférer**[4] *to prefer*
PRÉSENT	je mange tu manges il mange nous mangeons vous mangez ils mangent	je paie tu paies il paie nous payons vous payez ils paient	je préfère tu préfères il préfère nous préférons vous préférez ils préfèrent

[1] Verbes similaires: *se lever, se promener*
[2] Verbes similaires: *nager, voyager*
[3] Verbes similaires: *essayer, renvoyer, employer, envoyer*
[4] Verbes similaires: *célébrer, espérer, suggérer*

C. Verbes irréguliers

INFINITIF	**aller** *to go*	**avoir** *to have*	**conduire** *to drive*
PRÉSENT	je vais tu vas il va nous allons vous allez ils vont	j'ai tu as il a nous avons vous avez ils ont	je conduis tu conduis il conduit nous conduisons vous conduisez ils conduisent
PASSÉ COMPOSÉ	je suis allé(e)	j'ai eu	j'ai conduit
INFINITIF	**connaître** *to know*	**croire** *to believe*	**devoir** *to have to, to owe*
PRÉSENT	je connais tu connais il connaît nous connaissons vous connaissez ils connaissent	je crois tu crois il croit nous croyons vous croyez ils croient	je dois tu dois il doit nous devons vous devez ils doivent
PASSÉ COMPOSÉ	j'ai connu	j'ai cru	j'ai dû
INFINITIF	**dire** *to say*	**dormir** *to sleep*	**écrire** *to write*
PRÉSENT	je dis tu dis il dit nous disons vous dites ils disent	je dors tu dors il dort nous dormons vous dormez ils dorment	j'écris tu écris il écrit nous écrivons vous écrivez ils écrivent
PASSÉ COMPOSÉ	j'ai dit	j'ai dormi	j'ai écrit
INFINITIF	**être** *to be*	**faire** *to do, to make*	**lire** *to read*
PRÉSENT	je suis tu es il est nous sommes vous êtes ils sont	je fais tu fais il fait nous faisons vous faites ils font	je lis tu lis il lit nous lisons vous lisez ils lisent
PASSÉ COMPOSÉ	j'ai été	j'ai fait	j'ai lu

INFINITIF	**mettre** *to put*	**ouvrir**[1] *to open*	**partir** *to leave*
PRÉSENT	je mets tu mets il met nous mettons vous mettez ils mettent	j'ouvre tu ouvres il ouvre nous ouvrons vous ouvrez ils ouvrent	je pars tu pars il part nous partons vous partez ils partent
PASSÉ COMPOSÉ	j'ai mis	j'ai ouvert	je suis parti(e)
INFINITIF	**pouvoir** *to be able to*	**prendre**[2] *to take*	**recevoir** *to receive*
PRÉSENT	je peux tu peux il peut nous pouvons vous pouvez ils peuvent	je prends tu prends il prend nous prenons vous prenez ils prennent	je reçois tu reçois il reçoit nous recevons vous recevez ils reçoivent
PASSÉ COMPOSÉ	j'ai pu	j'ai pris	j'ai reçu
INFINITIF	**savoir** *to know*	**servir** *to serve*	**sortir** *to go out*
PRÉSENT	je sais tu sais il sait nous savons vous savez ils savent	je sers tu sers il sert nous servons vous servez ils servent	je sors tu sors il sort nous sortons vous sortez ils sortent
PASSÉ COMPOSÉ	j'ai su	j'ai servi	je suis sorti(e)
INFINITIF	**venir**[3] *to come*	**voir** *to see*	**vouloir** *to want*
PRÉSENT	je viens tu viens il vient nous venons vous venez ils viennent	je vois tu vois il voit nous voyons vous voyez ils voient	je veux tu veux il veut nous voulons vous voulez ils veulent
PASSÉ COMPOSÉ	je suis venu(e)	j'ai vu	j'ai voulu

[1] Verbes similaires: *couvrir, découvrir, offrir, souffrir*
[2] Verbes similaires: *apprendre, comprendre*
[3] Verbes similaires: *devenir, revenir*

D. Verbes avec *être* au passé composé

aller *(to go)*	je suis allé(e)
arriver *(to arrive)*	je suis arrivé(e)
descendre *(to go down, to get off)*	je suis descendu(e)
entrer *(to enter)*	je suis entré(e)
monter *(to go up)*	je suis monté(e)
mourir *(to die)*	je suis mort(e)
naître *(to be born)*	je suis né(e)
partir *(to leave)*	je suis parti(e)
passer *(to go by)*	je suis passé(e)
rentrer *(to go home)*	je suis rentré(e)
rester *(to stay)*	je suis resté(e)
retourner *(to return)*	je suis retourné(e)
revenir *(to come back)*	je suis revenu(e)
sortir *(to go out)*	je suis sorti(e)
tomber *(to fall)*	je suis tombé(e)
venir *(to come)*	je suis venu(e)

VOCABULAIRE FRANÇAIS-ANGLAIS

The *Vocabulaire français-anglais* contains all productive and receptive vocabulary from the text.

The numbers following each productive entry indicate the chapter and vocabulary section in which the word is introduced. For example, 2.2 means that the word first appeared in *Chapitre 2, Mots 2*. BV refers to the introductory *Bienvenue* lesson.

The following abbreviations are used in this glossary.

adj.	adjective
adv.	adverb
conj.	conjunction
dem. adj.	demonstrative adjective
dem. pron.	demonstrative pronoun
dir. obj.	direct object
f.	feminine
fam.	familiar
ind. obj.	indirect object
inf.	infinitive
inform.	informal
inv.	invariable
m.	masculine
n.	noun
pl.	plural
poss. adj.	possessive adjective
prep.	preposition
pron.	pronoun
sing.	singular
subj.	subject

A

à at, in, to, **3.1**
  à bord de on board, **7.2**
  à côté next door
  à côté de next to, **5**
  À demain. See you tomorrow., **BV**
  à demi-tarif half-price
  à destination de to (plane, train, etc.), **7.1**
  à domicile to the home
  à droite de to, on the right of, **5**
  à gauche de to, on the left of, **5**
  à l'avance in advance
  à l'étranger abroad, in a foreign country
  à l'heure on time, **8.1**
  à l'intérieur inside
  à la mode in style, 'in'
  à mi-temps part-time, **3.2**
  à mon avis in my opinion, **10.2**
  à partir de from . . . on; based on
  à peu près about
  à pied on foot, **5.2**
  à plein temps full-time, **3.2**
  à point medium-rare (meat), **5.2**
  à propos de concerning, as regards
  À quelle heure? At what time?, **2**
  À tout à l'heure. See you later., **BV**
absolument absolutely
absorber to absorb
accélérer to speed up, go faster, **12.1**
accepter to accept
l' **accessoire (m.)** accessory
l' **accident (m.)** accident, **14.2**
accompagné(e) (de) accompanied (by)
accueilli(e): bien accueilli(e) well-received
l' **achat (m.)** purchase (n.)
  faire des achats to shop, **10.1**
acheter to buy, **6.1**
l' **acidité (f.)** acidity
l' **acte (m.)** act, **16.1**
l' **acteur (m.)** actor (m.), **16.1**
actif, active active, **10**
l' **action (f.)** action
l' **activité (f.)** activity
l' **actrice (f.)** actress, **16.1**

l' **addition (f.)** check, bill (restaurant), **5.2**
admirer to admire
l' **adolescent(e)** adolescent, teenager
adopter to adopt
adorable adorable
adorer to love, **3.2**
l' **adresse (f.)** address
l' **adulte (m. et f.)** adult
adverse opposing, **13.1**
aérien(ne) air, flight (adj.), **9**
  les tarifs aériens airfares
l' **aérogare (f.)** terminal with bus to airport, **7.2**
l' **aéroport (m.)** airport, **7.1**
aérospatial(e) aerospace (adj.)
les **affaires (f. pl.)** business
affolé(e) panic-stricken
s'affronter to collide
africain(e) African
l' **âge (m.)** age, **4.1**
  Tu as quel âge? How old are you? (fam.), **4.1**
âgé(e) old
l' **agenda (m.)** datebook, **2.2**
l' **agent (m.)** agent (m. and f.), **7.1**
  l'agent (m.) de police police officer (m. and f.)
l' **agglomération (f.)** populated area
agité(e) agitated
agréable pleasant
l' **agriculteur (m.)** farmer (m. and f.)
aider to help
aimable nice (person), **1.2**
aimer to like, love, **3.2**
l' **air (m.)** air
  en plein air outdoor(s)
ajouter to add
l' **algèbre (f.)** algebra, **2.2**
l' **aliment (m.)** food
l' **alimentation (f.)** nutrition, diet
l' **Allemagne (f.)** Germany, **16**
allemand(e) German (adj.)
  l'allemand (m.) German (language)
aller to go, **5.1**
  aller à la pêche to go fishing, **9.1**
  aller pêcher to go fishing
  l'aller-retour (m.) round-trip ticket, **8**
  l'aller simple (m.) one-way ticket, **8.1**
l' **allergie (f.)** allergy, **15.1**
allergique allergic, **15.1**
alors so, then, well then

les **Alpes (f. pl.)** the Alps
l' **alpinisme (m.)** mountain climbing
l' **altitude (f.)** altitude
l' **amateur (m.): l'amateur d'art** art lover
aménager to renovate, transform
américain(e) American (adj.), **1.1**
l' **Américain(e)** American (person)
l' **Amérique (f.) du Nord** North America, **16**
l' **Amérique (f.) du Sud** South America, **16**
l' **ami(e)** friend, **1.2**
l' **amitié (f.)** friendship
amusant(e) funny, **1.1**
s'amuser to have fun, **11.2**
l' **an: avoir . . . ans** to be . . . years old, **4.1**
l' **anatomie (f.)** anatomy
ancien(ne) old
l' **angine (f.)** throat infection, tonsillitis, **15.1**
l' **anglais (m.)** English (language), **2.2**
  l'Anglais, l'Anglaise Englishman, Englishwoman
l' **Angleterre (f.)** England, **16**
l' **animal (m.)** animal
animé(e) lively, animated
l' **année (f.)** year, **4.1**
  l'année dernière last year, **13**
l' **anniversaire (m.)** birthday, **4.1**
  Bon (joyeux) anniversaire! Happy birthday!
  C'est quand, ton anniversaire? When is your birthday? (fam.), **4.1**
l' **annonce (f.)** announcement, **8.1**
  la petite annonce classified ad
annoncer to announce, **8.1**
l' **anorak (m.)** ski jacket, **14.1**
antérieur(e) previous, former
l' **anthropologie (f.)** anthropology
l' **antibiotique (m.)** antibiotic, **15.1**
l' **anticyclone (m.)** high pressure area
antillais(e) West Indian (adj.)
antipathique unpleasant (person), **1.2**
l' **Antiquité (f.)** ancient times
anxieux, anxieuse anxious
août (m.) August, **4.1**

apparenté: le mot apparenté cognate

l' **appartement (m.)** apartment, **4.2**

appeler to call

s' **appeler** to be called, be named, **11.1**

applaudir to applaud

apporter to bring

apprendre (à) to learn (to), **9.1**

apprendre à quelqu'un à faire quelque chose to teach someone to do something, **14.1**

l' **apprenti(e)** apprentice

appuyer sur le bouton to push the button

après after, **3.2**

l'après-midi (m.) afternoon, **2**

l' **arbitre (m.)** referee, **13.1**

l' **arbre (m.)** tree

l' **archipel (m.)** archipelago

l' **architecte (m. et f.)** architect

l' **architecture (f.)** architecture

l' **argent (m.)** money, **3.2**

l'argent liquide cash, **18.1**

l'argent de poche allowance

l' **Argentine (f.)** Argentina, **16**

l' **argot (m.)** slang

l' **aristocrate (m. et f.)** aristocrat

l' **arme (f.)** weapon

l' **armée (f.)** army

s' **arrêter** to stop, **12.1**

l' **arrivée (f.)** arrival, **7.2**

arriver to arrive, **3.1**; to happen

l' **arrondissement (m.)** district (in Paris)

l' **art (m.)** art, **2.2**

les **articles (m. pl.) de luxe** luxury items

les **articles (m. pl.) de sport** sporting goods

l' **artiste peintre (m. et f.)** painter

artistique artistic

l' **ascenseur (m.)** elevator, **4.2**

l' **asepsie (f.): pratiquer l'asepsie** to sterilize, disinfect

l' **Asie (f.)** Asia, **16**

aspiré(e) pulled in

l' **aspirine (f.)** aspirin, **15.1**

assez fairly, quite; enough

assez de (+ nom) enough (+ noun), **18**

l' **assiette (f.)** plate, **5.2**

ne pas être dans son assiette to be feeling out of sorts, **15.1**

assis(e) seated, **8.2**

l' **assistant(e)** assistant

l' **association (f.)** association

associer to associate

l' **assurance (f.)** insurance

l' **astronome (m. et f.)** astronomer

l' **atmosphère (f.)** atmosphere

attendre to wait (for), **8.1**

l' **attente: la salle d'attente** waiting room, **8.1**

l' **attention: faire attention** to pay attention, **6**; be careful, **9.1**

Attention! Careful! Watch out!

atterrir to land, **7.1**

l' **atterrissage (m.)** landing (plane)

attirer to attract

attraper un coup de soleil to get a sunburn, **9.1**

au at the, to the, in the, on the, **5**

au bord de la mer by the ocean; seaside, **9.1**

au contraire on the contrary

au-dessous: la taille au-dessous the next smaller size, **10.2**

au-dessus: la taille au-dessus the next larger size, **10.2**

au-dessus de above

au fond de at the bottom of

au moins at least

au revoir goodbye, **BV**

au sujet de about

l' **auberge (f.) de jeunesse** youth hostel

audacieux, audacieuse audacious, bold

augmenter to increase

aujourd'hui today, **2.2**

ausculter to listen with a stethoscope, **15.2**

aussi also, too, **1.1**; as (comparisons), **10**

l' **Australie (f.)** Australia, **16**

l' **auteur (m.)** author (m. and f.)

l' **auto-école (f.)** driving school, **12.2**

l' **autocar (m.)** bus, coach, **7.2**

l' **autoroute (f.)** highway

l'autoroute à péage toll highway, **12.2**

autour de around

autre other, **BV**

Autre chose? Anything else? (shopping), **6.2**

aux at the, to the, in the, **5**

l' **avance: à l'avance** in advance

en avance early, ahead of time, **8.1**

avancé(e) advanced

avant before, **7.1**

avant de (+ inf.) before (+ verb)

avant hier the day before yesterday, **13**

avec with, **5.1**

Avec ça? What else? (shopping), **6.2**

l' **aventure (f.)** adventure

l' **avion (m.)** airplane, **7.1**

en avion (by) plane, **7.1**

l' **avis (m.)** opinion

à mon avis in my opinion, **10.2**

avoir to have, **4.1**

avoir . . . ans to be . . . years old, **4.1**

avoir besoin de to need, **11.1**

avoir de la chance to be lucky

avoir faim to be hungry, **5.1**

avoir une faim de loup to be very hungry

avoir lieu to take place

avoir mal à to have a(n) . . . -ache, to hurt, **15.2**

avoir l'occasion de (+ inf.) to have the opportunity (+ inf.)

avoir raison to be right

avoir soif to be thirsty, **5.1**

avoir tendance à (+ inf.) to tend (+ inf.)

avril (m.) April, **4.1**

B

le **baccalauréat** French high school exam

le **bacon** bacon

bactérien(ne) bacterial, **15.1**

les **bagages (m. pl.)** luggage, **7.1**

les bagages à main carry-on luggage, **7.1**

la **baguette** loaf of French bread, **6.1**

le **bain** bath, **11.2**

le bain de soleil: prendre un bain de soleil to sunbathe, **9.1**

le **balcon** balcony, **4.2**

la **balle** ball (tennis, etc.), **9.2**; franc (slang), **18.2**

le **ballon** ball (soccer, etc.), **13.1**

la **banane** banana, **6.2**

la **bande dessinée** comic strip

la **banlieue** suburbs

la **banque** bank, **18.1**

le **banquier, la banquière** banker
baptiser to christen
Barcelone Barcelona, **16**
bas(se) low, **10**
   à talons bas low-heeled (shoes), **10**
le **base-ball** baseball, **13.2**
la **base: de base** basic
le **basket(-ball)** basketball, **13.2**
le **bateau** boat
le **bâtiment** building
le **bâton** ski pole, **14.1**
   bavarder to chat, **4.2**
   beau (bel) beautiful (m.), **4**
   Il fait beau. It's nice weather., **9.2**
   beaucoup a lot, **3.1**
   beaucoup de a lot of, many, **10.1**
la **beauté** beauty
les **Beaux-arts (m. pl)** fine arts
   beige beige, **10.2**
   belge Belgian (adj.)
   le/la Belge Belgian (person)
la **Belgique** Belgium
   belle beautiful (f.), **4**
le **béribéri** beriberi
le **besoin** need
   avoir besoin de to need, **11.1**
la **bêtise** stupid thing, nonsense
le **beurre** butter, **6.2**
le **bicentenaire** bicentennial
   bien fine, well, **BV**
     bien accueilli(e) well-received
     bien cuit(e) well-done (meat), **5.2**
     bien élevé(e) well-mannered
     bien sûr of course
   bientôt soon
   Bienvenue! Welcome!
la **bière** beer
le **billet** bill (currency), **18.1**; ticket, **7.1**
   le billet aller-retour round-trip ticket, **8.1**
la **biologie** biology, **2.2**
le/la **biologiste** biologist
   bizarre strange, odd
la **blague: Sans blague!** No kidding!
   blanc, blanche white, **10.2**
   bleu(e) blue, **10.2**
     bleu marine (inv.) navy blue, **10.2**
   blond(e) blond, **1.1**
   bloquer to block
le **blouson** jacket, **10.1**
le **bœuf** beef, **6.1**
la **boisson** beverage, **5.1**

la **boîte de conserve** can of food, **6.2**
   bon(ne) correct; good, **9**
     bon marché (inv.) inexpensive
   bonjour hello, **BV**
le **bonnet** ski cap, hat, **14.1**
   le bonnet de bain bathing cap
le **bord: à bord de** aboard (plane, etc.), **7.2**
   au bord de la mer by the ocean, seaside, **9.1**
   bordé(e) bordered
le **bordereau** receipt
la **bosse** mogul (ski), **14.2**
la **botanique** botany
la **botte** boot
la **bouche** mouth, **15.1**
la **boucherie** butcher shop, **6.1**
le **bouchon** traffic jam
   bouger to move
le **bouillon de poulet** chicken soup
la **boulangerie-pâtisserie** bakery, **6.1**
la **boule de neige** snowball, **14.2**
la **bouteille** bottle, **6.2**
la **boutique** shop, boutique
le **bouton** button; bud
la **brasse papillon** butterfly (swim stroke)
   Bravo! Good! Well done!
le **break** station wagon, **12.1**
le **Brésil** Brazil, **16**
la **Bretagne** Brittany
   breton(ne) Breton, from Brittany
la **brioche** sweet roll
   bronzé(e) tan
   bronzer to tan, **9.1**
le **bruit** noise
   brun(e) brunette, **1.1**; brown, **10.2**
le **bulletin de notes** report card
le **bulletin météorologique** weather report
le **bureau** desk, **BV**; office, bureau
   le bureau de change foreign exchange office, **18.1** (for foreign currency)
le **bus: en bus** by bus, **5.**
le **but** goal, **13.1**
   marquer un but to score a goal, **13.1**

C

   c'est it is, it's, **BV**
   C'est ça. That's right.

   C'est combien? How much is it?, **BV**
   C'est quand, ton anniversaire? When is your birthday? (fam.), **4.1**
   C'est quel jour? What day is it?, **2.2**
   C'est tout? Is that all?, **6.2**
   ça that (dem. adj.), **BV**
   Ça coûte cher. It's expensive.,
   Ça fait combien? How much is it?, **6.2**
   Ça fait . . . francs. That's . . . francs., **6.2**
   Ça fait mal. It hurts., **15.2**
   Ça va. Fine., OK., **BV**
   Ça va? How's it going?, How are you? (inform.), **BV**
la **cabine** cabin (airplane), **7.1**
le **cabinet** office (doctor's)
le **cadeau** gift, present, **10.2**
le **café** café; coffee, **5.1**
   le café au lait coffee with milk
le **cahier** notebook, **BV**
la **caisse** cash register, checkout counter, **6.2**
le **caissier, la caissière** cashier, **17.2**
le **calcium** calcium
le **calcul** calculation
la **calculatrice** calculator, **BV**
   calculer to calculate
   calme quiet, calm
   Calmez-vous. Calm down.
la **calorie** calorie
le/la **camarade** companion, friend
le **camp** side (in a sport or game), **13.1**
   le camp adverse opponents, other side, **13.1**
la **campagne** country(side)
le **Canada** Canada, **16**
   canadien(ne) Canadian (adj.), **9**
le **candidat, la candidate** candidate
le **canot** canoe
la **cantine** school restaurant
la **capitale** capital
le **car** bus (coach)
le **caractère: à caractère familial** family-style
la **caractéristique** characteristic
le **carnet** small book
la **carotte** carrot, **6.2**
le **carrefour** crossroads, **12.2**
la **carrière** career

la **carte** menu, **5.1**; map
   la carte d'anniversaire
     birthday card
   la carte de crédit credit
     card, **17.2**
   la carte de débarquement
     landing card, **7.2**
   la carte d'embarquement
     boarding pass, **7.1**
   la carte postale postcard
le **cas: en tout cas** in any case
le **casque** helmet
le **casse-cou** daredevil
la **cassette** cassette, **3.2**
la **catégorie** category
la **cathédrale** cathedral
la **cause** cause (n.)
   causer to cause
   ce (cet) (m.) this, that (m.), **8**
   ce que c'est what it is
   Ce n'est rien. You're wel-
     come., **BV**
la **ceinture de sécurité** seat belt,
   12.2
   célèbre famous, **1.2**
   célibataire single, unmarried
la **cellule** cell
   la cellule nerveuse nerve
     cell
   cent hundred, **5.2**
les **centaines (f. pl.)** hundreds
le **centre: le centre commercial**
   shopping center
   au centre de in the heart of
les **céréales (f. pl.)** cereal, grains
la **cérémonie** ceremony
   certain(e) certain
   pour certains for some
     people
   certainement certainly
   ces (pl.) these, those, **8**
   cette (f.) this, that, **8**
   chacun(e) each (one)
la **chaîne** T.V. channel
   la chaîne hôtelière hotel
     chain
la **chaise** chair, **BV**
le **chalet** chalet
la **chambre** room (in a hotel),
   17.1
   la chambre à un lit single
     room, **17.1**
   la chambre à deux lits
     double room, **17.1**
   la chambre à coucher bed-
     room, **4.2**
le **champ** field
   le champ de manœuvres
     parade ground
le **champion, la championne**
   champion

le **championnat** championship
la **chance** luck
   avoir de la chance to be
     lucky
   changer (de) to change, **8.2**; to
     exchange, **18.1**
   chanter to sing, **3.2**
le **chanteur, la chanteuse** singer
   chaque each, every, **16.1**
la **charcuterie** deli, **6.1**
   charger to put in charge
le **chariot** shopping cart
   charmant(e) charming
le **chat** cat, **4.1**
   avoir un chat dans la gorge
     to have a frog in one's
     throat, **15.2**
le **château** castle, mansion
   chaud(e) warm, hot
   Il fait chaud. It's hot
     (weather)., **9.2**
   chauffer to heat
les **chaussettes (f. pl.)** socks, **10.1**
les **chaussures (f. pl.)** shoes, **10.1**
   les chaussures de ski ski
     boots, **14.1**
   les chaussures de tennis
     sneakers, tennis shoes, **9.2**
la **chaux** quicklime
le **chef** head, boss
la **cheminée** chimney
la **chemise** shirt, **10.1**
le **chemisier** blouse, **10.1**
le **chèque (bancaire)** check, **18.1**
   le chèque de voyage
     traveler's check, **17.2**
   cher, chère dear; expensive, **10**
   Ça coûte cher. It's expensive.
   chercher to look for, seek, **5.1**
le **cheval (pl. les chevaux)** horse
les **cheveux (m. pl.)** hair, **11.1**
   chez at the home (business) of,
     5
   chez soi home
   chic chic, stylish
le **chien** dog, **4.1**
le **chiffre** number
le **Chili** Chile, **16**
la **chimie** chemistry, **2.2**
   chimique chemical
le/la **chimiste** chemist
la **Chine** China, **16**
   chinois(e) Chinese (adj.)
le **chirurgien** surgeon (m. and f.)
le **chocolat: au chocolat** choco-
     late (adj.), **5.1**
   choisir to choose, **7.1**
le **choix** choice
le **choléra** cholera
le **cholestérol** cholesterol

la **chose** thing
   pas grand-chose not much
   chouette great (inform.), **2.2**
la **chute: faire une chute** to fall,
   14.2
   ci-dessus above (adv.)
   ciao goodbye (inform.), **BV**
le **ciel** sky, **14.2**
la **cigale** grasshopper
le **cinéma** movie theatre, movies,
   16.1
le/la **cinéphile** movie buff
   cinq five, **BV**
   cinquante fifty, **BV**
le **cintre** hanger, **17.2**
la **circulation** traffic, **12.2**;
   circulation
   la circulation à double sens
     two-way traffic
   citer to cite, mention
le **citron pressé** lemonade, **5.1**
le **civilisé, la civilisée** civilized
   person
la **classe** class (people), **2.1**; class
   (course)
   la classe économique coach
     class (in plane)
le **classement** classification,
   classer to classify
la **clé** key, **12.1**
le **client, la cliente** customer,
   10.1
le **climat** climate
les **clous (m. pl.)** pedestrian
   crossing, **12.2**
le **club d'art dramatique** drama
   club
le **club de forme** health club,
   11.2
le **coca** Coca-Cola, **5.1**
le **cœur** heart
le **coffre** trunk (of car)
le **coin: du coin** neighborhood
   (adj.)
le **collaborateur, la collaboratrice**
   co-worker, associate
le **collant** pantyhose, **10.1**
le **collège** junior high, middle
   school
la **colonie de vacances** summer
   camp
   combattre to combat, fight
   combien (de) how much, how
     many, **6.2**
   C'est combien? How much
     is it?, **BV**
   Ça fait combien? How
     much is that?, **6.2**
   comble (adj.) packed
     (stadium), **13.1**

la **comédie** comedy, **16.1**
　　la comédie musicale
　　　musical comedy, **16.1**
comique funny, **1.2**
commander to order, **5.1**
comme like, as
le **commencement** beginning
commencer to begin
comment how; what
　　Comment vas-tu? How are
　　　you? (fam.), **BV**
　　Comment est . . . ? What
　　　is . . . like? (description),
　　　1.1
　　Comment t'appelles-tu?
　　　What's your name? (fam.),
　　　11.1
　　Comment vous appelez-
　　　vous? What's your name?
　　　(form.), **11.1**
commun(e) common
　　en commun in common
la **communauté** community
le **compact disc** compact disc,
　　3.2
la **compagnie aérienne** airline,
　　7.1
le **compartiment** compartment,
　　7.2
complet, complète full,
　　complete
le **complet** suit (man's), **10.1**
compléter to complete
le **comportement** behavior
composer to compose
composter to stamp, validate (a
　　ticket), **8.1**
comprendre to understand, **9.1**
le **comprimé** pill, **15.2**
compris(e) included (in the
　　bill)
　　Le service est compris. The
　　　tip is included., **5.2**
le **compte d'épargne** savings
　　account, **18.1**
le **comptoir** counter, **7.1**
le/la **concierge** concierge, caretaker
le **concours** competition, contest
le **conducteur, la conductrice**
　　driver, **12.1**
conduire to drive, **12.2**
la **conduite: des leçons de con-**
　　duite driving lessons, **12.2**
confiant(e) confident, **1.1**
le **confort** comfort
confortable comfortable
la **connaissance: faire la connais-**
　　sance de to meet
connaître to know, **16.2**
connu(e) known
la **conquête** conquest

conservateur, conservatrice
　　conservative
conserver to conserve
la **consigne** checkroom, **8.1**
　　la consigne automatique
　　　locker, **8.1**
consommer to consume
construit(e) built
la **consultation** consultation,
　　medical visit
le **contact: mettre le contact** to
　　start (a car), **12.1**
contaminer to contaminate
contenir to contain
content(e) happy, **1.1**
continu(e) continual, ongoing
continuer to continue
la **contractuelle** meter maid, **12.2**
le **contraire** opposite
　　au contraire on the contrary
la **contravention** traffic ticket,
　　12.2
contre against, **13.1**
　　par contre on the other
　　　hand, however
le **contrôle de sécurité** security
　　(airport), **7.1**
　　passer par le contrôle de
　　　sécurité to go through
　　　security (airport)
le **contrôleur** conductor, **8.2**
convenable correct
la **conversation** conversation
la **coopération** cooperation
le **copain** friend, pal (m.), **2.1**
la **copine** friend, pal (f.), **2.1**
la **coqueluche** whooping cough
le **corps** body
correspondre to correspond
corriger to correct
le **costume** costume, **16.1**
la **côte** coast
　　la Côte d'Azur French
　　　Riviera
　　la Côte d'Ivoire Ivory Coast,
　　　16
le **côté** side
　　côté couloir aisle (seat in
　　　airplane), **7.1**
　　côté fenêtre window (seat in
　　　airplane), **7.1**
se **coucher** to go to bed, **11.1**
la **couchette** bunk (on a train),
　　8.2
la **couleur** color, **10.2**
　　De quelle couleur est . . . ?
　　　What color is . . . ?, **10.2**
le **couloir** aisle, corridor, **8.2**
la **coupe** winner's cup, **13.2**
la **cour** courtyard, **4.2**; court

courageux, courageuse coura-
　　geous, brave
le **coureur** runner, **13.2**
　　le coureur cycliste racing
　　　cyclist, **13.2**
couronné(e) crowned
le **courrier** mail service
le **cours** course, class, **2.2**
　　le cours du change
　　　exchange rate, **18.1**
la **course** race, **13.2**
　　la course cycliste bicycle
　　　race
les **courses (f. pl.): faire les**
　　courses to go grocery shop-
　　ping, **6.1**
court(e) short, **10.2**
le **court de tennis** tennis court,
　　9.2
le **cousin, la cousine** cousin, **4.1**
le **couteau** knife, **5.2**
coûter to cost
　　Ça coûte cher. It's expensive.
la **coutume** custom
le **couturier** designer (of clothes),
　　10.1
　　couvert: Le ciel est couvert.
　　　The sky is overcast., **14.2**
le **couvert** table setting, **5.2**
　　mettre le couvert to set the
　　　table, **8**
la **couverture** blanket, **17.2**
couvrir to cover, **15**
le **crabe** crab, **6.1**
la **craie: le morceau de craie**
　　piece of chalk, **BV**
la **cravate** tie, **10.1**
le **crayon** pencil, **BV**
la **crèche** day-care center
créer to create
la **crème** cream, **6.1**
　　la crème solaire suntan
　　　lotion, **9.1**
le **crème** coffee with cream (in a
　　café), **5.1**
la **crémerie** dairy store, **6.1**
la **crêpe** crepe, pancake, **5.1**
la **crêperie** crepe restaurant
crevé(e) exhausted
la **crevette** shrimp, **6.1**
crier to shout
la **crise** crisis
le/la **critique** critic
　　critiquer to criticize
　　croire to believe, think, **10.2**
le **croisement** intersection, **12.2**
la **croissance** growth
le **croissant** croissant, crescent
　　roll, **6.1**
le **croque-monsieur** grilled ham
　　and cheese sandwich, **5.1**

croustillant(e) crusty
la **croyance** belief
le **cubisme** Cubism
la **cuillère** spoon, **5.2**
la **cuisine** kitchen, **4.2**
    faire la cuisine to cook, **6**
cuit(e): bien cuit(e) well-done
    (meat), **5.2**
la **culture** culture
culturel(le) cultural
la **cure** cure
le **cycle** cycle
    le cycle de l'eau water cycle
le **cyclisme** cycling, bicycle rid-
    ing, **13.2**
le/la **cycliste** cyclist

D

d'abord first (adv.), **11.1**
d'accord O.K., **3**
    être d'accord to agree, **2.1**
d'après according to
la **dame** lady
le **danger: en danger** in danger
dangereux, dangereuse dan-
    gerous
dans in, **BV**
la **danse** dance
    danser to dance, **3.2**
la **danseuse** dancer
la **date: Quelle est la date**
    aujourd'hui? What is today's
    date?, **4.1**
de from, **1.1**; of, belonging to,
    5
    de bonne heure early
    de côté aside, **17.2**
    de loin by far
    de nos jours today,
        nowadays
    de plus en plus more and
        more
    De quelle couleur est . . . ?
        What color is . . . ?, **10.2**
    de rêve dream (adj.)
    De rien. You're welcome
        (informal)., **BV**
    de temps en temps from
        time to time, occasionally
le **débarquement** landing,
    deplaning
débarquer to get off (an air-
    plane), **7.2**
déborder to overflow
debout standing, **8.2**
le **début** beginning (n.)
le **débutant, la débutante** begin-
    ner, **14.1**

le **décalage horaire** time
    difference
la **décapotable** convertible (car),
    12.1
décembre (m.) December, **4.1**
le **déchet** waste
décider (de) to decide (to)
déclarer to declare, call
décoller to take off (airplane),
    7.1
le **décor** set (for a play), **16.1**
le **décorateur (de porcelaine)**
    painter (of china)
la **découverte** discovery
découvrir to discover, **15**
décrire to describe
dédié(e) dedicated
défense de doubler no passing
    (traffic sign)
définir to define
la **définition** definition
le **degré** degree, **14.2**
    Il fait . . . degrés (Celsius).
        It's . . . degrees (Celsius).,
        14.2
dehors outside
    en dehors de outside (of)
déjà already, **14**
déjeuner to eat lunch, **5.2**
    le déjeuner lunch
délicieux, délicieuse delicious,
    10
le **delta** delta
demain tomorrow, **2.2**
    À demain. See you tomor-
        row., **BV**
demander to ask (for)
    se demander to wonder
demi(e) half
    à demi-tarif half-price
    et demie half past (time)
    le demi-cercle semi-circle;
        top of the key (on a
        basketball court), **13.2**
    le demi-kilo half a kilo
la **dent** tooth, **11.1**
    avoir mal aux dents to have
        a toothache, **15**
le **dentifrice** toothpaste, **11.1**
le **déodorant** deodorant, **11.1**
le **départ** departure, **7.1**
le **département d'outre-mer**
    French overseas department
dépendre (de) to depend (on)
dépenser to spend (money),
    10.1
la **dépression** low-pressure area
    (weather)
depuis since, for, **8.2**
dériver to derive

dernier, dernière last, **10**
derrière behind, **BV**
des some, any, **3**; **6**; of the,
    from the, **5**
désagréable unpleasant, **1.2**
descendre to get off, **8.2**; to
    take down, **8**; to go down,
    14.1
le **désert** desert
se **déshabiller** to get undressed
désirer to want
    Vous désirez? May I help
        you? (store); What would
        you like? (restaurant)
le **dessert** dessert
desservir to serve, fly to, etc.
    (transportation)
le **dessin** illustration
    le dessin animé cartoon,
        16.1
la **dessinatrice** illustrator
dessous: au-dessous smaller
    (size), **10.2**
dessus: au-dessus larger (size),
    10.2
la **destruction** destruction
le **détergent** detergent
détester to hate, **3.2**
deux two, **BV**
    les deux roues (f. pl.) two-
        wheeled vehicles
    tous (toutes) les deux both
deuxième second, **4.2**
    la Deuxième Guerre mondi-
        ale World War II
deuxièmement second of all,
    secondly
devant in front of, **BV**
le **développement** development
devenir to become, **16**
la **devise** currency
le **devoir** homework (assign-
    ment), **BV**
    faire les devoirs to do
        homework, **6**
le **diagnostic: faire un diagnostic**
    to diagnose, **15.2**
dicter to dictate
la **différence** difference
différent(e) different
difficile difficult, **2.1**
la **difficulté: être en difficulté** to
    be in trouble
dimanche (m.) Sunday, **2.2**
dîner to eat dinner, **4.2**
    le dîner dinner, **4.2**
la **diphtérie** diphtheria
diplômé(e): être diplômé(e) to
    graduate
dire to say, tell, **12.2**

la **direction** direction
diriger to direct
discuter to discuss
disparaître to disappear
le **disque** record, **3.2**
la **distance** distance
distingué(e) distinguished
le **distributeur automatique de billets** automated teller machine (ATM)
divisé(e) divided
le **divorce** divorce
dix ten, **BV**
dix-huit eighteen, **BV**
dix-neuf nineteen, **BV**
dix-sept seventeen, **BV**
le **docteur** doctor (title)
le **documentaire** documentary, **16.1**
le **dollar** dollar, **3.2**
le **domaine** domain, field
le **domicile: à domicile** to the home
donner to give, **3.2**
donner à manger à to feed
donner un coup de pied to kick, **13.1**
donner une fête to throw a party, **3.2**
donner sur to face, overlook, **17.1**
dormir to sleep, **7.2**
le **dortoir** dormitory
le **dos** back (body)
la **douane** customs, **7.2**
passer à la douane to go through customs, **7.2**
doublé(e) dubbed (movies), **16.1**
la **douche** shower
prendre une douche to take a shower, **11.1**
douloureux, douloureuse painful
douter to doubt
la **douzaine** dozen, **6.2**
douze twelve, **BV**
le **drame** drama, **16.1**
le **drap** sheet, **17.2**
le **drapeau** flag
dribbler to dribble (basketball), **13.2**
droite: à droite de to, on the right of, **5**
du of the, from the, **5**; some, any, **6**
du coin neighborhood (adj.)
du tout: pas du tout not at all
la **durée** length (of time)
durer to last

E

l' **eau (f.)** water
l'**eau minérale** mineral water, **6.2**
l' **échange (m.)** exchange
s'échapper to escape
l' **écharpe (f.)** scarf, **14.1**
l' **école (f.)** school, **1.2**
l'**école primaire** elementary school
l'**école secondaire** junior high, high school,
l' **écolier, l'écolière** pupil, schoolchild
l' **écologiste (m. et f.)** ecologist
les **économies (f. pl.): faire des économies** to save money, **18.2**
économique economical
la **classe économique** coach class (plane)
écouter to listen (to), **3.1**
l' **écran (m.)** screen, **7.1**
écrire to write, **12.2**
l' **écrivain (m.)** writer (m. and f.)
éducatif, éducative educational
l' **éducation (f.) civique** social studies, **2.2**
l' **éducation (f.) physique** physical education
efficace efficient
égaliser to tie (score)
l' **électricité (f.)** electricity
électrique electric
l' **élément (m.)** element
l' **élève (m. et f.)** student, **1.2**
élevé(e) high, **15.**
bien élevé(e) well brought-up
éliminer to eliminate
elle she, it, **1**; her (stress pron.), **9**
elles they (f.), **2**; them (stress pron.), **9**
l' **embarquement (m.)** boarding, leaving
embarquer to board (a plane, etc.), **7.2**
l' **embouteillage (m.)** traffic jam
émigrer to emigrate
l' **emploi (m.) du temps** schedule
l' **employé(e)** employee
emprunter to borrow, **18.2**
en of it, of them, etc., **18.2**; in; as
en avance early, ahead of time, **8.1**
en avion plane (adj.), by plane, **7.1**

en baisse coming down (in value)
en bas to, at the bottom
en ce moment right now
en classe in class
en commun in common
en dehors (de) outside (of)
en dehors de besides
en effet in fact
en exclusivité first run (movie)
en face de across from, opposite
en fait in fact
en fonction de in terms of, in accordance with
en général in general
en hausse going up (in value)
en haut de on top of
en plein(e) (+ nom) right in, on, etc. (+ noun)
en plein air outdoor(s)
en plus de besides, in addition
en première in first class, **8.1**
en provenance de arriving from (flight, train), **7.1**
en retard late, **8.2**
en seconde in second class, **8.1**
en solde on sale, **10.2**
en tout cas in any case
en version originale original language version, **16.1**
en ville in town, in the city
encore still (adv.); another; again
encourager to encourage
s'endormir to fall asleep, **11.1**
l' **endroit (m.)** place
l' **énergie (f.)** energy
énergique energetic, **1.2**
l' **enfant (m.)** child (m. and f.), **4.1**
enfin finally
l' **engrais (m.)** fertilizer
énormément enormously
l' **enquête (f.)** survey, opinion poll
enragé(e) rabid, enraged
enrhumé(e) to have a cold, **15.1**
l' **enseignement (m.)** teaching (n.)
ensemble together, **5.1**
ensuite then (adv.), **11.1**
entendre to hear, **8.1**
l' **enthousiasme (m.)** enthusiasm

entier, entière entire, whole, **10**

l' **entracte (m.)** intermission, **16.1**

entraîner to carry along

entre between, among, **9.2**

l' **entrée (f.)** entrance, **4.2**; admission

entrer to enter, **3.1**

l' **environnement (m.)** environment

envoyer to send, **13.1**

l' **épicerie (f.)** grocery store, **6.1**

l' **époque (f.)** period, times

l' **équilibre (m.)** balance

équilibré(e) balanced

l' **équipe (f.)** team, **13.1**

l' **équipement (m.)** equipment

l' **escalier (m.)** staircase, **17.1**

l' **espace (m.)** space

l' **Espagne (f.)** Spain, **16**

espagnol(e) Spanish (adj.)

l' **espagnol (m.)** Spanish (language), **2.2**

les **espèces (f. pl.): payer en espèces** to pay cash, **17.2**

l' **espionnage (m.)** spying (n.)

l' **essence (f.)** gas(oline), **12.1**

l' **essence ordinaire** regular gas

l' **essence super** super gas

l' **essence sans plomb** unleaded gas

essentiel(le) essential

essentiellement essentially

l' **est (m.)** east

estimer to consider

l' **estomac (m.)** stomach

et and, **1**

et toi? and you? (fam.), **BV**

établir to establish

l' **étage (m.)** floor (of a building), **4.2**

l' **étal (m.)** (market) stall

l' **état (m.)** state

les **États-Unis (m. pl.)** United States, **13.2**

l' **été (m.)** summer, **9.1**

en été in summer, **9.1**

éternuer to sneeze, **15.1**

étranger, étrangère foreign, **16.1**

à l'étranger abroad, in a foreign country

être to be, **2.1**

être à l'heure to be on time, **8.1**

être d'accord to agree, **2.1**

ne pas être dans son assiette to be feeling out of sorts, **15.2**

être en avance to be early, **8.1**

être en bonne (mauvaise) santé to be in good (poor) health, **15.1**

être en retard to be late, **8.2**

être enrhumé(e) to have a cold, **15.1**

être vite sur pied to be back on one's feet in no time, **15.2**

l' **être (m.) humain** human being

étroit(e) tight (shoes), narrow, **10.2**

l' **étudiant(e)** (university) student

étudier to study, **3.1**

européen(ne) European (adj.), **9**

eux them (m. pl. stress pron.), **9**

s' **évaporer** to evaporate

éventuellement possibly

évoquer to evoke

l' **examen (m.)** test, exam, **3.1**

passer un examen to take a test, **3.1**

réussir à un examen to pass a test, **7**

examiner to examine, **15.2**

excellent(e) excellent

exceptionnel(le) exceptional

l' **exemple (m.)** example

par exemple for example

s' **exercer** to practice

l' **expansion (f.)** expansion

l' **expédition (f.)** expedition

expliquer to explain

l' **explorateur (m.)** explorer

exposer to exhibit

l' **exposition (f.)** exhibit, show, **16.2**

l' **express (m.)** espresso, black coffee, **5.1**

exquis(e) exquisite

l' **extérieur (m.)** exterior, outside

extra terrific (informal), **2.2**

extraordinaire extraordinary

extrêmement extremely

F

fabriqué(e) made

fabriquer to make

fabuleux, fabuleuse fabulous

fâché(e) angry, **12.2**

facile easy, **2.1**

la **façon** way, manner

d'une façon générale in a general way

le **facteur** factor

la **facture** bill (hotel, etc.), **17.2**

facultatif, facultative elective

faire to do, make, **6.1**

faire des achats to shop, make purchases, **10.1**

faire de l'aérobic to do aerobics, **11.2**

faire l'annonce to announce

faire attention to pay attention, **6**; to be careful, **9.1**

faire une chute to fall, take a fall, **14.2**

faire la connaissance de to meet

faire les courses to do the grocery shopping, **6.1**

faire la cuisine to cook, **6**

faire les devoirs to do homework

faire un diagnostic to diagnose, **15.2**

faire du (+ nombre) to take size . . . , **10.2**

faire des économies to save money, **18.2**

faire enregistrer to check (luggage), **7.1**

faire des études to study, **6**

faire de l'exercice to exercise, **11.2**

faire du français (etc.) to study French (etc.), **6**

faire de la gymnastique to do gymnastics, **11.2**

faire du jogging to jog, **11.2**

faire le levé topographique to survey (land)

faire de la monnaie to make change, **18.1**

faire de la natation to swim, go swimming,

faire la navette to go back and forth

faire une ordonnance to write a prescription, **15.2**

faire partie de to be a part of

faire du patin to skate, **14.2**

faire du patin à glace to iceskate, **14.2**

faire du patin à roulettes to rollerskate

faire peur à to frighten

faire un pique-nique to have a picnic, **6**

faire de la planche à voile to go windsurfing, **9.1**

faire le plein to fill up (a gas tank), **12.1**

faire de la plongée sous-marine to go deep-sea diving, **9.1**

faire une promenade to take a walk, **9.1**
faire la queue to wait in line, **8.1**
faire un régime to go on a diet
faire du ski to ski, **14.1**
faire du ski nautique to waterski, **9.1**
faire du sport to play sports
faire du surf to go surfing, **9.1**
faire du surf des neiges to go snowboarding
faire les valises to pack (suitcases), **7.1**
faire un voyage to take a trip, **7.1**
le **fait** fact
la **famille** family, **4.1**
  la famille à parent unique single-parent family
le/la **fana** fan
fantaisiste whimsical
fantastique fantastic, **1.2**
fatigué(e) tired
fauché(e) broke (slang), **18.2**
faut: il faut (+ nom) (noun) is (are) necessary
  il faut + inf. one must, it is necessary to, **9.1**
faux, fausse false
favori(te) favorite, **10**
la **femme** woman, **2.1**; wife, **4.1**
la **fenêtre** window
  côté fenêtre (adj.) window (seat on plane, etc.), **7.1**
fermé(e) closed, **16.2**
la **fertilité** fertility
la **fête** party, **3.2**
  la Fête des Mères (Pères) Mother's (Father's) Day
le **feu** traffic light, **12.2**
  le feu orange yellow traffic light, **12.2**
  le feu rouge red light, **12.2**
  le feu vert green light, **12.2**
la **feuille** leaf
  la feuille de papier sheet of paper, **BV**
février (m.) February, **4.1**
la **fiche d'enregistrement** registration card (hotel), **17.1**
la **fièvre** fever, **15.1**
  la fièvre jaune yellow fever
  avoir une fièvre de cheval to have a high fever, **15.2**
la **figure** face, **11.1**
le **filet** net shopping bag, **6.1**; net (tennis, etc.), **9.2**; rack (train)

la **fille** girl, **BV**; daughter, **4.1**
le **film** film, movie, **16.1**
  le film d'amour love story, **16.1**
  le film d'aventures adventure movie, **16.1**
  le film étranger foreign film, **16.1**
  le film d'horreur horror film, **16.1**
  le film policier detective movie, **16.1**
  le film de science-fiction science-fiction movie, **16.1**
le **fils** son, **4.1**
fin(e) fine
finalement finally
fines herbes: aux fines herbes with herbs, **5.1**
finir to finish, **7**
fixe: à prix fixe at a fixed price
flambé(e) flaming
flâner to stroll
le **fleuve** river
flotter to float
la **fluctuation** fluctuation
le **foie** liver
  avoir mal au foie to have indigestion, **15**
la **fois** time (in a series)
le **fonctionnement** functioning (n.)
fonctionner to function, work
fond: au fond de at the bottom of
le **fondateur, la fondatrice** founder
fonder to found
le **foot(ball)** soccer, **13.1**
  le football américain football
la **force** force, power
le **forcing: faire le forcing** to put pressure on
la **forêt** forest
le **forfait-journée** lift ticket (skiing)
la **forme** form, shape
  la forme (physique) physical fitness
  le club de forme health club, **11.2**
  être en forme to be in shape, **11.2**
  rester en forme to stay in shape, **11.2**
  se mettre en forme to get in shape, **11.2**
former to form; to train
le **formulaire** form, data sheet
la **formule** formula

fort (adv.) hard, **9.2**
fort(e) strong; good
le **fort** fort
fou, folle crazy
le **foulard** scarf
la **foule: venir en foule** to crowd (into)
la **fourchette** fork, **5.2**
la **fourmi** ant
les **frais (m. pl.)** expenses, charges, **17.2**
le **franc** franc, **18.1**
français(e) French (adj.), **1.1**
  le français French (language), **2.2**
  le Français, la Française Frenchman, Frenchwoman
la **France** France, **16**
franchement frankly
francophone French-speaking
frapper to hit, **9.2**
freiner to brake, put on the brakes, **12.1**
fréquemment frequently
fréquent(e) frequent
fréquenter to frequent, patronize
le **frère** brother, **1.2**
le **fric** money, dough (slang), **18.2**
  avoir plein de fric to have lots of money (slang), **18.2**
les **frissons (m. pl.)** chills, **15.1**
les **frites (f. pl.)** French fries, **5.1**
froid(e) cold, **14.2**
  avoir froid to be cold
  Il fait froid. It's cold (weather)., **9.2**
le **fromage** cheese, **5.1**
le **front** front (weather)
la **frontière** border
le **fruit** fruit, **6.2**
  les fruits (m. pl.) de mer seafood
fumer to smoke
  fumeurs smoking (section), **7.1**
  non fumeurs no smoking (section), **7.1**
furieux, furieuse furious
la **fusée** rocket
le **futur** future

G

la **galaxie** galaxy
le **gagnant, la gagnante** winner, **13.2**
gagner to earn, **3.2**; to win, **9.2**
le **galet** pebble
le **Gange** Ganges River
le **gant** glove, **14.1**

le **gant de toilette** washcloth, **17.2**
le **garage** garage, **4.2**
le **garçon** boy, **BV**
garder to guard
le **gardien de but** goalie, **13.1**
la **gare** train station, **8.1**
garer la voiture to park the
car, **12.2**
gastronomique gastronomic,
gourmet
le **gâteau** cake, **6.1**
gauche: à gauche de to, on the
left of, **5**
le **gaz** gas
geler to freeze
Il gèle. It's freezing
(weather)., **14.2**
le **gendarme** police officer
général(e) general (adj.)
en général in general
le **général** general (n.), **7**
généralement generally
généraliser to generalize
généreux, généreuse generous,
10
la **générosité** generosity
le **genre** type, kind, **16.1**
les **gens (m. pl.)** people
gentil(le) nice (person), **9**
la **géographie** geography, **2.2**
la **géométrie** geometry, **2.2**
géométrique geometric
la **glace** ice cream, **5.1**; mirror,
11.1; ice, **14.2**
glisser to slip, slide
le **globe** globe
la **glucide** carbohydrate
le **golfe** gulf
la **gorge** throat, **15.1**
avoir la gorge qui gratte to
have a scratchy throat, **15.1**
avoir un chat dans la gorge
to have a frog in one's
throat, **15.2**
avoir mal à la gorge to have
a sore throat, **15.1**
le **gouvernement** government
grâce à thanks to
le **gradin** bleacher (stadium),
13.1
la **graisse** fat
la graisse animale animal
fat
le **gramme** gram, **6.2**
grand(e) tall, big, **1.1**
le **grand couturier** clothing
designer, **10.1**
le **grand magasin** department store, **10.1**

de grand standing (adj.)
luxury
les **Grands Lacs (m. pl.)** the
Great Lakes
la **Grande-Bretagne** Great
Britain, **16**
grandir to grow (up) (children)
la **grand-mère** grandmother, **4.1**
le **grand-père** grandfather, **4.1**
les **grands-parents (m. pl.)** grandparents, **4.1**
grave serious
la **Grèce** Greece
la **griffe** label
le **grill-express** snack bar (train)
la **grippe** flu, **15.1**
gris(e) gray, **10.2**
grossir to gain weight, **11.2**
la **Guadeloupe** Guadeloupe
la **guerre: la Deuxième Guerre
mondiale** World War II
le **guichet** ticket window, **8.1**; box
office, **16.1**
le **guide** guidebook, **12.2**
le **gymnase** gym(nasium), **11.2**
la **gymnastique** gymnastics, **2.2**
faire de la gymnastique to
do gymnastics, **11.2**

H

le **H.L.M.** low-income housing
habillé(e) dressy, **10.1**
s' **habiller** to get dressed, **11.1**
l' **habitant(e)** resident
habiter to live (in a city, house,
etc.), **3.1**
les **haricots (m. pl.) verts** green
beans, **6.2**
haut(e) high, **10.2**
avoir . . . mètres de haut to
be . . . meters high
du haut de from the top of
à talons hauts high-heeled
(shoes)
le **haut-parleur** loudspeaker, **8.1**
la **haute couture** high fashion
le **héros** hero
l' **heure (f.)** time (of day), **2**
à quelle heure? at what
time?, **2**
À tout à l'heure. See you
later., **BV**
de bonne heure early
être à l'heure to be on time,
8.1
Il est quelle heure? What
time is it?, **2**
heureux, heureuse happy, **10.2**
l' **hexagone (m.)** hexagon

hier yesterday, **13.1**
avant hier the day before
yesterday, **13**
hier matin yesterday morning, **13**
hier soir last night, **13**
l' **histoire (f.)** history, **2.2**
l' **hiver (m.)** winter, **14.1**
en hiver in winter, **14.2**
le **hockey** hockey
le hockey sur glace ice
hockey
la **Hollande** Holland, The Netherlands, **16**
l' **homme (m.)** man, **2.1**
les **honoraires (m. pl.)** fees
(doctor)
l' **hôpital (m.)** hospital
l' **horaire (m.)** schedule, time-
table, **8.1**
hors des limites out of
bounds, **9.2**
l' **hôtel (m.)** hotel, **17.1**
l' **hôtesse (f.) de l'air** flight
attendant (f.), **7.2**
huit eight, **BV**
humain(e) human
humide wet, humid,
humoristique humorous
l' **hydrate (m.) de carbone** carbohydrate
hystérique hysterical

I

idéal(e) ideal
l' **idée (f.)** idea
identifier to identify
il he, it, **1**
Il est quelle heure? What
time is it?, **2**
Il est . . . heure(s). It's . . .
o'clock., **2**
il faut (+ nom) (noun) is
(are) needed
il faut + inf. it is necessary,
one must, **9.1**
Il n'y a pas de quoi. You're
welcome., **BV**
il vaut mieux it is better
il y a there is, there are,
4.2
l' **île (f.)** island
illustré(e) illustrated
ils they (m.), **2**
l' **immeuble (m.)** apartment
building, **4.2**
l' **immigration (f.)** immigration,
7.2

passer à l'immigration to go through immigration (airport), **7.2**

impatient(e) impatient, **1.1**

important(e) important

les **Impressionnistes (m. pl.)** Impressionists (painters)

inauguré(e) inaugurated

inclure to include

inconnu(e) unknown

incroyable incredible

l' **Inde (f.)** India

l' **indication (f.)** cue

indiquer to indicate

l' **industrie (f.)** industry

infectieux, infectieuse infectious

l' **infection (f.)** infection, **15.1**

infiltrer to seep (into)

influencer to influence

l' **informatique (f.)** computer science, **2.2**

l' **inondation (f.)** flood

l' **institut (m.)** institute

l' **institution (f.)** institution

les **instructions (f. pl.)** instructions, **9.1**

l' **instrument (m.)** instrument

intelligent(e) intelligent, **1.1**

interdit(e) forbidden, prohibited

Il est interdit de stationner. Parking is prohibited., **12.2**

intéressant(e) interesting, **1.1**

intéresser to interest

s'intéresser à to be interested in

l' **intérieur (m.)** interior, inside

intérieur(e) domestic (flight) (adj.), **7.1**

international(e) international, **7.1**

inviter to invite, **3.2**

isoler to isolate

l' **Italie (f.)** Italy, **16**

italien(ne) Italian (adj.), **9**

J

jamais ever

ne ... jamais never

le **jambon** ham, **5.1**

janvier (m.) January, **4.1**

le **Japon** Japan, **16**

japonais(e) Japanese (adj.)

le **jardin** garden, **4.2**

jaune yellow, **10.2**

je I, **1.2**

Je t'en prie. You're welcome (fam.)., **BV**

je voudrais I would like, **5.1**

Je vous en prie. You're welcome (form.)., **BV**; please, I beg of you

le **jean** jeans, **10.1**

jeter to throw

le **jeu: les jeux de la lumière** play of light

jeudi (m.) Thursday, **2.2**

jeune young, **4.1**

les jeunes (m. pl.) young people

la jeune fille girl

le **jogging: faire du jogging** to jog, **11.2**

joli(e) pretty, **4.2**

jouer to play, to perform, **16.1**

jouer à (un sport) to play (a sport), **9.2**

le **joueur** player, **9.2**

le **jour** day, **2.2**

C'est quel jour? What day is it?, **2.2**

de nos jours today, nowadays

par jour a (per) day, **3**

tous les jours every day

le **journal** newspaper, **8.1**

le journal intime diary

le journal télévisé newscast

la **journée** day

juillet (m.) July, **4.1**

juin (m.) June, **4.1**

la **jupe** skirt, **10.1**

la **jupette** tennis skirt, **9.2**

le **Jura** Jura Mountains

le **jury** selection committee

jusqu'à (up) to, until, **13.2**

jusqu'en bas de la piste to the bottom of the trail

K

le **kilo(gramme)** kilogram, **6.2**

le **kilomètre** kilometer

le **kiosque** newsstand, **8.1**

le **kleenex** tissue, Kleenex, **15.1**

L

la the (f.), **1**; her, it (dir. obj.), **16**

là there

là-bas over there, **BV**

le **laboratoire** laboratory

le **lac** lake

les **Grands Lacs (m. pl.)** the Great Lakes

laisser to leave (something behind)

laisser un pourboire to leave a tip, **5.2**

le **lait** milk, **6.1**

la **laitue** lettuce, **6.2**

lancer to throw, **13.2**

la **langue** language, **2.2**

large loose, wide, **10.2**

le **latin** Latin, **2.2**

la **latitude** latitude

laver to wash, **11.1**

se laver to wash oneself, **11.1**

se laver les cheveux (la figure, etc.) to wash one's hair (face, etc.), **11**

le the (m.), **1**; him, it (dir. obj.), **16.1**

la **leçon** lesson, **9.1**

la leçon de conduite driving lesson, **12.2**

la **lecture** reading

légendaire legendary

la **légende** legend

le **légume** vegetable, **6.2**

lent(e) slow

lentement slowly

les the (pl.), **2**; them (dir. obj.), **16**

leur their (sing. poss. adj.), **5**

leur (to) them (ind. obj.), **17**

leurs their (pl. poss. adj.), **5**

levant rising

le **levé: faire le levé topographique** to survey

se **lever** to get up, **11.1**

le **lexique** vocabulary

libre free, **2.2**

le **lieu** place

avoir lieu to take place

la **ligne** line

les lignes de banlieue commuter trains

les grandes lignes main lines (trains)

la **limitation de vitesse** speed limit

les **limites (f. pl.)** boundaries (on tennis court), **9.2**

hors des limites out of bounds, **9.2**

la **limonade** lemon-lime drink

la **lipide** fat (n.)

lire to read, **12.2**

Lisbonne Lisbon

le **lit** bed, **8.2**

le **litre** liter, **6.2**

littéraire literary

la **littérature** literature, **2.2**

la **livre** pound, **6.2**

le **livre** book, **BV**

la **location** rental

loin de far from, **4.2**

les **loisirs (m. pl.)** leisure activities, **16**

Londres London

le **long de** along

long(ue) long, **10.2**

la **longueur** length

la **longitude** longitude

longtemps (for) a long time

lorsque while

louer to rent

lourd(e) heavy

lui him (m. sing. stress pron.), **9**; (to) him, (to) her (ind. obj.), **17.1**

la **lumière** light (n.)

lundi (m.) Monday, **2.2**

les **lunettes (f. pl.)** goggles, **14.1**

les **lunettes de soleil** sunglasses, **9.1**

lutter to fight

le **luxe** luxury

luxueux, luxueuse luxurious

le **lycée** high school, **1.2**

le **lycéen, la lycéenne** high school student

M

ma my (f. sing. poss. adj.), **4**

Madame (Mme) Mrs., Ms., **BV**

Mademoiselle (Mlle) Miss, Ms., **BV**

le **magasin** store, **3.2**

le **magazine** magazine, **3.2**

magnifique magnificent

mai (m.) May, **4.1**

maigrir to lose weight, **11.2**

le **maillot de bain** bathing suit, **9.1**

la **main** hand, **11.1**

maintenant now, **2**

mais but, **1**

Mais oui (non)! Of course (not)!

la **maison** house, **3.1**

le **maître** master

le **maître d'hôtel** maitre d', **5.2**

mal badly

avoir mal à to have a(n) . . . -ache, to hurt, **15.1**

Où avez-vous mal? Where does it hurt?, **15.2**

le/la **malade** sick person, **15.1**

malade sick, **15.1**

la **maladie** illness

malheureusement unfortunately

la **Manche** English Channel

la **manche** sleeve, **10.1**

à manches longues (courtes) long- (short-) sleeved, **10.1**

manger to eat

la **manière** manner, way

avoir de bonnes manières to have good manners

manquer: il en manque deux two are missing

se **maquiller** to put on make-up, **11.1**

le **marathon** marathon

le **marchand, la marchande (de fruits et légumes)** (produce) seller, **6.2**

la **marchandise** merchandise

le **marché** market, **6.2**

le **Marché Commun** Common Market

mardi (m.) Tuesday, **2.2**

la **marée** tide

le **mari** husband, **4.1**

le **mariage** marriage

marié(e) married

le **marin** sailor

le **Maroc** Morocco, **16**

la **marque** make (of car), **12.1**

marquer un but to score a goal, **13.1**

marron (inv.) brown, **10.2**

mars (m.) March, **4.1**

la **Martinique** Martinique

martiniquais(e) from Martinique

la **masse** mass

le **match** game, **9.2**

les **mathématiques (f. pl.)** mathematics

les **maths (f. pl.)** math, **2.2**

la **matière** subject (school), **2.2**; matter

le **matin** morning, in the morning, **2**

du matin A.M. (time), **2**

mauvais(e) bad; wrong

Il fait mauvais. It's bad weather., **9.2**

le **mazout** fuel oil

me (to) me (dir. and ind. obj.), **15.2**

le **médecin** doctor (m. and f.), **15.2**

chez le médecin at, to the doctor's, **15.2**

la **médecine** medicine (medical profession), **15**

médical(e) medical

le **médicament** medicine (remedy), **15.2**

meilleur(e) better (adj.), **10**

le **membre** member

même same (adj.), **2.1**; even (adv.)

le/la **mennonite** Mennonite

mental(e) mental

le **menu: le menu touristique** budget (fixed price) meal

la **mer** sea, **9.1**

la **mer des Caraïbes** Caribbean Sea

la **mer Méditerranée** Mediterranean Sea

merci thank you, **BV**

mercredi (m.) Wednesday, **2.2**

la **mère** mother, **4.1**

le **méridien** meridian

merveilleux, merveilleuse marvelous, **10.2**

mes my (pl. poss. adj.), **4**

la **mesure** measurement

mesurer to measure

le **métabolisme** metabolism

la **météo** weather forecast

la **météorologie** meteorology, the study of weather

météorologique meteorological

le **métier** profession

le **mètre** meter

métrique metric

le **métro** subway, **4.2**

en métro by subway, **5.2**

la **station de métro** subway station, **4.2**

mettre to put (on), to place, **8.1**; to put on (clothes), **10**; to turn on (appliance), **10**

mettre au point to come out with, develop

mettre de l'argent de côté to put money aside, save, **18.2**

se **mettre en forme** to get in shape, **11.1**

mettre le contact to start the car **12.1**

mettre le couvert to set the table, **8**

le **Mexique** Mexico, **16**

la **mi-temps** half (sporting event)

le **microbe** microbe

la **microbiologie** microbiology

le **microscope** microscope

midi (m.) noon, **2.2**

militaire military

le **militaire** soldier
mille (one) thousand, **6.2**
les **milliers (m. pl.)** thousands
le **minéral** mineral
le **ministère** ministry
minuit (m.) midnight, **2.2**
la **mission** mission
moche terrible, ugly, **2.2**
le **modèle** model
moderne modern
moderniser to modernize
modeste modest, reasonably
  priced
moi me (stress pron.), **9**
moins less
  moins . . . que less . . . than
  Il est une heure moins dix.
    It's ten to one (time)., **2**
  au moins at least
le **mois** month, **4.1**
le **moment: en ce moment** right
  now
mon my (m. sing. poss. adj.),
  4
le **monde** world
  beaucoup de monde a lot of
    people, **13.1**
  tout le monde everyone,
    everybody, **BV**
le **moniteur, la monitrice** instructor, **9.1**; camp counselor
la **monnaie** change; currency,
  18.1
  faire de la monnaie to make
    change, **18.1**
Monsieur (M.) Mr., sir, **BV**
la **montagne** mountain, **14.1**
  à la montagne in the
    mountains
monter to go up, get on, in,
  8.2; to take upstairs, **17.1**
  monter une pièce to put on
    a play, **16.1**
montrer to show, **17.1**
moral(e) moral
le **morceau de craie** piece of
  chalk, **BV**
mordu(e) bitten
mort(e) dead
la **mort** death
mortel(le) fatal
Moscou Moscow
le **mot** word
  le mot apparenté cognate
le **motard** motorcycle cop, **12.2**
le **moteur** engine (car, etc.), **12.1**
la **moto** motorcycle, **12.1**
le **mouchoir** handkerchief, **15.1**
mourir to die, **17**
la **moutarde** mustard, **6.2**
le **mouvement** movement

mouvementé(e) eventful
moyen(ne) average, inter-
  mediate
le **moyen de transport** mode of
  transportation
municipal(e) municipal
musclé(e) muscular
le **musée** museum, **16.2**
la **musique** music, **2.2**
la **mythologie** mythology

N

n'est-ce pas? isn't it, doesn't it
  (he, she, etc.)?, **1.2**
nager to swim, **9.1**
  nager la brasse papillon to
    do the butterfly (swim
    stroke)
le **nageur, la nageuse** swimmer
naître to be born, **17**
la **nappe** tablecloth, **5.2**
la **natation** swimming, **9.1**
la **nation** nation
national(e) national
la **nature** nature
nature plain (adj.), **5.1**
ne . . . jamais never, **12**
ne . . . pas not, **1.2**
ne . . . personne no one,
  nobody, **12.2**
ne . . . rien nothing, **12.2**
né: il est né he was born
nécessaire necessary
négatif, négative negative
la **neige** snow, **14.2**
  Il neige. It's snowing., **14.2**
nerveux, nerveuse nervous
  les cellules nerveuses nerve
    cells
neuf nine, **BV**
neutraliser to neutralize
le **neveu** nephew, **4.1**
le **nez** nose, **15.1**
  avoir le nez qui coule to
    have a runny nose, **15.1**
ni . . . ni neither . . . nor
la **nièce** niece, **4.1**
le **niveau** level
  vérifier les niveaux to check
    under the hood, **12.1**
noir(e) black, **10.2**
  le tableau noir blackboard,
    3.1
le **nom** name, **16.2**; noun
le **nombre** number, **5.2**
nombreux, nombreuse
  numerous
nommer to name, mention
non no

non fumeurs no smoking
  (section), **7.1**
non seulement not only
le **nord** north
normal(e) normal
normalement normally, usually
nos our (pl. poss. adj.), **5**
la **nostalgie** nostalgia
la **note** bill (currency), **17.2**;
  grade
notre our (sing. poss. adj.), **5**
nourrir to feed
la **nourriture** food, nutrition
nous we, **2**; us (stress pron.),
  9; (to) us (dir. and ind. obj.),
  15
nouveau (nouvel) new (m.), **4**
nouvelle new (f.), **4**
les **nouvelles (f. pl.)** news
novembre (m.) November, **4.1**
le **nuage** cloud, **9.2**
la **nuit** night
le **numéro** number
  **Quel est le numéro de télé-
    phone de . . . ?** What is
    the phone number of . . . ?,
    5.2

O

obéir(à) to obey, **7**
l' **objet (m.)** object
obligatoire mandatory
obliger to oblige
obtenir to obtain
occupé(e) busy, **2.2**
occuper to occupy
l' **océan (m.)** ocean
octobre (m.) October, **4.1**
l' **odeur (f.)** scent, smell
l' **œil (m., pl. yeux)** eye
l' **œuf (m.)** egg, **6.2**
  l'œuf sur le plat fried egg
l' **œuvre (f.)** work (of art), **16**
officiel(le) official
offrir to offer, give, **15**
l' **oignon (m.)** onion, **6.2**
l' **omelette (f.)** omelette, **5.1**
  l'omelette aux fines herbes
    omelette with herbs, **5.1**
  l'omelette nature plain
    omelette, **5.1**
on we, they, people, **3**
  On y va (?) Let's go; Shall
    we go?, **5.**
l' **oncle (m.)** uncle, **4.1**
onze eleven, **BV**
l' **opéra (m.)** opera, **16.1**
opérer to operate
opposer to oppose, **13.1**

l' **or** (m.) gold
orange (inv.) orange (color), **10**
l' **orange** (f.) orange (n.), **6.2**
l' **Orangina** (m.) orange soda, **5.1**
ordinaire regular (gasoline), **12.1**
l' **ordinateur** (m.) computer, **BV**
l' **ordonnance** (f.) prescription, **15.2**
   faire une ordonnance to write a prescription, **15.2**
l' **oreille** (f.) ear, **15.1**
   avoir mal aux oreilles to have an earache, **15.**
l' **oreiller** (m.) pillow, **17.2**
les **oreillons** (m. pl.) mumps
organisé(e) organized
l' **organisme** (m.) organism
l' **origine** (f.): **à l'origine** originally
original(e) original
orner to decorate
l' **os** (m.) bone
ôter to take off (clothing)
ou or, **1.1**
où where, **BV**
oublier to forget
l' **ouest** (m.) west
oui yes, **1**
ouvert(e) open, **16**
l' **ouverture** (f.) opening
l' **ouvrier** (m.) worker
ouvrir to open, **15**
ovale oval
l' **oxygène** (m.) oxygen

P

le **pain** bread, **6.1**
la **paire** pair, **10**
le **palais** palace
le **panier** basket, **13.2**
le **panneau** backboard (basketball), **13.2**; road sign
panoramique panoramic
le **pantalon** pants, **10.1**
la **papeterie** stationery store
le **papier** paper, **6**
   le papier hygiénique toilet paper, **17.2**
   la feuille de papier sheet of paper, **BV**
le **paquet** package, **6.2**
par dessus over (prep.), **13**
par exemple for example
par jour a (per) day, **3**
par semaine a (per) week, **3.2**
le **paragraphe** paragraph

le **parallèle** parallel
le **parc** park (n.), **11.2**
parce que because, **9.1**
parcourir to travel, go through
pardon excuse me, pardon me
le **parebrise** windshield, **12**
les **parents** (m. pl.) parents, **4.1**
parfait(e) perfect
parisien(ne) Parisian, **9**
le **parking** parking lot
le **parlement** parliament
parler to speak, talk, **3.1**
   parler au téléphone to talk on the phone, **3.2**
parmi among
participer (à) to participate (in)
particulièrement particularly
la **partie** game, match, **9.2**; part
   la partie en simple (en double) singles (doubles) match (tennis), **9.2**
   faire partie de to be a part of
partir to leave, **7.1**
partout everywhere
pas not
   pas de no (+ noun)
   Pas de quoi. You're welcome (inform.), **BV**
   pas du tout not at all
   pas mal not bad, **BV**
   pas mal de quite a few
le **passager, la passagère** passenger, **7.1**
le **passé** past (n.)
le **passeport** passport, **7.1**
passer to spend (time), **3**; **to pass, go through, 7.2**; to show (a movie), **16.1**
   passer à la douane to go through customs, **7.2**
   passer à l'immigration to go through immigration
   passer par le contrôle de sécurité to go through security (airport), **7**
   passer un examen to take an exam, **3.1**
   passer un film to show a movie, **16.1**
passionné(e) de excited by
passionner to excite
le **pâté** pâté, **5.1**
patient(e) patient (adj.), **1.1**
le **patin à glace** ice skate (n.), **14.2**
   faire du patin to skate, **14.2**
   faire du patin à glace to iceskate, **14.2**

   faire du patin à roulettes to rollerskate
le **patinage** skating, **14.2**
le **patineur, la patineuse** skater, **14.2**
la **patinoire** skating rink, **14.2**
le/la **pauvre** poor thing, **15.1**
pauvre poor, **15.1**
le **pavillon** small house, bungalow
payer to pay, **6.1**
   payer en espèces to pay cash, **17.**
le **pays** country, **7.1**
les **Pays-Bas** (m. pl.) the Netherlands, **16**
le **paysage** landscape
le **peigne** comb
   se peigner to comb (one's hair), **11.1**
peindre to paint
le/la **peintre** painter, artist, **16.2**
la **peinture** painting (n.), **16.2**
péjoratif, péjorative pejorative, disparaging
le **penalty** penalty (soccer)
pendant during, for (time), **3.2**
   pendant que while
la **pénicilline** penicillin, **15.2**
penser to think, **10.1**
la **pension** small hotel
perdre to lose, **8.2**
   perdre patience to lose patience, **8.2**
   perdre des kilos to lose weight
le **père** father, **4.1**
la **périphérie** outskirts
la **perle** pearl
permettre to permit, allow, **14**
le **permis** permit
   le permis de conduire driver's license, **12.2**
le **personnage** character
la **personne** person
   ne . . . personne no one, nobody
personnel(le) personal
le **personnel de bord** flight attendants, **7.2**
personnellement personally, **16.2**
la **perte** loss
peser to weigh
petit(e) short, small, **1.1**
   la petite annonce classified ad
   le petit déjeuner breakfast, **9**
   prendre le petit déjeuner to eat breakfast, **9**

le **petit-fils** grandson, **4.1**
la **petite-fille** granddaughter, **4.1**
le **pétrolier** oil tanker
peu (de) few, little, **18**
    un peu (de) a little
la **pharmacie** pharmacy, **15.2**
le **pharmacien, la pharmacienne**
    pharmacist, **15.2**
la **photo** photograph
la **phrase** sentence
la **physique** physics, **2.2**
    physique physical
        la forme physique physical
            fitness, **13**
la **pièce** room, **4.2**; play, **16.1**;
    coin, **18.1**
le **pied** foot, **13.1**
    à pied on foot, **5.2**
la **pierre** stone
le **piéton, la piétonne** pedestrian,
    12.2
le/la **pilote** pilot
le/la **pilote de ligne** airline pilot
    piloter to pilot
la **piscine** pool, **9.2**
    la piscine couverte indoor
        pool
la **piste** track, **13.2**; ski trail, **14.1**
    pittoresque picturesque
le **placard** closet, **17.2**
la **place** seat (plane, etc.), **7.1**;
    parking space, **12.2**; place
la **plage** beach, **9.1**
la **plaine** plain (n.)
le **plan** map
la **planche à voile: faire de la**
    planche à voile to windsurf,
    9.1
la **plante** plant
    les plantes aquatiques
        aquatic vegetation
le **plastique: en plastique** plastic
    (adj.)
le **plateau** plateau
    plein(e) full, **13.1**
        avoir plein de fric to have
            lots of money (slang), **18.2**
        en pleine zone tempérée
            right in the temperate zone
        faire le plein to fill up (a gas
            tank), **12.1**
    pleut (inf. pleuvoir): Il pleut.
        It's raining., **9**
la **plongée sous-marine: faire de**
    la plongée sous-marine to
    go deep-sea diving, **9.1**
    plonger to dive, **9.1**
la **pluie** rain
    les pluies (f. pl.) acides
        acid rain
la **plupart (des)** most (of), **8.2**

le **pluriel** plural
plus more (comparative), **10**
    plus tard later
    en plus de in addition to
plusieurs several, **18**
le **pneu** tire, **12.1**
    le pneu à plat flat tire **12.1**
la **poche** pocket, **18.1**
la **poésie** poetry
le **poème** poem
le/la **poète** poet
le **poids** weight
le **point** point; period
la **pointure** size (shoes), **10.2**
    Vous faites quelle pointure?
        What (shoe) size do you
        take?, **10.2**
le **poisson** fish, **6.1**
la **poissonnerie** fish store, **6.1**
le **pôle** pole
la **poliomyélite** polio
    polluer to pollute
la **pollution** pollution
la **pomme** apple, **6.2**
la **pomme de terre** potato, **6.2**
le/la **pompiste** gas station attendant,
    12.1
    populaire popular, **1.2**
la **porcelaine** porcelaine, china
le **port: le port de pêche** fishing
    port
la **porte** gate (airport), **7.1**; door,
    17.1
le **porte-monnaie** change purse,
    18.1
le **portefeuille** wallet, **18.1**
    porter to wear, **10.1**
le **porteur** porter, **8.1**
le **portrait** portrait
le **Portugal** Portugal, **16**
    poser une question to ask a
        question, **3.1**
la **possibilité** possibility
le **pot** jar, **6.2**
le **pouce** inch, thumb
le **poulet** chicken, **6.1**
    pour for; in order to, **2**
le **pourboire** tip (restaurant), **5.2**
    laisser un pourboire to
        leave a tip, **5.2**
le **pourcentage** percentage
    pourquoi why, **9.1**
    pourtant yet, still, nevertheless
    pouvoir to be able to, **6**
    pratiquer un sport to play a
        sport, **11.2**
    précieux, précieuse precious
    précis(e) precise, exact
        à l'heure précise right on
            time
    préféré(e) favorite

préférer to prefer, **5**
le **préfixe** prefix
premier, première first, **4.1**
    en première in first class,
        8.1
premièrement first of all
les **tout premiers** very first
    prendre to take, **9.1**
        prendre des kilos to gain
            weight
        prendre le petit déjeuner to
            eat breakfast, **9**
        prendre le train (etc.) to
            take the train (etc.), **9**
        prendre part à to take part
            in
        prendre possession de to
            take possession of
        prendre rendez-vous to
            make an appointment
        prendre un bain (une
            douche) to take a bath
            (shower), **11.1**
        prendre un bain de soleil to
            sunbathe, **9.1**
        prendre un billet to buy a
            ticket, **9**
        prendre un pot to have a
            drink
    préparer to prepare, **4.2**
    près de near, **4.2**
    prescrire to prescribe **15.2**
    présenter to present, introduce
la **préservation** preservation
    presque almost
    pressé(e) in a hurry
la **pression artérielle** blood
    pressure
    prêt(e) ready
        prêt-à-porter ready-to-wear
            (adj.), **10**
        le rayon prêt-à-porter
            ready-to-wear department,
            10.1
    prêter to lend, **18.2**
la **preuve** proof
    prévoir to predict
    primaire: l'école (f.) primaire
        elementary school,
    principal(e) main, principal
le **printemps** spring, **13.2**
    pris(e) taken, **5.1**
    privé(e) private
le **prix** price, cost, **10.1**
        à prix fixe at a fixed price
    probablement probably
le **problème** problem, **11.2**
    prochain(e) next, **8.2**
le **produit** product
le/la **prof** teacher (inform.), **2.1**

le **professeur (m.)** teacher (m. and f.), **2.1**

professionnel(le) professional

profiter de to take advantage of, profit from

profond(e) deep

le **programme** TV program

le **progrès** progress

progressif, progressive progressive

le **projet** project, plan

la **promenade: faire une promenade** to take a walk, **9.1**

se **promener** to walk, **11.2**

proposer to suggest

propre clean; own (adj.)

protéger to protect

la **protéine** protein

provenance: en provenance de arriving from (train, plane, etc.), **7.1**

provençal(e) from Provence, the south of France

les **provisions (f. pl.)** groceries

prudemment carefully, **12.2**

le **public** public (n.)

la **publicité** advertisement

les **Puces: le Marché aux Puces** flea market

puissant(e) powerful

le **pull** sweater, **10.1**

punir to punish, **7**

pur(e) pure

la **pureté** purity

la **pyramide** pyramid

Q

Qu'est-ce que c'est? What is it?, **BV**

Qu'est-ce qu'il a? What's wrong with him?, **15.1**

le **quai** platform (railroad), **8.1**

la **qualité** quality

quand when, **3.1**

quarante forty, **BV**

le **quart: et quart** a quarter past (time), **2**

moins le quart a quarter to (time), **2**

le **quartier** neighborhood, district, **4.2**

quatorze fourteen, **BV**

quatre four, **BV**

quatre-vingt-dix ninety, **5.2**

quatre-vingts eighty, **5.2**

quel(le) which, what, **7**

Quel est le numéro de téléphone de . . . ? What is the phone number of . . . ?, **5.2**

Quelle est la date aujourd'hui? What is today's date?, **4.1**

Quel temps fait-il? What's the weather like?, **9.2**

quelque some

quelque chose à manger something to eat, **5.1**

quelquefois sometimes, **5**

quelques some, **8.2**

la **question: poser une question** to ask a question, **3.1**

la **queue: faire la queue** to wait in line, **8.1**

qui who, **BV**; whom, **11.**; which, that

Qui ça? Who (do you mean)?, **BV**

Qui est-ce? Who is it?, **BV**

quinze fifteen, **BV**

quitter to leave (a room, etc.), **3.1**

quoi what (after prep.), **14**

R

raconter to tell (about)

le **racquet(-ball)** racquetball

la **radio** radio, **3.2**

radioactif, radioactive radioactive

la **rage** rabies

raide steep, **14.2**

la **raison** reason

ralentir to slow down

le **randonneur, la randonneuse** hiker

rapide quick, fast

le **rapport** relationship; report

rapporter to report

la **raquette** racket, **9.2**

rare rare

se **raser** to shave, **11.1**

le **rasoir** razor, shaver

rassembler to collect, gather together

le **rayon** department (in a store), **10.1**

la **réaction** reaction

réaliser to realize (an ambition), achieve

la **réalité** reality

la **réception** front desk (hotel), **17.1**

le/la **réceptionniste** desk clerk, **17.1**

recevoir to receive, **18.1**

la **recherche: faire de la recherche** to do research

recommandé(e) recommended

reconnu(e) recognized

la **récréation** recess

récrire to rewrite

récupérer to claim (luggage), **7.2**

refléter to reflect

regarder to look at, **3.1**

se **regarder** to look at oneself, look at one another

la **région** region

la **règle** rule

le **règlement** rule

régler to direct (traffic)

regretter to be sorry

régulier, régulière regular

régulièrement regularly

relativement relatively

le **relevé de compte** statement (bank), **18**

remarquer to notice

rembourser to pay back, reimburse, **18.2**

remplir to fill out, **7.2**

la **rencontre** meeting

rencontrer to meet

le **rendez-vous: prendre rendez-vous** to make an appointment

rendre to give back, **18.2**

les **renseignements (m. pl.)** information

rentrer to go home, **3.1**

renvoyer to return (tennis ball), **9.2**

la **répartition** distribution

le **repas** meal

répéter to repeat

répondre to answer, **8**

la **réponse** answer

se **reposer** to rest

repoussé(e) pushed back

représenter to represent

la **reprise** reshowing

reproduire to reproduce

la **république** republic, democracy

la **réserve** reserve, supply

réservé(e) reserved

réserver to reserve

le **réservoir** gas tank, **12.1**

résidentiel(le) residential

la **résistance** resistance

respecter to respect

la **respiration** breathing

respirer (à fond) to breathe (deeply), **15.2**

ressembler à to resemble

ressentir to feel

le **restaurant** restaurant, **5.2**

la **restauration** food service

rester to stay, remain, **17**

rester en forme to stay in shape, **11.1**

le **retard** delay

    en retard late, **8.2**

retomber to fall back down

le **retour** return

    à votre retour when you return

la **retransmission** rebroadcast

réunir to bring together

réussir(à) to succeed, to pass (exam), **7**

le **rêve** dream (n.)

se **réveiller** to wake up, **11.1**

la **révélation** revelation

revenir to come back, **16**

rêver to dream

la **révolution** revolution

révolutionner to revolutionize

le **rez-de-chaussée** ground floor, **4.2**

le **rhume** cold (illness), **15.1**

    avoir un rhume to have a cold, **15.1**

riche rich

la **richesse** wealth

le **rideau** curtain, **16.1**

    le lever du rideau at curtain time (theatre)

Rien d'autre. Nothing else., **6.2**

rigoler to joke around, **3.2**

    Tu veux rigoler! Are you kidding?!

le **rite** rite, ritual

la **rivière** river

la **robe** dress, **10.1**

le **roi** king

le **rôle** role

le **roman** novel

    le roman policier detective novel, mystery

rond(e) round

rose pink, **10.2**

le **rosier** rosebush

la **roue** wheel, **12.1**

    la roue de secours spare tire, **12.1**

    les deux roues two-wheeled vehicles

rouge red, **10.2**

la **rougeole** measles

le **rouleau de papier hygiénique** roll of toilet paper, **17.2**

rouler (vite) to go, drive (fast) **12.1**

la **route** road, **12.1**

    En route! Let's go!

la **rubéole** German measles

la **rue** street, **3.1**

le **rugby** rugby

rural(e) rural

le/la **Russe** Russian (person)

S

s'il te plaît please (fam.), **BV**

s'il vous plaît please (form.), **BV**

sa his, her (f. sing. poss. adj.), **4**

le **sable** sand

le **sac** bag, **6.1**; pocketbook, purse, **18.1**

le **sac à dos** backpack, **BV**

saignant(e) rare (meat), **5.2**

la **saison** season

    la belle saison summer

la **salade** salad, **5.1**

le **salaire** salary

la **salle à manger** dining room, **4.2**

la **salle d'attente** waiting room, **8.1**

la **salle de bains** bathroom, **4.2**

la **salle de cinéma** movie theatre, **16.1**

la **salle de classe** classroom, **2.1**

la **salle de séjour** living room, **4.2**

le **Salon** official art show

salut hi, **BV**

samedi (m.) Saturday, **2.2**

le **sandwich** sandwich, **5.1**

sans without, **12.1**

    sans aucun doute without a doubt

    Sans blague! No kidding!

    sans plomb unleaded, **12.1**

la **santé** health, **15.1**

    être en bonne (mauvaise) santé to be in good (poor) health, **15.1**

la **saucisse de Francfort** hot dog, **5.1**

le **saucisson** sausage, **6.1**

sauf except, **16.2**

sauver to save

le **savant** scientist

savoir to know (information), **16.2**

le **savon** soap, **11.1**

scandalisé(e) scandalized, shocked

la **scène** stage; scene, **16.1**

les **sciences (f. pl.)** science, **2.2**

    les sciences humaines social sciences

    les sciences naturelles natural sciences

le **scorbut** scurvy

le **score** score, **9.2**

le **sculpteur** sculptor (m. and f.), **16.2**

la **sculpture** sculpture, **16.2**

la **séance** show (movie) **16.1**

sec, sèche dry

se **sécher** to dry (off), **17.2**

la **sécheresse** dryness, drought

secondaire: l'école (f.) secondaire junior high, high school

la **seconde** second (time)

    en seconde in second class, **8.1**

seize sixteen, **BV**

le **séjour** stay (n.)

selon according to

la **semaine** week, **2.2**; allowance

    par semaine a (per) week, **3.2**

sembler to seem

le **Sénégal** Senegal, **16**

le **sens** direction; meaning

    sens interdit (m.) wrong way (traffic sign)

    sens unique (m.) one way (traffic sign)

se **sentir** to feel (well, etc.), **15.1**

séparer to separate

sept seven, **BV**

septembre (m.) September, **4.1**

la **série** series

sérieux, sérieuse serious, **10**

serré(e) tight, **10.2**

le **serveur, la serveuse** waiter, waitress, **5.1**

le **service** tip; service, **5.2**

    Le service est compris. The tip is included., **5.2**

la **serviette** napkin, **5.2**; towel, **17.2**

servir to serve (food), **7.2**; to serve (a ball in tennis, etc.), **9.2**

ses his, her (pl. poss. adj.), **5**

seul(e) alone; single; only (adj.)

    tout(e) seul(e) all alone, by himself/herself

seulement only (adv.)

sévère strict

le **sexe** sex

le **shampooing** shampoo

le **short** shorts, **9.2**

si if; yes (after neg. question)

le **SIDA (Syndrome Immuno-Déficitaire Acquis)** AIDS

le **siècle** century

le **siège** seat, **7.1**

siffler to (blow a) whistle, **13.1**

le **signal** sign

signer to sign, **18.1**
signifier to mean
simplement simply
sincère sincere, **1.2**
situé(e) located
six six, **BV**
le **ski** ski (n.), skiing (n.), **14.1**
    le **ski alpin** downhill skiing, **14.1**
    le **ski de fond** cross-country skiing, **14.1**
    faire du ski to ski, **14.1**
    faire du ski nautique to water-ski, **9.1**
le **skieur, la skieuse** skier, **14.1**
social(e) social
la **société** society
la **sociologie** sociology
la **sœur** sister, **1.2**
soi: chez soi home
la **soie: en soie** silk (adj.)
le **soir** evening, in the evening, **2**
    du soir P.M. (time), **2**
la **soirée** evening
soit is, exists (subjunctive)
soixante sixty, **BV**
soixante-dix seventy, **5.2**
le **sol** ground, **13.2**
les **soldes (f. pl.)** sale (in a store), **10.2**
le **soleil** sun
    le **soleil levant** rising sun
    Il fait du soleil. It's sunny., **9.2**
    soluble dans l'eau water-soluble
    soluble dans la graisse fat-soluble
sombre dark
la **somme** sum
le **sommeil** sleep
le **sommet** summit, mountaintop, **14.1**
    son his, her (m. sing. poss. adj.), **4**
la **sorte** sort, kind
la **sortie** exit, **7.1**
    sortir to go out, take out, **7**
    souffrir to suffer, **15.2**
la **soupe à l'oignon** onion soup, **5.1**
la **source** source
sous under
les **sous-titres (m. pl.)** subtitles, **16.1**
souvent often, **5**
se **spécialiser** to specialize
le **spectacle** show
le **spectateur** spectator, **13.1**
la **splendeur** splendor
splendide splendid

le **sport: faire du sport** to play sports
    pratiquer un sport to play a sport
    le **sport collectif** team sport
    le **sport d'équipe** team sport
    les **sports d'hiver** winter sports, skiing, **14.1**
    sport casual (clothes) (adj.), **10.1**
sportif, sportive athletic
le **stade** stadium, **13.1**
la **station balnéaire** seaside resort, **9.1**
la **station de métro** subway station, **4.2**
la **station de sports d'hiver** ski resort, **14.1**
la **station-service** gas station, **12.1**
le **stationnement** parking
    stationnement interdit no parking (traffic sign)
    stationner to park, **12.2**
    Il est interdit de stationner. No parking (traffic sign), **12.2**
la **statue** statue
steak frites steak and French fries, **5.2**
le **steward** flight attendant (m.), **7.2**
stop stop (traffic sign)
strict(e) strict
le **stylo** (ballpoint) pen, **BV**
se **succéder** to follow one another
le **succès** success
le **sud** south
le **sud-est** southeast
suffir to suffice, be enough
suisse Swiss (adj.)
la **Suisse** Switzerland
suivant(e) following (adj.)
suivre to follow
le **sujet** subject
super terrific, super, **2.2**; super (gasoline), **12.1**
superbe superb
la **superficie** area (geography)
le **supermarché** supermarket, **6.1**
supersonique supersonic
le **supplément** surcharge (train fare)
    payer un supplément to pay a surcharge (train)
sur on, **BV**
sûr(e) sure
la **surface** surface
surgelé(e) frozen, **6.2**
surtout especially, above all
surveiller to watch, **12.2**

le **survêtement** warmup suit, **11.2**
le **sweat-shirt** sweatshirt, **10.1**
sympathique nice (person), **1.2**
le **symptôme** symptom
le **syndicat d'initiative** tourist office
le **synonyme** synonym
le **système** system

T

ta your (f. sing. poss. adj.), **4**
la **table** table, **BV**
le **tableau** blackboard, **BV**; painting, **16.2**
    le **tableau des départs et arrivées** arrival and departure board
la **taille** size (clothes), **10.2**
    la **taille au-dessous** next smaller size, **10.2**
    la **taille au-dessus** next larger size, **10.2**
    Vous faites quelle taille? What size do you take?, **10.2**
le **tailleur** suit (woman's), **10.1**
le **talon** heel, **10.2**
    à talons hauts (bas) high- (low-) heeled (shoes)
la **tante** aunt, **4.1**
tard late
    plus tard later
le **tarif** fare
    les **tarifs aériens** airfares
la **tarte** pie, tart, **6.1**
    la **tarte aux fruits** fruit tart, pie
la **tasse** cup, **5.2**
le **taux** level, rate
le **taxi** taxi, **7.2**
    te (to) you (fam.) (dir. and ind. obj.), **15.2**
technique technical
technologiquement technologically
le **tee-shirt** T-shirt, **9.2**
la **télé** TV, **3.2**
    à la télé on TV
le **téléphone** telephone
le **télésiège** chairlift, **14.1**
la **température** temperature, **14.1**
le **temps** weather, **9.2**
    de temps en temps from time to time
    Quel temps fait-il? What's the weather like?, **9.2**
la **tendance: avoir tendance à** to tend (+ inf.)
le **tennis** tennis, **9.2**

les **tennis (f. pl.)** sneakers
le **terminal** terminal
le **terrain de football** soccer field, **13.1**
la **terrasse** terrace, **4.2**
    la **terrasse d'un café** sidewalk café, **5.1**
la **terre** earth, land
    la **Terre** the Earth
la **Terre-Neuve** Newfoundland
    terrible terrible; terrific (inform.), **2.2**
le **territoire** territory
le **tétanos** tetanus
la **tête** head, **13.1**
    avoir mal à la tête to have a headache, **15.1**
le **thé citron** tea with lemon, **5.1**
le **théâtre** theater, **16.1**
la **théorie** theory
    Tiens! Hey! Well! Look! **10.1**
le **tilleul** linden tree
    timide timid, shy, **1.2**
    toi you (sing., stress pron.), **9**
la **toilette: faire sa toilette** to wash and groom oneself, **11.1**
les **toilettes (f. pl.)** bathroom, **4.2**
la **tomate** tomato, **6.2**
    tomber to fall, **17**
    ton your (m. sing. poss. adj.), **4**
la **tonne** ton
le **topographe** topographer (m. and f.)
    tôt early
    total(e) total
    toucher to cash (a check), **18.1**; to touch
    toujours always, **5**
la **tour Eiffel** Eiffel Tower
le **tour: À votre tour.** (It's) your turn.
le/la **touriste** tourist
    tous, toutes all, every, **7**
    tous (toutes) les deux both
    tout(e) the whole, the entire, **7**
    C'est tout? Is that all?, **6.2**
    tout autour de all around (prep.)
    tout de suite right away
    tout le monde everyone, everybody, **BV**
    tout(e) seul(e) all alone, **5.2**
    les tout premiers (m.) the very first
    toxique toxic
la **tragédie** tragedy, **16.1**
le **train** train, **8.1**
    le train à grande vitesse (TGV) high-speed train

le **trajet** distance
    transporter to transport
le **travail** work
    travailler to work, **3.1**
    travailleur, travailleuse hard-working
    traverser to cross, **12.2**
    treize thirteen, **BV**
    trente thirty, **BV**
    très very, **1.2**
le **tricolore** French flag
la **trigonométrie** trigonometry, **2.2**
    trois three, **BV**
    troisième third, **4.2**
    trop too (excessive), **10.2**
    trop de too many, too much
le **trophée** trophy
    tropical(e) tropical, **9**
le **trottoir** sidewalk, **12.2**
le **trouble digestif** digestive trouble
    trouver to find, **5.1**; to think (opinion), **10.2**
se **trouver** to be located, found
    tu you (fam., subj. pron.), **1**
la **tuberculose** tuberculosis
    tuer to kill
la **Tunisie** Tunisia, **16**
le **type** guy (informal)
le **typhoïde** typhoide
    typique typical

U

    un, une a, one, **BV**
    unir to unite
    unisexe unisex
l' **unité (f.)** unit
    universitaire university (adj.)
l' **université (f.)** university
l' **ustensile (m.)** utensil
    utiliser to use
    en utilisant using

V

les **vacances (f. pl.)** vacation
    en vacances on vacation
le **vaccin** vaccination (shot)
la **vaccination** vaccination
    vacciner to vaccinate
    vachement really (informal)
la **vague** wave, **9.1**
la **valeur** value
la **valise** suitcase **7.1**
    faire les valises to pack, **7.1**
la **vallée** valley, **14.1**
la **vanille: à la vanille** vanilla (adj.), **5.1**

la **vapeur d'eau** water vapor
la **variation** variation
    varié(e) varied
    varier to vary
la **variété** variety
    vaste vast, enormous
    vaut: il vaut mieux it's better
la **vedette** star (actor or actress), **16.1**
le **végétal** vegetable, plant
    végétarien(ne) vegetarian
le **vélo** bicycle, **13.2**
    à vélo by bicycle
    le vélo tout terrain (VTT) mountain bike
le **vélodrome** bicycle racing track
le **vélomoteur** moped, **12.1**
le **vendeur, la vendeuse** salesperson, **10.1**
    vendre to sell, **8.1**
    vendredi (m.) Friday, **2.2**
    venir to come, **16**
    venir de to have just
    venir en tête to rate above
le **vent** wind, **14.2**
    Il fait du vent. It's windy., **9.2**
la **vente** sale
le **ventre** abdomen, stomach, **15.1**
    avoir mal au ventre to have a stomach-ache, **15.1**
    au ventre de in the depths of
le **ver à soie** silkworm
le **verbe** verb
    vérifier to check, verify, **7.1**
    vérifier les niveaux to check under the hood, **12.1**
    véritable real
le **verre** glass, **5.2**
    vers around (time); towards
le **versement** deposit
la **version originale** original language version (of a movie), **16.1**
    vert(e) green, **10.2**
    vertical(e) vertical
la **veste** (sports) jacket, **10.1**
    vestimentaire: normes vestimentaires dress code
le **veston** (suit) jacket
les **vêtements (m. pl.)** clothes, **10.1**
la **viande** meat, **6.1**
la **victoire** victory
le **vide** vacuum, space
    vide empty
la **vidéo(cassette)** videocassette, **3.2**

la **vie** life
  vieille old (f.), **4.1**
  vieux (vieil) old (m.), **4.1**
  vif, vive bright (color)
  vigilant(e) vigilant, watchful
la **villa** house
le **village** village, small town
la **ville** city, town
le **vin (rouge, blanc)** (red, white)
  wine
  vingt twenty, **BV**
  violent(e) violent
  viral(e) viral, **15.1**
la **virgule** comma
le **virus** virus
la **visite** visit
  visiter to visit (a place), **16.2**
la **vitamine** vitamin
  vite fast (adv.), **12.2**
la **vitrine** (store) window
  Vive . . . ! Long live . . . !,
    Hooray for . . . !
  vivre to live (exist)
  voici here is, here are, **1.1**
la **voie** track (railroad), **8.1**; lane
  (of a road), **12.1**
  voilà there is, there are
  (emphatic)
  voir to see, **10.1**
le **voisin, la voisine** neighbor, **4.2**

la **voiture** car, **4.2**
  la voiture-lit sleeping car,
    8.2
  la voiture-restaurant dining
    car
  la voiture de sport sports
    car, **12.1**
  en voiture by car, **5.2**; "All
    aboard!," **8**
  monter en voiture to board
    the train, **8**
le **vol** flight, **7.1**
le **volley-ball** volleyball, **13.2**
le **volume** volume
  vos your (pl. poss. adj.), **5**
  votre your (sing. poss. adj.), **5**
  voudrais: je voudrais I would
    like, **5.1**
  vouloir to want, **6.1**
  vous you (sing. form., pl.), **2**;
    you (stress pron.), **9**; (to) you
    (dir. and ind. obj.), **15**
le **voyage** trip
  faire un voyage to take a
    trip, **7.1**
  voyager to travel, **8.1**
le **voyageur, la voyageuse** traveler,
  passenger, **8.1**
  vrai(e) true, real
  vraiment really, **2.1**

la **vue** view
la **vulgarité** vulgarity

W

le **walkman** walkman, **3.2**
le **week-end** weekend, **2.2**

Y

  y there, **5.2**; **18.2**
le **yaourt** yogurt, **6.1**
les **yeux (m. pl; sing. œil)** eyes,
  15.1
  avoir les yeux qui piquent
    to have stinging eyes, **15.1**

Z

  zéro zero, **BV**
la **zone** area, zone, section, **7.1**
  la zone tempérée temperate
    zone
  en pleine zone tempérée
    right in the temperate zone
la **zoologie** zoology
  zut! darn!, **12.2**

VOCABULAIRE ANGLAIS-FRANÇAIS

The *Vocabulaire anglais-français* contains all productive and receptive vocabulary from the text.

The numbers following each productive entry indicate the chapter and vocabulary section in which the word is introduced. For example, 2.2 means that the word first appeared in *Chapitre 2, Mots 2*. *BV* refers to the introductory *Bienvenue* lesson.

The following abbreviations are used in this glossary.

adj.	adjective
adv.	adverb
conj.	conjunction
dem. adj.	demonstrative adjective
dem. pron.	demonstrative pronoun
dir. obj.	direct object
f.	feminine
fam.	familiar
ind. obj.	indirect object
inf.	infinitive
inform.	informal
inv.	invariable
m.	masculine
n.	noun
pl.	plural
poss. adj.	possessive adjective
prep.	preposition
pron.	pronoun
sing.	singular
subj.	subject

A

a un, une, **1**
  a day (week) par jour (semaine), **3.2**
  a lot beaucoup, **3.1**
abdomen le ventre, **15.1**
accident l'accident (m.), **14.2**
act l'acte (m.), **16.1**
active actif, active, **10**
actor l'acteur (m.), **16.1**
actress l'actrice (f.), **16.1**
aerobics: to do aerobics faire de l'aérobic, **11.2**
after après, **3.2**
afternoon l'après-midi (m.), **2**
against contre, **13.1**
age l'âge (m.), **4.1**
agent (m. and f.) l'agent (m.), **7.1**
to **agree** être d'accord, **2.1**
air aérien(ne) (adj.), **9**
  air terminal l'aérogare (f.), **7.1**
airline la compagnie aérienne, **7.1**
airplane l'avion (m.), **7.1**
airport l'aéroport (m.), **7.1**
aisle le couloir (n.), **8.2**
  aisle seat (une place) côté couloir, **7.1**
algebra l'algèbre (f.), **2.2**
all tous, toutes, **7**
  all alone tout(e) seul(e), **5.2**
  all right d'accord (agreement), **3**
  Is that all? C'est tout?, **6.2**
allergic allergique, **15.1**
allergy l'allergie (f.), **15.1**
already déjà, **14**
also aussi, **1.1**
always toujours, **5**
American américain(e) (adj.), **1.1**
among entre, **9.2**
and et, **1**
  and you? et toi? (fam.), **BV**
angry fâché(e), **12.2**
announcement l'annonce, (f.), **8.1**
to **answer** répondre, **8**
antibiotic l'antibiotique (m.), **15.1**
Anything else? Autre chose?, **6.2**
apartment l'appartement (m.), **4.2**
apartment building l'immeuble (m.), **4.2**
apple la pomme, **6.2**
April avril (m.), **4.1**

arrival l'arrivée (f.), **7.2**
to **arrive** arriver, **3.1**
arriving from (flight) en provenance de, **7.1**
art l'art (m.), **2.2**
to **ask (for)** demander, **5**
  to ask a question poser une question, **3.1**
aspirin l'aspirine (f.), **15.1**
at à, **3.1**
  at the au, aux, **5**
  at the home (business) of chez, **5**
  at what time? à quelle heure?, **2**
athletic sportif, sportive, **10**
August août (m.), **4.1**
aunt la tante, **4.1**
autumn l' automne (m.), **13.2**

B

backboard (basketball) le panneau, **13.2**
backpack le sac à dos, **BV**
bacterial bactérien(ne), **15.1**
bag le sac, **6.1**
bakery la boulangerie-pâtisserie, **6.1**
balcony le balcon, **4.2**
ball la balle (tennis, etc.), **9.2**; le ballon (soccer, etc.), **13.1**
banana la banane, **6.2**
bank la banque, **18.1**
baseball le base-ball, **13.2**
basket le panier, **13.2**
basketball le basket(-ball), **13.2**
bathing suit le maillot (de bain), **9.1**
bathroom la salle de bains, (f.), les toilettes (f. pl.), **4.2**
to **be** être, **2.1**
  to be able to pouvoir, **6**
  to be better soon être vite sur pied, **15.2**
  to be born naître, **17**
  to be called s'appeler, **11.1**
  to be careful faire attention, **9.1**
  to be early être en avance, **8.1**
  to be hungry avoir faim, **5.1**
  to be in shape être en forme, **11.2**
  to be late être en retard, **8.2**
  to be on time être à l'heure, **8.1**
  to be out of sorts ne pas être dans son assiette, **15.2**
  to be thirsty avoir soif, **5.2**

  to be . . . years old avoir . . . ans, **4.1**
beach la plage, **9.1**
beautiful beau (bel), belle, **4**
because parce que, **9.1**
to **become** devenir, **16**
bed le lit, **8.2**
to **go to bed** se coucher, **11.1**
bedroom la chambre à coucher, **4.2**
beef le bœuf, **6.1**
before avant, **7.1**
beginner le débutant, la débutante, **14.1**
behind derrière, **BV**
beige beige, **10.2**
to **believe** croire, **10.2**
better meilleur(e) (adj.), **10**
between entre, **9.2**
beverage la boisson, **5.2**
bicycle le vélo, **13.2**
  bicycle racer le coureur cycliste, **13.2**
  by bicycle à vélo, **5.2**
big grand(e), **1.1**
bill le billet (currency), **18.1**; la facture, **17.2**
biology la biologie, **2.2**
birthday l'anniversaire (m.), **4.1**
  When is your birthday? C'est quand, ton anniversaire? (fam.), **4.1**
black noir(e), **10.2**
blackboard le tableau, **BV**
blanket la couverture, **17.2**
bleacher le gradin, **13.1**
blond blond(e), **1.1**
blouse le chemisier, **10.1**
to **blow a whistle** siffler, **13.1**
blue bleu(e), **10.2**
  navy blue bleu marine (inv.), **10.2**
to **board** embarquer (plane), **7.2**; monter (train), **8.2**
boarding pass la carte d'embarquement, **7.1**
book le livre, **BV**
born: to be born naître, **17**
to **borrow** emprunter, **18.2**
bottle la bouteille, **6.2**
boundaries (on a tennis court) les limites (f. pl.), **9.2**
box office le guichet, **16.1**
boy le garçon, **BV**
to **brake** freiner, **12.2**
bread le pain, **6.1**
  loaf of French bread la baguette, **6.1**
to **breathe (deeply)** respirer (à fond), **15.2**

broke (slang) fauché(e), **18.2**
brother le frère, **1.2**
brown brun(e), marron (inv.), **10.2**
brunette brun(e), **1.1**
to brush (one's teeth, hair, etc.) se brosser (les dents, les cheveux, etc.), **11.1**
bunk (on a train) la couchette, **8.2**
bus l'autocar (m.), **7.2**, le bus, **5.2**
    by bus en bus, **5.2**
busy occupé(e), **2.2**
but mais, **1**
butcher shop la boucherie, **6.1**
butter le beurre, **6.2**
to buy acheter, **6.1**
    to buy a ticket prendre un billet, **7**

C

cabin (plane) la cabine, **7.1**
café le café, **5.1**
cake le gâteau, **6.1**
calculator la calculatrice, **BV**
can of food la boîte de conserve, **6.2**
Canadian canadien(ne), **7**
cap (ski) le bonnet, **14.1**
car la voiture, **4.2**
    sports car la voiture de sport, **12.2**
carefully prudemment, **12.2**
carrot la carotte, **6.2**
carry-on luggage les bagages (m. pl.) à main, **7.1**
cartoon le dessin animé, **16.1**
cash l'argent liquide (m.), **18.1**
    to cash (a check) toucher (un chèque), **18.1**
cash register la caisse, **6.2**
cashier le caissier, la caissière, **17.2**
cassette la cassette, **3.2**
casual (clothes) sport (adj. inv.), **10.1**
cat le chat, **4.1**
chair la chaise, **BV**
chairlift le télésiège, **14.1**
chalk: piece of chalk le morceau de craie, **BV**
change la monnaie, **18.1**
    to make change faire de la monnaie, **18.1**
to change changer (de), **8.2**
change purse le porte-monnaie, **18.1**
to chat bavarder, **4.2**

to check vérifier, **7.1**; faire enregistrer (luggage), **7.1**
    to check under the hood vérifier les niveaux, **12.2**
    to check out (of a hotel) libérer une chambre, **17.2**
check (n.) l'addition (f.) (in a restaurant), **5.2**; le chèque (bancaire), **18.1**
    traveler's check le chèque de voyage, **17.2**
checkout counter la caisse, **6.2**
checkroom la consigne, **8.1**
cheese le fromage, **5.1**
chemistry la chimie, **2.2**
chicken le poulet, **6.1**
child l'enfant (m. et f.), **4.1**
chills (n.) les frissons (m. pl.), **15.1**
chocolate (adj.) au chocolat, **5.1**
to choose choisir, **7.1**
to claim (luggage) récupérer, **7.2**
class la classe (people), **2.1**; le cours (course), **2.2**
classroom la salle de classe, **2.1**
closed fermé(e), **16.2**
closet le placard, **17.2**
clothes les vêtements (m. pl.), **10.1**
clothing designer le grand couturier, **10.1**
cloud le nuage, **9.2**
Coca-Cola le coca, **5.1**
coffee le café, **5.1**
    black coffee l'express (m.), **5.1**
    coffee with cream (in a café) le crème, **5.1**
coin la pièce, **18.1**
cold froid(e) (adj.), **14.2**; le rhume (illness), **15.1**
    to have a cold être enrhumé(e), **15.1**
    It's cold (weather). Il fait froid., **9.2**
color la couleur, **10.2**
    What color is . . . ? De quelle couleur est . . . ?, **10.2**
to comb (one's hair) se peigner, **11.1**
to come venir, **16**
to come back revenir, **16**
comedy la comédie, **16.1**
    musical comedy la comédie musicale, **16.1**
comic strip la bande dessinée, **16**

compact disc le compact disc, **3.2**
compartment le compartiment, **7.2**
computer l'ordinateur (m.), **BV**
computer science l'informatique (f.), **2.2**
conductor (train) le contrôleur, **8.2**
confident confiant(e), **1.1**
convertible (car) la décapotable, **12.2**
to cook faire la cuisine, **6**
corridor le couloir, **8.2**
costume le costume, **16.1**
to cough tousser, **15.1**
counter le comptoir, **7.1**
country le pays, **7.1**
course le cours, **2.2**
courtyard la cour, **4.2**
cousin le cousin, la cousine, **4.1**
to cover couvrir, **15**
crab le crabe, **6.1**
cream la crème, **6.1**
credit card la carte de crédit, **17.2**
crepe la crêpe, **5.1**
croissant le croissant, **6.1**
to cross traverser, **12.2**
crossroads le carrefour, **12.2**
cup la tasse, **5.2**
    winner's cup la coupe, **13.2**
currency la monnaie, **18.1**
curtain le rideau, **16.1**
customer le client, la cliente, **10.1**
customs la douane, **7.2**
    to go through customs passer à la douane, **7.2**
cycling le cyclisme, **13.2**
cyclist le coureur cycliste (in a race), **13.2**

D

dairy store la crémerie, **6.1**
to dance danser, **3.2**
darn! zut!, **12.2**
date: What is the date today? Quelle est la date aujourd'hui?, **4.1**
datebook l'agenda (m.), **2.2**
daughter la fille, **4.1**
day le jour, **2.2**
    a (per) day par jour, **3**
    What day is it? C'est quel jour?, **2.2**
December décembre (m.), **4.1**

degree: It's . . . degrees Celsius. Il fait . . . degrés Celsius., **14.2**
delicatessen la charcuterie, **6.1**
delicious délicieux, délicieuse,
10
deodorant le déodorant, **11.1**
department store le grand
magasin, **10.1**
departure le départ, **7.1**
to deposit verser, **18.1**
to descend descendre, **14.1**
desk le bureau, **BV**
desk clerk le/la réceptionniste,
17.1
diagnosis: to make a diagnosis faire un diagnostic, **15.2**
to die mourir, **17**
difficult difficile, **2.1**
dining car la voiture-
restaurant, **8.2**
dining room la salle à manger,
4.2
dinner le dîner, **4.2**
to eat dinner dîner, **4.2**
to discover découvrir, **15**
district le quartier, **4.2**; l'arrondissement (m.) (in Paris)
to dive plonger, **9.1**
diving: to go deep-sea diving
faire de la plongée sous-
marine, **9.1**
to do faire, **6.1**
to do the shopping faire les
courses, **6.1**
doctor le médecin (m. et f.),
15.2
documentary le documentaire,
16.1
dog le chien, **4.1**
dollar le dollar, **18.1**
domestic (flight) intérieur(e),
7.1
door la porte, **17.1**
dozen la douzaine, **6.2**
drama le drame, **16.1**
dress la robe, **10.1**
dressed: to get dressed
s'habiller, **11.1**
dressy habillé(e), **10.1**
to dribble (a basketball) dribbler,
13.2
to drive conduire, **12.2**
driver le conducteur, la conductrice, **12.2**
driver's license le permis de
conduire, **12.2**
driving lesson la leçon de conduite, **12.2**
driving school l'auto-école (f.),
12.2

to dry (off) se sécher, **17.2**
dubbed (movie) doublé(e), **16.1**
during pendant, **3.2**

E

each (adj.) chaque, **16.1**
ear l'oreille (f.), **15.1**
earache: to have an earache
avoir mal aux oreilles, **15.1**
early: to be early être en
avance, **8.1**
to earn gagner, **3.2**
easy facile, **2.1**
to eat manger, **5**
to eat breakfast prendre le
petit déjeuner, **7**
to eat dinner dîner, **4.2**
to eat lunch déjeuner, **5.2**
egg l'œuf (m.), **6.2**
eight huit, **BV**
eighteen dix-huit, **BV**
eighty quatre-vingts, **5.2**
elevator l'ascenseur (m.), **4.2**
eleven onze, **BV**
energetic énergique, **1.2**
English (language) l'anglais
(m.), **2.2**
to enter entrer, **3.1**
entire entier, entière, **10**
entrance l'entrée (f.), **4.2**
espresso l'express (m.), **5.1**
European (adj.) européen(ne),
7
evening le soir, **2**
in the evening (P.M.) du soir,
2
every tous, toutes, **7**; chaque,
16.1
everybody, everyone tout le
monde, **BV**
everywhere partout
exam l'examen (m.), **3.1**
to take an exam passer un
examen, **3.1**
to pass an exam réussir à
un examen, **7**
to examine examiner, **15.2**
except sauf, **16.2**
to exchange (money) changer,
18.1
exchange office (for foreign
currency) le bureau de
change, **18.1**
exchange rate le cours du
change, **18.1**
to exercise faire de l'exercice, **11.2**
exhibit l'exposition (f.), **16.2**
exit la sortie, **7.1**
expenses les frais (m. pl.), **17.2**

expensive cher, chère, **10.1**
eye l'œil (m., pl. yeux), **15.1**
to have stinging eyes avoir
les yeux qui piquent, **15.1**

F

face la figure, **11.1**
to face donner sur, **17.1**
to fall faire une chute, **14.2**; tomber, **17**
to fall asleep s'endormir, **11.1**
fall l'automne (m.) (season),
13.2
family la famille, **4.1**
famous célèbre, **1.2**
fantastic fantastique, **1.2**
far from loin de, **4.2**
fast vite, **12.2**
father le père, **4.1**
favorite favori(te), **10**
February février (m.), **4.1**
to feel se sentir (feel well, etc.),
15.1
to feel out of sorts ne pas
être dans son assiette, **15.2**
fever la fièvre, **15.1**
to have a high fever avoir
une fièvre de cheval, **15.2**
few peu (de), **18**
fifteen quinze, **BV**
fifty cinquante, **BV**
to fill out remplir, **7.2**
to fill up faire le plein (gas tank),
12.2
film le film, **16.1**
love story (movie) le film
d'amour, **16.1**
adventure film/movie le
film d'aventures, **16.1**
foreign film le film étranger,
16.1
horror film/movie le film
d'horreur, **16.1**
detective film/movie le film
policier, **16.1**
science fiction film/movie
le film de science-fiction,
16.1
finally enfin, **11.1**
to find trouver, **5.1**
fine ça va, bien, **BV**
to finish finir, **7**
first premier, première (adj.),
4.2; d'abord (adv.), **11.1**
in first class en première, **8.1**
fish le poisson, **6.1**
fish store la poissonnerie, **6.1**
fishing: to go fishing aller à la
pêche, **9.1**

fitness (physical)   la forme physique, **11**
five   cinq, **BV**
flight   le vol, **7.1**
   flight attendant   l'hôtesse (f.) de l'air, le steward, **7.2**
floor (of a building)   l'étage (m.), **4.2**
flu   la grippe, **15.1**
foot   le pied, **13.1**
   on foot   à pied, **5.2**
for (time)   depuis, **8.2**
forbidden   interdit(e), **12.2**
foreign   étranger, étrangère, **16.1**
fork   la fourchette, **5.2**
forty   quarante, **BV**
four   quatre, **BV**
fourteen   quatorze, **BV**
franc   le franc, **18.1**
France   la France, **16**
free   libre, **2.2**
freezing: It's freezing (weather).   Il gèle, **14.2**
French   français(e) (adj.), **1.1**; le français (language), **2.2**
French fries   les frites (f. pl.), **5.2**
Friday   vendredi (m.), **2.2**
friend   l'ami(e), **1.2**; le copain, la copine (pal), **2.1**
from   de, **1.1**
   from the   du, de la, de l', des, **5**
frozen   surgelé(e), **6.2**
fruit   le fruit, **6.2**
full   plein(e), **13.1**
   full-time   à plein temps, **3.2**
fun: to have fun   s'amuser, **11.2**
funny   amusant(e), **1.1**; comique, **1.2**

G

to gain weight   grossir, **11.2**
game   le match, **9.2**
garage   le garage, **4.2**
garden   le jardin, **4.2**
gas(oline)   l'essence (f.), **12.1**
   regular (gas)   (de l'essence) ordinaire, **12.1**
   super (gas)   (de l'essence) super, **12.1**
   unleaded (gas)   (de l'essence) sans plomb, **12.1**
gas station   la station-service, **12.2**
   gas station attendant   le/la pompiste, **12.2**
gas tank   le réservoir, **12.2**
gate (airport)   la porte, **7.1**

geography   la géographie, **2.2**
geometry   la géométrie, **2.2**
to get a sunburn   attraper un coup de soleil, **9.1**
to get in shape   se mettre en forme, **11.1**
to get off   descendre, **8.2**
to get on   monter, **8.2**
to get up   se lever, **11.1**
gift   le cadeau, **10.2**
girl   la fille, **BV**
to give   donner, **3.2**
   to give back   rendre, **18.2**
glass   le verre, **5.2**
glove   le gant, **14.1**
to go   aller, **5.1**
   to go (in a car, etc.)   rouler, **12.2**
   to go deep-sea diving   faire de la plongée sous-marine, **9.1**
   to go down   descendre, **14.1**
   to go fast   rouler vite, **12.2**
   to go fishing   aller à la pêche, **9.1**
   to go home   rentrer, **3.1**
   to go out   sortir, **7**
   to go to bed   se coucher, **11.1**
   to go through customs,   passer à la douane, **7.2**
   to go up   monter, **17.1**
   to go windsurfing   faire de la planche à voile, **9.1**
   Shall we go?   On y va?, **5**
goal   le but, **13.1**
goalie   le gardien de but, **13.1**
goggles (ski)   les lunettes (f. pl.), **14.1**
good   bon(ne), **7**
goodbye   au revoir, ciao (inform.), **BV**
gram   le gramme, **6.2**
granddaughter   la petite-fille, **4.1**
grandfather   le grand-père, **4.1**
grandmother   la grand-mère, **4.1**
grandparents   les grands-parents (m. pl.), **4.1**
grandson   le petit-fils, **4.1**
gray   gris(e), **10.2**
great   chouette (inform.), **2.2**
green   vert(e), **10.2**
green beans   les haricots (m. pl.) verts, **6.2**
grilled ham and cheese sandwich   le croque-monsieur, **5.1**
grocery store   l'épicerie (f.), **6.1**
ground   le sol, **13.2**

ground floor   le rez-de-chaussée, **4.2**
guide(book)   le guide, **12.2**
gym(nasium)   le gymnase, **11.2**
gymnastics   la gymnastique, **2.2**
   to do gymnastics   faire de la gymnastique, **11.2**

H

hair   les cheveux (m.pl.), **11.1**
half   demi(e)
   half past (time)   et demie, **2**
ham   le jambon, **5.1**
hand   la main, **11.1**
handkerchief   le mouchoir, **15.1**
hanger   le cintre, **17.2**
happy   content(e), **1.1**; heureux, heureuse, **10.2**
hard (adv.)   fort, **9.2**
hat   le bonnet, **14.1**
to hate   détester, **3.2**
to have   avoir, **4.1**
   to have a(n) . . . -ache   avoir mal à (aux) . . . , **15.2**
   to have a cold   être enrhumé(e), **15.1**
   to have a picnic   faire un pique-nique, **6**
   to have to   devoir, **18.2**
he   il, **1**
head   la tête, **13.1**
headache: to have a headache   avoir mal à la tête, **15.1**
health   la santé, **15.1**
   to be in good (poor) health   être en bonne (mauvaise) santé, **15.1**
   health club   le club de forme, **11.2**
to hear   entendre, **8.1**
heel   le talon, **10.2**
   high (low)-heeled (shoes)   à talons hauts (bas), **10.2**
hello   bonjour, **BV**
her   elle (stress pron.), **9**; la (dir. obj.), **16**; lui (ind. obj.), **17.1**; sa, son (poss. adj.), **4**; ses (poss. adj.), **5**
here is, here are   voici, **1.1**
hi   salut, **BV**
high   élevé(e), **15**; haut(e), **10.2**
   high school   le lycée, **1.2**
highway   l'autoroute (f.), **12**
him   le (dir. obj.), **16.1**; lui (stress pron.), **9**; lui (ind. obj.), **17.1**
his   sa, son, **4**; ses, **5**
history   l'histoire (f.), **2.2**

to **hit** frapper, **9.2**
homework (assignment) le devoir, **BV**
   to do homework faire les devoirs, **6**
hot: It's hot (weather). Il fait chaud., **9.2**
hot dog la saucisse de Francfort, **5.1**
hotel l'hôtel (m.), **17.1**
house la maison, **3.1**
how: How are you? Ça va? (inform.); Comment vas-tu? (fam.); Comment allez-vous? (form.), **BV**
   How beautiful they are! Qu'elles (ils) sont belles (beaux)!
how much combien, **6.2**
   How much is it? C'est combien?, **6.2**
   How much is that? Ça fait combien?, **5.2**
   How's it going? Ça va?, **BV**
hundred cent, **5.2**
to **hurt** avoir mal à, **15.1**
   It hurts. Ça fait mal., **15.2**
   Where does it hurt (you)? Où avez-vous mal?, **15.2**
husband le mari, **4.1**

I

I je, **1**
ice la glace, **14.2**
ice cream la glace, **5.1**
ice skate (n.) le patin à glace, **14.2**
   (ice) skating (n.) le patinage, **14.2**
   to (ice) skate faire du patin (à glace), **14.2**
immigration l'immigration (f.), **7.2**
impatient impatient(e), **1.1**
in dans, **BV**; à, **3.1**
   in back of derrière, **BV**
   in front of devant, **BV**
   in first (second) class en première (seconde), **8.1**
inexpensive bon marché (inv.), **10.1**
infection l'infection (f.), **15.1**
instructor le moniteur, la monitrice, **9.1**
intelligent intelligent(e), **1.1**
interesting intéressant(e), **1.1**
intermission l'entracte (m.), **16.1**

international international(e), **7.1**
intersection le croisement, **12.2**
to **invite** inviter, **3.2**
it (dir. obj.) le, la, **16.1**
   it is, it's c'est, **BV**
   It's expensive. Ça coûte cher., **7.2**
   it is necessary (+ inf.) il faut (+ inf.), **9.1**
Italian italien(ne), **7**
Italy l'Italie (f.), **16**

J

jacket le blouson, **10.1**
   (suit) jacket la veste, **10.1**
   ski jacket l'anorak (m.), **14.1**
January janvier (m.), **4.1**
jar le pot, **6.2**
jeans le jean, **10.1**
to **jog** faire du jogging, **11.2**
to **joke around** rigoler, **3.2**
July juillet (m.), **4.1**
June juin (m.), **4.1**

K

key la clé, **12.2**; (basketball) le demi-cercle, **13.2**
to **kick** donner un coup de pied, **13.1**
kilogram le kilo, **6.2**
kind (n.) le genre, **16.1**
kitchen la cuisine, **4.2**
kleenex le kleenex, **15.1**
knife le couteau, **5.2**
to **know** connaître (be acquainted with), savoir (information), **16.2**

L

to **land** atterrir, **7.1**
landing card la carte de débarquement, **7.2**
lane (of a road) la voie, **12.2**
language la langue, **2.2**
last dernier, dernière, **10**
   last night hier soir, **13**
   last year l'année (f.) dernière, **13**
late: to be late être en retard, **8.2**
Latin le latin, **2.2**
to **learn (to)** apprendre (à), **9.1**
to **leave** partir, **7**
   to leave (a room, etc.) quitter, **3.1**

to leave (something behind) laisser, **5.2**
   to leave a tip laisser un pourboire, **5.2**
left: to the left of à gauche de, **5**
lemonade le citron pressé, **5.1**
to **lend** prêter, **18.2**
lesson la leçon, **9.1**
lettuce la laitue, **6.2**
level le niveau, **12.2**
to **like** aimer, **3.2**
   I would like je voudrais, **5.1**
line: to wait in line faire la queue, **8.1**
to **listen (to)** écouter, **3.2**
   to listen with a stethoscope ausculter, **15.2**
liter le litre, **6.2**
literature la littérature, **2.2**
to **live (in a city, house, etc.)** habiter, **3.1**
living room la salle de séjour, **4.2**
lobby le hall, **17.1**
locker la consigne automatique, **8.1**
long long(ue), **10.2**
to **look at** regarder, **3.1**
to **look for** chercher, **5.1**
to **lose** perdre, **8.2**
   to lose patience perdre patience, **8.2**
   to lose weight maigrir, **11.2**
lot: a lot of beaucoup de, **10.1**
   a lot of people beaucoup de monde, **13.1**
loudspeaker le haut-parleur, **8.1**
to **love** aimer, **3.2**
low bas(se), **10**
luggage les bagages (m. pl.), **7.1**
   carry-on luggage les bagages à main, **7.1**

M

ma'am madame, **BV**
magazine le magazine, **3.2**
maitre d' le maître d'hôtel, **5.2**
to **make** faire, **6.1**
   make (of car) la marque, **12.2**
man l'homme (m.), **10.1**
March mars (m.), **4.1**
market le marché, **6.2**
marvelous merveilleux, merveilleuse, **10.2**
match (singles, doubles) (tennis) la partie (en simple, en double), **9.2**

math les maths (f. pl.), **2.2**
May mai (m.), **4.1**
me me (dir. and ind. obj.), **15.2**; moi (stress pron.), **1.2**
meat la viande, **6.1**
medicine la médecine (medical profession), **15**; le médicament (remedy), **15.2**
medium-rare (meat) à point, **5.2**
menu la carte, **5.1**
merchant le marchand, la marchande, **6.2**
    produce merchant le marchand, la marchande de fruits et légumes, **6.2**
meter maid la contractuelle, **12.2**
midnight minuit (m.), **2.2**
milk le lait, **6.1**
mineral water l'eau (f.) minérale, **6.2**
mirror la glace, **11.1**
Miss (Ms.) Mademoiselle (Mlle), **BV**
mogul la bosse, **14.1**
Monday lundi (m.), **2.2**
money l'argent (m.), **3.2**
    to have lots of money avoir plein de fric (slang), **18.2**
month le mois, **4.1**
moped le vélomoteur, **12.2**
morning le matin, **2**
    in the morning (A.M.) du matin, **2**
Morocco le Maroc, **16**
most (of) la plupart (des), **8.2**
mother la mère, **4.1**
motorcycle la moto, **12.2**
    motorcycle cop le motard, **12.2**
mountain la montagne, **14.1**
mouth la bouche, **15.1**
movie le film, **16.1**
    movie theater le cinéma, la salle de cinéma, **16.1**
Mr. Monsieur (M.), **BV**
Mrs., Ms. Madame (Mme), **BV**
museum le musée, **16.2**
music la musique, **2.2**
must devoir, **18.2**
mustard la moutarde, **6.2**
my ma, mon, **4**; mes, **5**

N

name le nom, **16.2**
    What is your name? Tu t'appelles comment? (fam.), **11.1**

napkin la serviette, **5.2**
narrow étroit(e), **10.2**
near près de, **4.2**
necessary: it is necessary (+ inf.) il faut (+ inf.), **9.1**
to **need** avoir besoin de, **11.1**
neighbor le voisin, la voisine, **4.2**
neighborhood (n.) le quartier, **4.2**
nephew le neveu, **4.1**
net le filet, **9.2**
    net bag le filet, **6.1**
never ne . . . jamais, **12**
new nouveau (nouvel), nouvelle, **4**
newspaper le journal, **8.1**
newsstand le kiosque, **8.1**
next prochain(e), **8.2**
    next to à côté de, **5**
nice (person) aimable, sympathique, **1.2**; gentil(le), **9**
niece la nièce, **4.1**
nine neuf, **BV**
nineteen dix-neuf, **BV**
ninety quatre-vingt-dix, **5.2**
no one, nobody ne . . . personne, **12.2**
No parking permitted. Il est interdit de stationner., **12.2**
no smoking (section) (la zone) non fumeurs, **7.1**
noon midi (m.), **2.2**
nose le nez, **15.1**
    to have a runny nose avoir le nez qui coule, **15.1**
not ne . . . pas, **1**
    not bad pas mal, **BV**
notebook le cahier, **BV**
nothing ne . . . rien, **12.2**
    nothing else rien d'autre, **6.2**
novel le roman, **16**
November novembre (m.), **4.1**
now maintenant, **2**
number le numéro, **5.2**
    What is the phone number of . . . ? Quel est le numéro de téléphone de . . . ? **5.2**

O

to **obey** obéir (à), **7**
o'clock: it's . . . o'clock il est . . . heure(s), **2.2**
October octobre (m.), **4.1**
of de, **5**
    of the du, de la, de l', des, **5**
to **offer** offrir, **15**

often souvent, **5**
OK ça va (health); d'accord (agreement), **BV**
old vieux (vieil), vieille, **4.1**
    How old are you? Tu as quel âge? (fam.), **4.1**
omelette (with herbs/plain) l'omelette (f.) (aux fines herbes/nature), **5.1**
on sur, **BV**
    on board à bord de, **7.2**
    on foot à pied, **5.2**
    on time à l'heure, **8.1**
one un, une, **1**
    one-way ticket l'aller simple (m.), **8.1**
onion l'oignon (m.), **6.2**
    onion soup la soupe à l'oignon, **5.1**
open ouvert(e), **16.2**
    to open ouvrir, **15.2**
opera l'opéra (m.), **16.1**
opinion: in my opinion à mon avis, **10.2**
to **oppose** opposer, **13.1**
opposing adverse, **13.1**
or ou, **1.1**
orange l'orange (fruit) (f.), **6.2**; orange (color) (inv.), **10.2**
    orange soda l'Orangina (m.), **5.1**
to **order** commander, **5.1**
    original language version (of a film) la version originale, **16.1**
other autre, **BV**
our notre, nos, **5**
out of bounds hors des limites, **9.2**
over (prep.) par dessus, **13.2**
    over there là-bas, **BV**
overcast (cloudy) couvert(e), **14.2**
to **overlook** donner sur, **17.1**
to **owe** devoir, **18.2**

P

to **pack (suitcases)** faire les valises, **7.1**
package le paquet, **6.2**
packed (stadium) comble, **13.1**
painter le/la peintre, **16.2**
painting la peinture; le tableau, **16.2**
pair la paire, **10.1**
pal le copain, la copine, **2.1**
pancake la crêpe, **5.1**
pants le pantalon, **10.1**
pantyhose le collant, **10.1**

paper: sheet of paper la feuille
de papier, BV
parents les parents (m. pl.), 4.1
Parisian parisien(ne), 7
park le parc, 11.2
    to park the car garer la voi-
    ture, 12.2
parking: no parking Il est
    interdit de stationner., 12.2
part-time à mi-temps, 3.2
party la fête, 3.2
to pass passer, 7.2
passenger le passager, la pas-
    sagère, 7.1; le voyageur, la
    voyageuse (train), 8
passport le passeport, 7.1
pâté le pâté, 5.1
patient patient(e), 1.1
to pay payer, 6.1
    to pay attention faire atten-
    tion, 6
    to pay back rembourser,
    18.2
    to pay cash payer en
    espèces, 17.2
pedestrian le piéton, la
    piétonne, 12.2
    pedestrian crossing les
    clous (m. pl.), 12.2
pen le stylo, BV
pencil le crayon, BV
penicillin la pénicilline, 15.1
to permit permettre, 14
person la personne, 17.1
personally personnellement,
    16.2
pharmacist le pharmacien, la
    pharmacienne, 15.2
pharmacy la pharmacie, 15.2
physical education l'éducation
    (f.) physique, 2.2
physics la physique, 2.2
picture le tableau, 16.1
pie la tarte, 6.1
pill le comprimé, 15.2
pillow l'oreiller (m.), 17.2
pink rose, 10.2
to place mettre, 8.1
plain (adj.) nature, 5.1
plate l'assiette (f.), 5.2
platform (railroad) le quai, 8.1
to play, perform jouer, 16
    to play (a sport) jouer à,
    9.2; pratiquer un sport,
    11.2
play la pièce, 16.1
    to put on a play monter une
    pièce, 16.1
player le joueur, 9.2
please s'il vous plaît (form.),
    s'il te plaît (fam.), BV

pocket la poche, 18.1
pocketbook, purse le sac, 18.1
pool la piscine, 9.2
poor pauvre, 15.1
    poor thing le/la pauvre, 15.1
popular populaire, 1.2
porter le porteur, 8.1
potato la pomme de terre, 6.2
pound la livre, 6.2
to prepare préparer, 4.2
to prescribe prescrire, 15.2
prescription l'ordonnance (f.),
    15.2
    to write a prescription faire
    une ordonnance, 15.2
pretty joli(e), 4.2
price le prix, 10.1
problem le problème, 11.2
to punish punir, 7
to put (on) mettre, 8.1
    to put money aside mettre
    de l'argent de côté, 18.2
    to put on makeup se
    maquiller, 11.1

Q

quarter: quarter after (time) et
    quart, 2
    quarter to (time) moins le
    quart, 2
question: to ask a question
    poser une question, 3.1
quite assez, 1

R

race la course, 13.2
racket la raquette, 9.2
radio la radio, 3.2
raining: It's raining. Il pleut.,
    9.2
rare (meat) saignant(e), 5.2
to read lire, 12.2
ready-to-wear department le
    rayon prêt-à-porter, 10.1
really vraiment, 2.1
to receive recevoir, 18.1
reception desk la réception,
    17.1
record le disque, 3.2
red rouge, 10.2
referee l'arbitre (m.), 13.1
registration card (at a hotel
    desk) la fiche d'enregistre-
    ment, 17.1
regular ordinaire (gasoline),
    12.2
to reserve réserver, 17
restaurant le restaurant, 5.2

to return (tennis ball, etc.) ren-
    voyer, 9.2
right: to the right of à droite
    de, 5
right away tout de suite, 11.1
road la route, 12.2
role le rôle, 16
room la pièce, 4.1; la chambre
    (in a hotel), 17.1
    single room la chambre à
    un lit, 17.1
    double room la chambre à
    deux lits, 17.1
round-trip ticket le billet aller-
    retour, 8.1
runner le coureur, 13.2

S

salad la salade, 5.1
sales les soldes (f. pl.), 10.2
salesperson le vendeur, la ven-
    deuse, 10.1
same même, 2.1
sand le sable, 9.1
sandwich le sandwich, 5.1
    grilled ham and cheese
    sandwich le croque-
    monsieur, 5.1
Saturday samedi (m.), 2.2
sausage le saucisson, 6.1
to save money faire des écono-
    mies, 18.2
savings account le compte
    d'épargne, 18.1
to say dire, 12.2
scarf l'écharpe (f.), 14.1
scene la scène, 16.1
schedule l'horaire (m.), 8.1
school l'école (f.), 1.2
    high school le lycée, 1.2
science les sciences (f. pl.), 2.2
score le score, 9.2
    to score a goal marquer un
    but, 13.1
screen l'écran (m.), 7.1
sculptor le sculpteur (m. et f.),
    16.2
sculpture la sculpture, 16.2
sea la mer, 9.1
    by the sea au bord de la
    mer, 9.1
seashore le bord de la mer, 9.1
seaside resort la station bal-
    néaire, 9.1
seat le siège, 7.1
    seat (on an airplane, at
    movies, etc.) la place, 7.1
seat belt la ceinture de
    sécurité, 12.2

seated assis(e), **8.2**
second (adj.) deuxième, **4.2**
section la zone, **7.1**
smoking (no smoking) section la zone (non) fumeurs
security (airport) le contrôle de sécurité, **7.1**
to **see** voir, **10.1**
See you later. À tout à l'heure., **BV**
See you tomorrow. À demain., **BV**
to **sell** vendre, **8.1**
to **send (hit)** envoyer, **13.1**
September septembre (m.), **4.1**
to **serve** servir, **7.2**
service le service, **5.2**
service station la station-service, **12.2**
service station attendant le/la pompiste, **12.2**
set (for a play) le décor, **16.1**
to set the table mettre le couvert, **8**
seven sept, **BV**
seventeen dix-sept, **BV**
seventy soixante-dix, **5.2**
several plusieurs, **18.2**
Shall we go? On y va?, **5**
to **shave** se raser, **11.1**
she elle, **1**
sheet le drap, **17.2**
sheet of paper la feuille de papier, **BV**
shirt la chemise, **10.1**
shoes les chaussures (f. pl.), **10.1**
shop la boutique, **10.1**
to shop faire des achats, **10.1**
short petit(e), **1.1**; court(e), **10.2**
shorts le short, **9.2**
show la séance (movies), **16.1**
to **show** montrer, **17.1**
to show a movie passer un film, **16.1**
shrimp la crevette, **6.1**
shy timide, **1.2**
sick malade, **15.1**
sick person le/la malade, **15.2**
side le camp (in a sporting event), **13.1**
sidewalk le trottoir, **12.2**
sidewalk café la terrasse (d'un café), **5.1**
to **sign** signer, **18.1**
since depuis, **8.2**
sincere sincère, **1.2**

to **sing** chanter, **3.2**
sir monsieur, **BV**
sister la sœur, **1.2**
six six, **BV**
sixteen seize, **BV**
sixty soixante, **BV**
size la taille (clothes); la pointure (shoes), **10.2**
the next larger size la taille au-dessus, **10.2**
the next smaller size la taille au-dessous, **10.2**
to take size . . . faire du (nombre), **10.2**
What size do you take? Vous faites quelle pointure (taille)?, **10.2**
skate (ice) le patin à glace, **14.2**
to (ice) skate faire du patin (à glace), **14.2**
skater le patineur, la patineuse, **14.2**
skating (n.) la patinage, **14.2**
skating rink la patinoire, **14.2**
ski (n.) le ski, **14.1**
to ski faire du ski, **14.1**
ski boot la chaussure de ski, **14.1**
ski jacket l'anorak (m.), **14.1**
ski pole le bâton, **14.1**
ski resort la station de sports d'hiver, **14.1**
skiing (n.) le ski, **14.1**
downhill skiing le ski alpin, **14.1**
cross-country skiing le ski de fond, **14.1**
skier le skieur, la skieuse, **14.1**
skirt la jupe, **10.1**
sky le ciel, **14.2**
to **sleep** dormir, **7.2**
sleeping car la voiture-lit, **8.2**
sleeve la manche, **10.2**
long- (short-) sleeved à manches longues (courtes), **10.2**
small petit(e), **1.1**
smoking (section) (la zone) fumeurs, **7.1**
snack bar (train) le grill-express, **8**
sneakers les chaussures (f. pl.) de tennis, **9.2**
to **sneeze** éternuer, **15.1**
snowball la boule de neige, **14.2**
snowing: It's snowing. Il neige., **14.2**
soap le savon, **11.1**
soccer le foot(ball), **13.1**

soccer field le terrain de football, **13.1**
socks les chaussettes (f. pl.), **10.1**
some quelques (pl.), **8.2**
somebody, someone quelqu'un, **12.2**
something to eat quelque chose à manger, **5.1**
sometimes quelquefois, **5**
son le fils, **4.1**
sore throat avoir mal à la gorge **15.1**
space (parking) la place, **12.2**
Spanish (language) l'espagnol (m.), **2.2**
to **speak** parler, **3.1**
to speak on the telephone parler au téléphone, **3.2**
spectator le spectateur, **13.1**
speed limit la limitation de vitesse, **12.2**
to **speed up** accélérer, **12.2**
to **spend** dépenser (money), **10.1**
spoon la cuillère, **5.2**
sporty (clothes) sport (adj. inv.), **10.1**
spring (season) le printemps, **13.2**
stadium le stade, **13.1**
stage la scène, **16.1**
staircase l'escalier (m.), **17.1**
to **stamp (a ticket)** composter, **8.1**
standing debout, **8.2**
star (actor or actress) la vedette, **16.1**
to start the car mettre le contact, **12.2**
station wagon le break, **12.2**
statue la statue, **16.2**
to **stay in shape** rester en forme, **11.1**
steak and French fries le steak frites, **5.2**
steep raide, **14.1**
stomach le ventre, **15.1**
stomachache avoir mal au ventre, **15.1**
to **stop** s'arrêter, **12.2**
store le magasin, **3.2**
street la rue, **3.1**
student l'élève (m. et f.), **1.2**
to **study** étudier, **3.1**; faire des études, **6**
to study French (math, etc.) faire du français (des maths, etc.), **6**
subject la matière (school), **2.2**
subtitles les sous-titres (m. pl.), **16.1**
subway le métro, **4.2**

by subway en métro, **5.2**
  subway station la station de métro, **4.2**
to **succeed** réussir (à), **7**
to **suffer** souffrir, **15.2**
  suit le complet (men's), le tailleur (women's), **10.1**
  (suit) jacket la veste, **10.1**
  suitcase la valise, **7.1**
  summer l'été (m.), **9.1**
  summit le sommet, **14.1**
to **sunbathe** prendre un bain de soleil, **9.1**
  Sunday dimanche (m.), **2.2**
  sunglasses les lunettes (f. pl.) de soleil, **9.1**
  sunny: It's sunny. Il fait du soleil., **9.2**
  suntan lotion la crème solaire, **9.1**
  super extra, super (inform.), **2.2**
  super (gasoline) (de l'essence) super, **12.2**
  supermarket le supermarché, **6.1**
to **surf** faire du surf, **9.1**
  sweater le pull, **10.1**
  sweatshirt le sweat-shirt, **10.1**
  sweatsuit le survêtement, **11.2**
to **swim** nager, **9.1**
  swimming (n.) la natation, **9.1**

T

T-shirt le tee-shirt, **9.2**
table la table, **BV**
  table setting le couvert, **5.2**
  to set the table mettre le couvert, **5.2**
  tablecloth la nappe, **5.2**
to **take** prendre, **9.1**
  to take a bath (a shower) prendre un bain (une douche), **11.1**
  to take an exam passer un examen, **3.1**
  to take off (airplane) décoller, **7.1**
  to take size (number) faire du (+ nombre), **10.2**
  to take something upstairs monter, **17.1**
  to take the train (plane, etc.) prendre le train (l'avion, etc.), **7**
  to take a trip faire un voyage, **7.1**
  to take a walk faire une promenade, **9.1**
  taken pris(e), **5.1**

to **talk** parler, **3.1**
  to talk on the phone parler au téléphone, **3.1**
to **tan** bronzer, **9.1**
  tart la tarte, **6.1**
  taxi le taxi, **7.2**
  tea with lemon le thé citron, **5.1**
to **teach someone to do something** apprendre à quelqu'un à faire quelque chose, **14.1**
  teacher le professeur; le/la prof (inform.), **2.1**
  team l'équipe (f.), **13.1**
  television la télé, **3.2**
to **tell** dire, **12.2**
  temperature la température, **15.1**
  ten dix, **BV**
  tennis le tennis, **9.2**
  tennis court le court de tennis, **9.2**
  tennis shoes les chaussures (f. pl.) de tennis, **9.2**
  tennis skirt la jupette, **9.2**
  terrible terrible, **2.2**
  terminal (bus to airport) l'aérogare (f.), **7.2**
  terrace la terrasse, **4.2**
  test l'examen (m.), **3.1**
  to take a test passer un examen, **3.1**
  to pass a test réussir à un examen, **7**
thank you merci, **BV**
that (dem. adj.) ce (cet), cette, **8**
  That's expensive. Ça coûte cher., **18**
  that is to say c'est-à-dire, **16.1**
the la, le, **1**; les, **2**
theater le théâtre, **16.1**
their leur, leurs, **5**
them elles, eux, (stress pron.), **9**; les (dir. obj.), **16**; leur (ind. obj.), **17**
then (adv.) ensuite, **11.1**
there y, **5**
there is, there are il y a, **4.2**; voilà (emphatic), **BV**
these ces (m. and f. pl.), **8**
they elles, ils, **2**
to **think** penser, **10.2**
third troisième, **4.2**
thirteen treize, **BV**
thirty trente, **BV**
this (dem. adj.) ce (cet), cette, **8**
those (dem. adj.) ces (m. and f. pl.), **8**
thousand mille, **6.2**

three trois, **BV**
throat la gorge, **15.1**
  to have a frog in one's throat avoir un chat dans la gorge, **15.2**
  to have a scratchy throat avoir la gorge qui gratte, **15.1**
  to have a throat infection avoir une angine, **15.1**
to **throw** lancer, **13.2**
Thursday jeudi (m.), **2.2**
ticket le billet, **7.1**
  one-way ticket l'aller simple (m.), **8.1**
  round-trip ticket le billet aller-retour, **8.1**
  ticket window le guichet, **8.1**
  traffic ticket la contravention, **12.2**
tie la cravate, **10.1**
tight serré(e); étroit(e) (shoes), **10.2**
time l'heure (f.) (of day), **2**
  At what time? À quelle heure?, **2**
  to be on time être à l'heure, **8.1**
  What time is it? Il est quelle heure?, **2**
timid timide, **1.2**
tip (restaurant) le pourboire, **5.2**
  to leave a tip laisser un pourboire, **5.2**
  The tip is included. Le service est compris., **5.2**
tire le pneu, **12.2**
  flat tire le pneu à plat, **12.2**
  spare tire la roue de secours, **12.2**
to **à**, **3.1**; à destination de (flight, etc.), **7.1**
  to the au, aux, **5**
  to the left of, à gauche de, **5**
  to the right of à droite de, **5**
today aujourd'hui, **2.2**
together ensemble, **5.1**
toilet (bathroom) les toilettes (f. pl.), **4.2**
  toilet paper: roll of toilet paper le rouleau de papier hygiénique, **17.2**
toll highway l'autoroute (f.) à péage, **12.2**
tomato la tomate, **6.2**
tomorrow demain, **2.2**
  See you tomorrow. À demain., **BV**
too aussi (also), **1.1**; trop (excessively), **10.2**

tooth la dent, 11.1
toothpaste le dentifrice, 11.1
towel la serviette, 17.2
track la piste (race), 13.2; la voie (train), 8.1
traffic la circulation, 12.2
  traffic light le feu, 12.2
  green (traffic) light le feu vert, 12.2
  red (traffic) light le feu rouge, 12.2
  yellow (traffic) light le feu orange, 12.2
tragedy la tragédie, 16.1
trail la piste, 14.1
  slalom trail la piste de slalom, 14.1
train le train, 8.1
  train station la gare, 8.1
traveler le voyageur, la voyageuse, 8.1
trigonometry la trigonométrie, 2.2
Tuesday mardi (m.), 2.2
TV la télé, 3.2
twelve douze, BV
twenty vingt, BV
two deux, BV
type (n.) le genre, 16.1

U

uncle l'oncle (m.), 4.1
under sous, BV
to **understand** comprendre, 9.1
United States les États-Unis (m. pl.), 9.1
unleaded sans plomb, 12.2
unpleasant désagréable, antipathique (person), 1.2
up to jusqu'à, 13.2
us nous, 7

V

valley la vallée, 14.1
vanilla (adj.) à la vanille, 5.1
vegetable le légume, 6.2
very très, 1.1
videocassette la vidéo(cassette), 3.2
viral viral(e), 15.1
volleyball le volley-ball, 13.2

W

to **wait (for)** attendre, 8.1
  to wait in line faire la queue, 8.1

waiter le serveur, 5.1
waiting room la salle d'attente, 8.1
waitress la serveuse, 5.1
to **wake up** se réveiller, 11.1
to **walk** se promener, 11.2
Walkman le walkman, 3.2
wallet le portefeuille, 18.1
to **want** vouloir, 6.1
warmup suit le survêtement, 11.2
to **wash (one's face, hair, etc.)** se laver (la figure, les cheveux, etc.), 11.1
  to wash and groom oneself faire sa toilette, 11.1
washcloth le gant de toilette, 17.2
to **watch** surveiller, 12.2
water l'eau (f.), 6.2
to **water-ski** faire du ski nautique, 9.1
wave la vague, 9.1
we nous, 2
to **wear** porter, 10.1
weather le temps, 9.2
  It's bad weather. Il fait mauvais., 9.2
  It's nice weather. Il fait beau., 9.2
  What's the weather like? Quel temps fait-il?, 9.2
Wednesday mercredi (m.), 2.2
week la semaine, 2.2
  a (per) week par semaine, 3.2
weekend le week-end, 2.2
weight: to gain weight grossir, 11.2
  to lose weight maigrir, 11.2
well bien, BV
well-done (meat) bien cuit(e), 5.2
what quel(le), 7; qu'est-ce que, 13; quoi, 14
  What else? (shopping) Avec ça?, 6.2
  What is it? Qu'est-ce que c'est?, BV
  What is . . . like? Comment est . . . ? (description), 1.1
wheel la roue, 12.2
when quand, 3.1
  When is your birthday? C'est quand, ton anniversaire? (fam.), 4.1
where où, BV
which quel(le) (interrrogative adj.), 7

to **whistle (blow a whistle)** siffler, 13.1
white blanc, blanche, 10.2
who qui, BV
  Who (do you mean)? Qui ça?, BV
  Who is it? Qui est-ce?, BV
whom qui, 14
why pourquoi, 9.1
wide large, 10.2
wife la femme, 4.1
to **win** gagner, 9.2
wind le vent, 14.2
  window (seat in airplane) côté fenêtre, 7.1
to **windsurf** faire de la planche à voile, 9.1
windy: It's windy. Il fait du vent., 9.2
winner le gagnant, la gagnante, 13.2
winter l'hiver (m.), 14.1
with avec, 5.1
without sans, 12.2
to **work** travailler, 3.2
  work l'œuvre (f.) (of art), 16.2
to **write** écrire, 12.2
wrong: What's wrong with him? Qu'est-ce qu'il a?, 15.1

Y

year l'année (f.), 4.1
yellow jaune, 10.2
yes oui, BV
yesterday hier, 13.1
  the day before yesterday avant hier, 13
  yesterday morning hier matin, 13
yogurt le yaourt, 6.1
you te (dir. and ind. obj.), 15; toi (stress pron.), 9; tu, (subj. pron.) (fam.), 1; vous (sing. form. and pl.), 2
  You're welcome. De rien., Je t'en prie., Pas de quoi (fam.).; Ce n'est rien., Il n'y a pas de quoi., Je vous en prie (form.)., BV
young jeune, 4.1
your ta, ton, tes (fam.), 4; votre, vos (form.), 5

Z

zero zéro, BV

INDEX GRAMMATICAL

interrogative adjective *quel*, 182, (7)

interrogative words, 308 (12)

interrogatives   (see **questions**)

inversion, 130 (5); 308 (12)

irregular verbs   present tense: *aller*, 129 (5); *apprendre*, 235 (9); *avoir*, 96 (4); *comprendre*, 235 (9); *conduire*, 305 (12); *connaître*, 406 (16); *devenir*, 412 (16); *devoir*, 474 (18); *dire*, 305 (12); *dormir*, 184 (7); *écrire*, 305 (12); *être*: singular forms, 25 (1); plural forms, 46 (2); *faire*, 157 (6); *lire*, 305 (12); *mettre*, 207 (8); *offrir*, 384 (15); *ouvrir* 384 (15); *partir*, 184 (7); *prendre*, 235 (9); *pouvoir*, 160 (6); *recevoir*, 474 (18); *revenir*, 412 (16); *savoir*, 406 (16); *servir*, 184 (7); *sortir*, 184 (7); *souffrir*, 384 (15); *venir*, 412 (16); *vouloir*, 160 (6); *passé composé* of irregular verbs: 360 (14); 442, 444 (17)

-*ir* verbs   (see **present tense** and *passé composé*)

liaison, 45 (2); 343 (13)

lire   present tense, 305 (12); *passé composé*, 360 (14)

mettre   present tense, 207 (8); *passé composé*, 360 (14)

moins . . . que, 261 (10)

mourir   *passé composé*, 444 (17)

naître   *passé composé*, 444 (17)

negation   *ne . . . pas*, 27 (1); *ne . . . jamais, ne . . . personne, ne . . . rien*, 307 (12); of indefinite articles, 76 (3); of the partitive, 155 (6)

nouns   gender, 21 (1); plural of, 45 (2); ending in -*al*: singular and plural, 183 (7)

nouveau, 101 (4)

number   of adjectives, 50 (2); of definite articles, 45 (2); of indefinite articles, 76 (3); of nouns, 45 (2)

numbers   cardinal numbers 0-60, 9 (BV); 61-100, 126 (5); 101-1,000, 151 (6); ordinal numbers, 92 (4); with *en*, 473 (18)

object pronouns   (see **direct object pronouns, indirect object pronouns**, *en, y*)

ouvrir   present tense, *passé composé*, 384 (15); verbs like, 384 (15)

partir   present tense, 184 (7); *passé composé*, 442 (17)

partitive   154 (6); in the negative, 155 (6); replaced by *en*, 471 (18); vs. definite article, 154 (6)

passé composé   with *avoir*: regular -*er*, -*ir*, -*re* verbs, 338 (13); irregular verbs, 360 (14); with *être*: 442 (17); verbs conjugated with *avoir* or *être*: 446 (17); (see also **irregular verbs** and individual verb entries)

past participles   of regular verbs, 338 (13); of irregular verbs, 360 (14); agreement of with subject, 442 (17)

past time expressions, 339 (13)

plural   of adjectives, 50 (2); of adjectives like *beau, nouveau, vieux*, 101 (4); of adjectives and nouns ending in -*al*, 183 (7); of definite articles, 45 (2); of indefinite articles, 76 (3); of nouns, 45 (2); of subject pronouns 46 (2)

plus . . . que, 261 (10)

possession   with *de*, 132 (5) (see also **possessive adjectives**)

possessive adjectives   *mon, ton, son*, 98 (4); *notre, votre, leur*, 134 (5)

pouvoir   present tense, 160 (6); *passé composé*, 360 (14)

prendre   present tense, 235 (9); *passé composé*, 360 (14)

prepositions   in questions with *qui* and *quoi*, 363 (14); with geographical names, 410, 413 (16); with stress pronouns, 237 (9)

present tense   of -*er* verbs, 73 (3); of -*ir* verbs like *finir*, 180 (7); of -*ir* verbs like *dormir*, 184, (7); of -*re* verbs, 203 (8); of reflexive verbs, 282 (11); of verbs with spelling changes, 284 (11); (see also **irregular verbs** and individual verb entries)

pronouns   direct object pronouns: *le, la, les*, 408 (16); direct object pronouns: *me, te, nous, vous*, 382 (15); *en*, 471 (18); indirect object pronouns: *lui, leur*, 448 (17); indirect object pronouns: *me, te, nous, vous*, 382 (15); *on*, 72 (3); reflexive pronouns, 282 (11); stress pronouns, 237 (9); subject pronouns: singular, 25 (1); plural, 46 (2); *y*, 129 (5); 468, 470 (18)

pronunciation   accents, 497; accent and intonation, 28 (1); alphabet, 497; elision, 22, 27 (1); 343 (13) liaison, 45 (2); 343 (13); pronunciation of final consonants, 54 (2); pronunciation of regular adjectives, 23 (1); pronunciation of sounds:
/é/ *et* /è/: *élève*, 79 (3)
/ā /: *grand*, 103 (4)
/r/: *verre*, 136 (5)
/œ/ *et* /œ̀/: *des œufs, un œuf*, 163 (6)
/l/: *l'île*, 187 (7)
/ō/ *et* /ē/: *son train*, 209 (8)
/y/ *et* /y/ + *voyelle*: *soleil, maillot*, 240 (9)
/sh/ *et* /zh/: *chemise orange*, 265 (10)
/s/ *et* /z/: *poisson, poison*, 289 (11)
/wa/: *trottoir*, 310 (12)
/r/: *radio*, 364 (14)
/ü/: *température*, 389 (15)
/ü/ *et* /u/: *une roue*, 414 (16)
/ó/ *et* /ò/: *Hôtel de Bordeaux*, 451 (17)
/p/, /t/ *et* /k/: *payer avec une carte de crédit*, 477 (18)

quantity   expressions of, 150 (6); 151 (18)

quel, quelle, quels, quelles, 182 (7)

qu'est-ce que   interrogative, 341 (13); in exclamations, 341 (13)